What do you call Madiba w  white wine?

Persona non Graça.

＊

What does Zuma stand for?

Zero Understanding of Medical Affairs.

＊

Vusi finally cracks an appointment to see his psychiatrist in Sandton.

'Doc,' he says, 'you've got to help me. Everywhere I go, I find myself overcome by this terrible urge to steal things.'

The doc nods his head, and scrawls out a prescription.

'Try these tablets for the next two weeks,' he says. 'And if they don't work, get me a video recorder and a colour TV.'

＊

Wat het die blond gesê toe sy die oggend onder die koei wakker word?

'Is julle vier manne nog steeds hier?'

＊

Knock-knock.
Who's there?
Fivaz.
Fivaz who?
Fivazholes working on the case, and they still can't solve the crime.

＊

A man walks into a bar with a crocodile on a leash. The man asks the bartender, 'Do you serve lawyers here?' Not wanting to lose any business, the bartender grits his teeth and says, 'Sure we do.'

'Great,' says the man. 'Give me a beer, and my crocodile will have a lawyer.'

＊

'Vusi,' says the teacher, 'make me a sentence containing the word contagious.'

'That's easy,' says Vusi. 'They kicked Baas Louis out of SARFU, and it will take the contagious to get back in again.'

✻

On which hand does Naas have a tattoo of a cow?

On de udder hand.

✻

'Is jy getroud?'

'Nee, as ek probleme wil hê, koop ek 'n Alfa.'

✻

'You look stukkend, ou Jeremy,' said Leon to his pal. 'What's wrong?'

'No man, I'm suffering from syncopation.'

'Syncopation?'

'Ja. Uneven movement from bar to bar.'

✻

Die onderwyser vra vir klein Mike: 'Wat is die Salvation Army?'

En Mike antwoord: 'Dis die militêre vleuel van die Rhema Kerk.'

✻

There's good news and bad news about the wonder drug, Viagra. The bad news is that you have to be rich to be able to afford it. And the good news? If you're hard up, you don't need it.

✻

Meraai sien die nuwe sexy buurvrou wat met 'n G-string aan in die tuin rondloop, en sê vir Gatiep, 'As ek soe gelyk het, het ek nie my voete by die hys ytgesit nie.'

Gatiep sê, 'Meraai, as djy soe gelyk het, het ek ook nie my voete by die hys ytgesit nie.'

✻

What's the difference between a saloon and an elephant's fart?

One is a bar-room. The other is a BARRROOOOOOM!

✻

LEON SCHUSTER'S LEKKER THICK SOUTH AFRICAN JOKE BOOK

LEON SCHUSTER

ZEBRA

ZEBRA

First published by Zebra Press
(an imprint of the Struik New Holland Publishing Group (Pty) Ltd.)
PO Box 5563, Rivonia 2128
Tel: +27 11 807 2292
Fax: +27 11 803 1783

First edition 1998
Second edition 2000

ISBN 1 86872 251 1

Designer: Micha McKerr
Cover artwork and concept: Weyni Deysel
Cover design: Micha McKerr

Set in Neue Helvetica 11/13pt

Reproduction by Positive Proof cc
Printed and bound by NBD, Drukkery Street, Goodwood, Western Cape

CONTENTS

Introduction.   xi

A
Affairs   1
Affirmative Action   6
Airlines   11
Alcoholics Anonymous   14
Amabokkebokke   14
ANC   23
Animal Kingdom   24
Animals in Bars   28
Army   31
Aussies   33
AWB   38

B
Bachelors   40
Baas Louis   43
Bafana Bafana   46
Bicycles   49
Blondes   50
Boere   57
Boobs   59
Boxing   62
Brothels   64
Bumper Stickers   65
Bushmen.   68
Buthelezi   71

C
Cannibals   73
Cars & Trucks   74
Cellphones   77
Chickens.   77
Chinese.   79

Condoms 81
Corruption. 84
Courts. 85
Cowboys & Indians 90
Crime Wave 93
Crocodiles. 99

D

Darkest Africa 100
Dentists. 102
Dieting 103
Divorce 104
Doctors. 106
Dogs. 113
Drunks 115

E

Elephants 120

F

Farmers 121
Farts 126
Fashion. 128
Finance. 129
Fishing 131
Flashers 134

G

Gambling 135
Gammat, Gatiep & Meraai. 137
Gardening. 142
Golf. 142
Guide-dogs. 157
Gynaes 158

H

Hansie & The Boys 159
Heaven and & The Other Place 164

Hijack!. 167
Holidays 168
Honeymoons. 169
Hospitals. 171
Hotels 172
Hunting. 175

I
Innocents Abroad 179
Irish. 181

J
Jewish 186

K
Kids 195
Knock-knock. 199
Kugels. 203

L
Lawyers 204

M
Madiba 207
Marriage 208
Mayors & Mayoresses. 215
Midlife Crisis 216
Mike 217
Misunderstandings 224
Moffies 226
Mothers-in-law 229
Movies 231
Musicians & Their Instruments. 233

N
Naas. 236
New South Africa 241
No Job, No Food, No Money 244

Nuns 247

O
Old Toppies 248
Oom PW 259
Ou Doc 260

P
Parenthood 262
Parrots 268
Pet Shops 269
Police 271
Politicians 272
Pommies 275
Priests 276
Psychiatrists 277
Pubs & Bars 278

R
Rabbis 282
Racial Discrimination 285
Rainbow Nation 287
Riddle-Me-Ree 290
Royal Visit 294
Rugby 297

S
Salesmen 304
Schooldays 307
Sex 312
Skydiving 319
Snuff 320
Spietkops 321

T
Tall Tales 324
Tennis 325
Titanic 326

V

Ventriloquists 327
Viagra 328
Vrystaat 332

W

Weddings 333
Winnie 342
Workers 342

Y

Your Momma! 344

Z

Zoos 347
Zuma 349

Schuster Unplugged! 355

INTRODUCTION

Hello, howzit, sanibonani, and welcome one and all to the lekkerest, thickest, and most South African joke book in the history of lekker thick joke books. Within these 400-odd (very odd) pages, you'll find the full cast of crazy characters who make this Rainbow Nation of ours tick, and sometimes even tock.

You'll find ou Van, the celebrated boertjie with the comb in his pocket and the cellphone in his sock. You'll find Mike and Kallie and Jimmy, the ex-heavyweight boxers with the famously featherweight IQs. (Only joking, hey boys. You're actually much closer to bantamweights.)

You'll find Gammat and Gatiep and Meraai, Mitchell's Plein's most talked-about, joked-about threesome. You'll find Abie and Soozee and Murphy and McTavish and Vusi and Rajbaansa and ET and Naas and Madiba and Buthelezi and Gary and Joost and Baas Louis and Dr Zuma and Hansie and the Boys and ... ag, you'll find the whole blerrie lot, man.

When this Boertjie from Bloemfontein (that's me) and this Rooinek Boerejoodjie from Potch (that's Gus Silber) went to work on this lekker thick book, we wanted to make sure that we included every possible sector of the populace in our bid to be Equal Opportunity Offenders. So if there's any sector or sub-group we've somehow forgotten to offend, we apologise – no offence meant, hey.

Me and ou Gus slaved away on this book for the better part of a year, going through much agony, sweat, and tears of laughter in the process. For me, the book provided an ideal excuse to dig into my favourite drawer in the house – my joke drawer.

There I found the bulk of these jokes that will hopefully tickle your funnybone. They were scribbled on the back of hundreds of credit card slips, thousands of business cards, napkins, pages from other okes' diaries, and one even on a cute little pair of pink panties. Don't get the wrong idea: I got the joke and the panties from this oke who owns a pub in P.E. For some reason, he collects panties – I suppose the scientific term for that is a 'pantiemologist'.

Anyway, I was trying to give up smoking at the time, and I asked this oke for a smoke, and then another, and then another. After the tenth cigarette, the oke handed me the panties, on which he wrote: 'Schuster is like a pantie – always on the bum.'

So wie moet ek bedank vir die boek? Eerstens, al julle Gogos en Gogino's van die Reënboognasie, want dis waar die oorgrote meerderheid van die jokes vandaan kom.

Ek is mal oor 'n goeie joke, en sê nooit 'ek het hom al gehoor' as 'n ou vir my 'n grap vertel nie. Ek lag maar, want ek sien hoe hy lekkerkry as ek sy storie geniet. My vrou en my pêlle sê ek's 'n tweegesig as ek so lekker lag en hulle weet ek ken die grap, maar joke vertel is vir mense 'n vorm van stress-ontlading, en daar is geen groter plesier vir enige iemand as jy uit jou maag vir sy grap lag nie.

So hoekom sal ek die ou sy plesiertjie ontneem? Onthou dit.

'n Groot dankie aan my ou pêlle, almal van hulle, maar veral vir Smuts van Klapmuts, Willem Brandslang, Piet de Beer, my ouboet in Bloem wat eintlik in showbiz kon gewees het, my skerp moeder in Westerbloem, Daantjie Niehaus, Lads, André Scholtz, Olla Bolla, Louw en Sarah, ou Weyni Verbrysel (Deysel), daai aartshumoris wat hierdie heerlike voorblad geteken het, my humor-koningpêl ou Fanna Rautenbach, Brandt en sy pêl Willie van Pretoorja, Madeonsh, Mike Schutte, Irv, en veral Laals, Bammie, Sussie, Ernie, Bernie en Shella Vella wat oor die afgelope ses maande so getrou na my jokes geluister het.

Thanks a stack also to Kelly McGillivray for her assistance in the joke 'research-and-development' department, and to Kate and Nicholas and all the other Zebras for making the book possible, and to Colin Plen and David Thompson for all their lekker thick jokes. And thanks to Gussie for doing it with 'passie', and for helping to make this book so baie lekker en so wragtag thick.

Onthou, as ek iemand vergeet het, het ek jou in elk geval bo by die Reënboognasie ingesluit!

Finally: Naas, please don't sue me when you read the jokes about yourself. (You'll find them neatly and conveniently gathered under the category labelled NAAS.) Incidentally, the one about the outjie who klapped you after a match against Province has to be one of my all-time favourites.

It's called SNOTKLAP. Quickly! Flip the pages to NAAS and take a look for yourself.

Onthou Naas, op die ou einde van die dag is dit net 'n joke on de udder hand.

Lekker lag, almal!

Leon Schuster
September 1998

AFFAIRS

UNDER THE BED

Mike, Jimmy and Kallie are having a couple of dops at Mike's butchery one Friday after work.

'I'm worried about my wife,' says Kallie. 'I think she's having an affair with a cricket player.'

'Howzat?' asks Jimmy.

'Well,' says Kallie, 'on Tuesday night, I came home and found a cricket bat under our bed.'

'Hmmm,' says Jimmy, 'makes sense. Then I was right all the time, thinking that my wife has been having an affair with a rugby player.'

'What makes you think that?' asks Kallie.

'Well, on Wednesday night I came home and found a pair of togs under our bed.'

Hearing this, Mike puts his drink down and slams his fist against his forehead. He gazes at his pals with a sudden look of revelation on his face.

'Oh shit,' he says. 'Then that means my wife is definitely having an affair with a horse.'

'A horse?' say Jimmy and Kallie, looking at each other and then at Mike in amazement.

'Ja,' says Mike. 'Last night I came home and found a jockey under our bed.'

TEARFUL FAREWELL

Mrs Goldberg is on her deathbed, and her husband is holding her hand with tears streaming down his face. She says, 'Harry …'

He says, 'Don't talk.'

She says, 'Harry, I have to talk. I have to confess.'

Harry says, 'It's all right. Everything's all right.'

She says, 'No, no. I want to die in peace. I have to confess that I've been unfaithful to you.'

He says, 'Don't worry, I know all about it. Why else would I have poisoned you?'

LOVE THY NEIGHBOUR

Julio knocks on his neighbour's door and says, 'Hey Carlos, do you like-a da woman weeth-a da beeg fat stomach sticking alla da way out?'

Carlos says: 'No.'

'Do you like-a da woman weeth-a da teets hanging almost-a down to her knees?'

Carlos says: 'No.'

'Do you like-a da woman whose-a heeps are da size-a da Grand Canyon?'

Carlos says: 'No.'

'Then-a why do you keep screwing my wife?'

AFFAIR COMMENT

'So what can you tell me about current affairs?' the guy asks the blonde on their first date.

'Nothing,' says the blonde. 'I've never had an affair with a currant.'

IT TAKES TWO

This woman is having a quiet conversation on the phone. 'That's okay honey,' she says. 'No problem. I hope you have a good time. See you later'. Then she puts down the receiver.

'Who was that?', asks the man lying beside her in bed. 'My husband,' she replies.

'What did he want?'

'Nothing. He just wanted to say he would be home late today. He's out somewhere playing snooker with you and some of his other colleagues.'

SWEET CHARITY

Mrs Van comes home from her shopping expedition to find her husband in bed with another woman. Van leaps up from under the covers. 'Sweetie-pie,' he says, 'I can explain!'

Mrs Van stands there with her arms folded and smoke coming out of her ears. Van explains.

'You see, I was coming home from the golf course, when I saw this poor helpless girl on the side of the road. So I gave her a ride and asked her where she was going. She said she had nowhere to go and hadn't eaten anything in three days. I felt so sorry for her that I brought her home and gave her something to eat. While she was eating, I noticed she had no shoes, so I gave her a pair of yours that you don't use anymore. Then I noticed her clothes were worn, so I gave her one of your dresses that you don't use anymore. As she was ready to leave, she turned to me and said, "Is there anything else your wife doesn't use anymore?"'

SHORT SHRIFT

Van comes home from a day at the golf course to find his wife in bed with a midget. Van erupts.

'What is it with you!' he yells. 'We've been through this over and over! We've spent hours at the marriage counsellor! You've made promises and promises! And now this … just when I was starting to believe I could trust you again!'

Mrs Van looks meekly at her husband, while the shamefaced midget ducks out of the room.

'I know,' says Mrs Van. 'But at least I'm cutting down!'

UNDER THE TABLE

A man and a beautiful woman are having dinner in a fancy restaurant. Their waitress, taking another order at a table a few steps away, suddenly notices that the man is sliding further and further down his chair. The woman at the table looks unconcerned. Finally, the man disappears altogether from view.

The waitress goes over to the table and says, 'Pardon me, Madam, but I think your husband just slid under the table.'

The woman looks up calmly and says, 'No, he didn't. He just walked in the door.'

HOME AFFAIRS

'n Voormalige NP minister was 'n haan onder die henne. Een aand ontvang hy 'n oproep van 'n erg ontstelde dame. 'Ek is swanger!' gil sy.

Daar's 'n stilte voor die minister vra, 'Wie praat?'

IN EN UIT

Van dieselfde minister het sy sekretaresse eendag vir 'n vriendin gesê, 'My baas trek vreeslik mooi aan.'

Toe sê haar vriendin, 'Ja, en net so vinnig uit.'

HARD BARGAIN

Van comes home early from the pub and finds Mike and Mrs Van in bed together. They're not sleeping. Van whips out his Magnum, cocks it, and points the barrel at his former best buddy.

'Okay,' says Van. 'I see your new 4×4 is parked in the driveway. How much did you pay for it?'

'Two hundred and fifty grand,' says Mike. 'Why?'

'Because I want to buy it from you.'

Van pulls a R100 note from his pocket and shows it to Mike.

'Deal?'

Mike is about to stammer in protest, when Van slowly increases the pressure of his finger on the trigger.

'Deal,' says Mike.

Later that evening, Mike enters the threshold of his own home, minus his brand-new 4×4.

'Where's the 4×4?' shrieks Mrs Mike.

'Ag, I sold it to some oke for R100,' shrugs Mike.

'Bliksem,' says Mrs Mike. 'He must have seen you coming.'

O SHUCKS

Wanneer is 'n man regtig in die moeilikheid?

As sy skelm uitvind hy't 'n date met sy verloofde en albei is op pad om dit vir sy vrou te vertel.

SPARE RIBS

What was the first thing Eve did when Adam came home late one night?

She counted his ribs.

BEWARE THE TOKOLOSH

Vusi comes home early from work one day, and finds his young son in tears.

'What's the matter, my little one?' asks Vusi. And the little one says, 'The Tokolosh is in Mom's cupboard.'

Vusi tells his son that there is no such thing as the Tokolosh. But the kid is inconsolable.

'Come,' says Vusi. 'Let's go and take a look in the cupboard together.'

Up the stairs they go, and into the bedroom, where an alarmed-looking Mrs Vusi is sitting up in bed. Vusi nods a cordial greeting and opens the cupboard door. No Tokolosh.

Instead, Vusi finds himself face-to-face with a man who is not wearing a single item of clothing.

'Haai! Shame on you!' says Vusi. 'Don't you have anything better to do than run around scaring little kids?'

WEG MET MOTTE

Die ou word op heterdaad met sy buurman se vrou betrap. Hy spring uit die bed uit, en staan daar en bewe in sy Adamsgewaad. 'Wie's jy?!' skree die buurman woedend.

'Ek is … eee … o ja, ek is van die mottebestrydings-eenheid.'

'O ja? En waar's jou klere?' vra die buurman.

Hy kyk vinnig af, sit sy hande voor sy parte en sê, 'Bastards!'

HAVING A NICE TIME

Van writes a postcard to his wife during his overseas trip. 'I'm enjoying Florence to the full,' it says.

His wife writes back: 'Good. Because I'm enjoying Frank.'

MOAN AND GROAN

Poor Rachel was devastated when she found out about Hymie's affair.

'Why Hymie, why oh why?' Rachel sobbed bitterly.

'I wanted ecstasy, Rachel,' said Hymie. 'I wanted someone with passion – someone who could moan and groan when we made love.'

Rachel decides she's going to win Hymie back, come hell or high water. That night she puts on her sexiest negligée, prepares dinner by candlelight and places two bottles of red wine on the table.

Later that night, Hymie is humping away, when Rachel suddenly remembers his deep-rooted needs and desires. 'Oy Hymie,' she moans and groans, 'I went to Sandton to buy groceries today, they stole my purse, they broke into my car, the maid didn't turn up for work … you wouldn't believe what a day I've been having …'

AFFIRMATIVE ACTION

INTELLIGENCE TEST

Although some would see it as menial labour, Mike and Kallie really dig their jobs. One day, they're digging a trench for a sewerage pipe on the outskirts of Jo'burg, when Mike turns to Kallie and says, 'Hey, how come we're down here, working our arses off, and Vusi is up there, sipping his blerrie Coke in the shade?'

Kallie shrugs. 'Because Vusi is our supervisor, I suppose.'

But Mike isn't happy with this. He grabs his shovel, climbs out of the trench, and says, 'Vusi!'

'Yebo?'

'How come me and Kallie are working our arses off down there, and you're sitting up here with your blerrie Coke in the shade?'

Vusi checks Mike out. 'It's because I've got intelligence, and you haven't.'

'Intelligence?' says Mike. 'What's that?'

'Here, let me show you.'

Vusi un-parks himself from the tree. He stands up, and places his hand on the trunk.

'Here,' he says. 'Hit my hand as hard as you can with your shovel.'

'Are you crazy?' says Mike. 'You're my supervisor!'

'I know. That's why I'm telling you to hit my hand as hard as you can with your shovel.'

'Okay,' shrugs Mike. 'You asked for it.'

WHAAAAMMM! Just before the shovel finds its mark, Vusi pulls his hand away. Mike vibrates like a tub of jelly for about five minutes.

'Now that's intelligence,' says Vusi, going back to his Coke and his place in the shade. Mike climbs back into the trench.

'Well?' asks Kallie, 'What did he say?'

'He says we're working down here, and he's sitting up there, because he's got intelligence and we haven't.'

'Intelligence?' says Kallie. 'What's that?'

'Here, let me show you,' says Mike. He looks around for a tree. There isn't one. He puts his hand in front of his face.

'Okay,' he says, 'now take your shovel and hit me as hard as you can.'

TRAIN SMASH

Vusi applies for a job as a signalman on the Railways. Although his CV is impressive, the inspector decides to give him a practical test.

'Okay, Vusi,' says the inspector, pointing at the signal box, 'what would you do if you realised that two trains were heading for each other on the same track?'

Quick as a flash, Vusi answers: 'I would switch the points for one of the trains.'

'And what if the lever broke?' asks the inspector.

'Then I'd dash out of the signal box,' says Vusi, 'and I'd use the manual lever over there.'

'But what if the manual lever had been struck by lightning?'

'Then,' says Vusi, 'I'd run back into the signal box and phone the next signal box.'

'And what if the phone was engaged?'

'Well in that case,' continues Vusi, 'I'd rush out of the box and use the public emergency phone at the level crossing.'

'What if the phone had been vandalised?'

'Then I'd run into town and fetch my uncle Jacob.'

This stops the inspector in his tracks, so he asks, 'Why would you want to do that?'

And Vusi says, 'Because my uncle Jacob has never seen a train crash.'

WE DIDN'T INVENT FLYING ...

Overheard on an airliner somewhere over the Rainbow Nation ...

Air hostess to passenger: 'What can I get you to drink, sir?'

Passenger no 1: 'I'd like a dry white wine, thank you.'

Air hostess: 'I'm sorry, sir, we only have wet white wine.'

Passenger no 1: 'That'll do.'

Air hostess: 'And for you, sir?'

Passenger no 2: 'Ditto for me.'

Air hostess: 'I am sorry, sir, but we do not have any Ditto.'

Passenger no 2: 'What? Well, bring me a Captain Morgan.'

Air hostess: 'Sorry, sir, the captain is Van Vuuren, and he's busy flying the plane right now.'

Passenger no 2: 'Look, just get me a Grand Cru, okay?'

Air hostess: 'I am very sorry, sir, but the Grand Cru, they don't fly. Can I get you anything else?'

Passenger no 2: 'Ag, just bring me a blerrie cup of coffee.'

Air hostess: 'How would you like it, sir?'

Passenger no 2: 'Decaffeinated.'

WE SOMMER JUST PERFEKTED IT ...

Later, dinner is served. The air hostess approaches Andrew Hudson, the cricketing hero.

Air hostess: 'What would you like for dinner, sir – the duck or the chicken?'

Andrew: 'Duck, please.'

Air hostess: 'Haven't you had enough of those?'

Andrew: 'I'm sorry?'

Air hostess: 'Yes, I would be sorry too. So what's it going to be – duck or chicken?

Andrew: 'What's the duck like?'

Air hostess: 'It's like the chicken, but he can swim. Next please.'

Shane Warne: 'Sheep's head.'

Air hostess: 'How would you like it?'

Shane: 'The Aussie way.'

Air hostess: 'Okay, we'll take the brains out. Next please.'

Naas: 'I'd like those same meatballs I had last time.'

Air hostess: 'The matchacos balls from the Spanish Bull?'

Naas: 'Yes please.'

Half an hour later.

Air hostess: 'How's your balls?'

Naas: 'Let me just check … ya, they're still kicking, thanks.'

Air hostess: 'I mean the matchacos balls.'

Naas: 'Terrible. The portions were so much smaller than last time. What happened?

Air hostess: 'Well, you have to remember, sir, sometimes the bull wins.'

AFFIRMATIVE BOWLER

For many years, the SA Cricket Board had been searching for an outstanding fast bowler from a previously disadvantaged community. Eventually they found Makhaya Ntini, and everyone was happy. Everyone, that is, except Ali Bacher.

'Ntini is good,' Ali thought to himself, 'but he's not the greatest the world has ever seen. I need the world's greatest affirmative bowler and I won't stop searching till I've found him.'

Ali's cricket-developing mission took him into darkest Africa: Zimbabwe, Uganda, Kenya, Libya, Rwanda and even Morocco. Nothing.

Then one night it happened. Watching CNN in his hotel room after an exhausting day in Casablanca, Ali spotted this 19-year African-American who was involved in a major riot in the East End of LA. He was built like a fortress, with biceps as big as watermelons.

He walked down the war-torn main street of East End Los Angeles Terminator-style, armed with a bandolier of hand grenades slung over his shoulder. He took a grenade, started wiping it furiously against his tattered blue jeans, and with a perfect fast-bowling action he bowled the grenade to an anti-riot policeman 150 meters off.

The grenade travelled like a missile, completely taking off the policeman's head, helmet and all. Ali was amazed, seeing visions of a headless Shane Warne at the crease.

Our young hero saw a looter 200 meters off, exiting a

burning TV store with a huge ghettoblaster on his shoulder – something he had always desired. He took another grenade and bowled the ultimate fast delivery, ripping the looter to pieces and sending the ghettoblaster sky-high.

With a dive that would put Jonty to shame he caught the ghettoblaster in mid-air with his left hand, while bowling another perfect delivery straight into the exhaust of a police car 300 meters off with the right.

Ali knew that he had found his man. He offered him six ghettoblasters and a contract the young American couldn't refuse. Our hero outshone Donald, Proctor and Ntini, and won the five-day series against Australia on Aussie turf, taking 9/27.

The bowler phoned his dad, elated, much richer and a world-renowned cricketing star. His father's attitude shattered the young affirmative bowler.

'You have deserted us!' the father said. 'Since you went on this Australian tour, we have been robbed three times, your mother has been hijacked twice, your youngest brother was stabbed and robbed of his money at an automatic teller.' The father paused briefly, and then he said: 'Why oh why did you ever convince us to come with you to this damn Gauteng?'

AIRLINES

FLY UNITED

Little Pietie and his ma are flying South African Airways to Bloemfontein. Pietie looks out of the window and says, 'Ma, if big dogs have baby dogs and big cats have baby cats, why don't big planes have baby planes?'

His ma thinks about this for a moment, and comes up with the perfect answer. 'Go and ask the air hostess.'

So Pietie goes up to the air hostess and says, 'Tannie, if big dogs have baby dogs and big cats have baby cats, why don't big planes have baby planes?'

The air hostess checks him out and says, 'Did your mommy tell you to ask me, little boy?'

Pietie nods his head.

And the air hostess says, 'Because South African Airways always pulls out on time.'

FLY ME

The head stewardess finally realises that the plane she is on is going to crash. She rushes into the cockpit to see the pilot. She rips off her shirt and she says, 'Make me feel like a woman for the last time!' So the pilot rips off his shirt and says, 'All right, iron this!'

BRING ME THE PEPPA

Vusi rushed out of the toilet in the Boeing 747 and cornered the air hostess: 'I want peppa, please.'

Air hostess: 'Certainly, sir. White pepper or black pepper?'

Vusi: 'No, toilet peppa.'

Later, Vusi was relaxing on board when he called the same air hostess: 'Can I have the peppa, please?'

Air hostess: 'Toilet peppa?'

Vusi: 'No, the newspeppa.'

She hands him *The Star*.

Vusi: 'No, the black peppa.'

Air hostess: 'You said the newspeppa.'

Vusi: 'Yes. But not the white peppa.'

Air hostess: 'Oooh! You mean the black peppa.'

(She hands him a copy of the *Sowetan*)

INSTRUCTION MANUAL

Captain Vusi has just got his commercial pilot's license and is on his first 747 flight from Cape Town to Durban. He takes the microphone and greets his passengers, 'Excuse me, ladies and gentlemen, this is your Captain Vusi Dlamini speaking.'

Half the passengers get off.

There's a dominee on board. He turns around and tells everyone to be calm. Then he requests a Bible from the air hostess. It's not in its usual place in the rack at the front of the plane. The air hostess scurries around trying to find it, but it's nowhere to be seen. She decides to tell a little white lie.

'I'm sorry,' she says, walking out of the cockpit. 'The Captain is busy reading the Bible.'

So the other half got off.

AUTOMATIC PILOT

Die kaptein het pas sy passasiers op vlug SAL 642 na London ingelig oor die weersomstandigdhede, die hoogte en al daai nonsies, maar vergeet om die 'af'-knoppie van die aankondigingstelsel te druk. Hy lê gemaklik terug in sy sitplek, sit sy hande agter sy kop en strek lekker uit terwyl sy stem klokhelder oor die luidprekers in die grote Boeing deurkom.

'Pottie,' sê hy vir sy vlugingenieur, 'jy kan maar oorgaan automatic pilot toe. Ek gaan gou sk***t, dan gaan ek daai sexy lugwaardinnetjie met die bobcut en die blou ogies in my slaapkajuit plattrek.'

Die passasiers verstik amper aan hulle biltong en peanuts, en uit pure skok laat val die sexy lugwaardinnetjie 'n bottel Swartland Blanc Fumé op 'n swierige Sandton antie se kop.

Sy sny 'n lyn na die kajuit, en net voor sy by die deur instorm gryp 'n oom haar aan haar skirt se pant en sê, 'Jy hoef nie so haastig te wees nie, juffrou. Die kaptein het gesê hy gaan eers sk***t.'

LIGHTS OUT

It was a long, tiresome flight through the night. As the sun began to rise, the air hostesses switched on the cabin lights for breakfast.

'Switch off the f****ng lights!' shouted a male

passenger who had drunk heavily and made a pig of himself the previous night.

The air hostess took a look at this oke and said calmly, 'These are the breakfast lights, sir. The f****ng lights are much dimmer and you snored right through them.'

ALCOHOLICS ANONYMOUS

DRINK UP

In the quest to conquer the rising spectre of alcohol abuse, Alcoholics Anonymous dispatches its best Man With No Name to set up a display in a shopping mall. He waits until a small crowd has gathered, and then he holds a glass of crystal-clear water in the air.

He shows the crowd a wriggling worm, and then he lets go. The worm swims happily around in the water. Then he picks up another glass. This one is full of whisky. Plop! The worm goes into the whisky.

After a couple of seconds, the worm is struggling. Then the worm struggles no more, as it curls up and sinks to the bottom of the glass. Kaput.

'Now what does this little demonstration teach us?' asks the man from AA.

And Vusi, who has been watching with eyes a-boggle, pipes up from the back of the crowd: 'If I drink whisky, I won't get worms!'

AMABOKKEBOKKE

WHEN YOU GOTTA GO

Along with hundreds of thousands of other South Africans, I'll never forget that glorious moment when the

Boks won the World Cup at Ellis Park in '95. It was a feeling next to none when my World Cup Song, 'Hie' kommie Bokke' was played over and over again, seemingly giving the Boks renewed courage every time it thundered over the speakers.

When Stransky scored the historic drop goal that clinched the match, I jumped out of my seat and shouted, 'Stransky, you're the best Jew since Moses!'

I sneaked into the after-match celebrations at Gallagher Estate, because I didn't receive an invite. I went over to poor old Sean Fitzpatrick, who didn't look as if he had much to celebrate.

Of course, if we were to believe his story, it was all the fault of some waitress called Suzie, who had somehow spiked the team's food with a powerful laxative. A kak excuse, I told Fitzy.

'Why don't you go and inspect Zinzan Brooke's underpants,' said Fitzy. 'You'll be able to see the skid-marks for yourself.' I declined the offer, suggesting that the player be called Zinzan ONNERBROOKS from now on.

I also advised Fitzy to change the team's name from All Blacks to Brooklaxs, and the war cry from 'Haka' to 'Kaka'. For some strange reason, Fitzy didn't think this was funny.

'Have you ever tried playing rugby with a big fart?' he asked. 'No,' I said, 'I can't recall ever playing rugby with you.'

Poor Fitzy looked pained as he confided, 'You know, I had this terrible urge throughout the whole game to leave the field and take a shit.'

'Well then,' I said, 'why didn't you just take Jeff Wilson and leave?'

Fitzy just bared his teeth at me in what I took to be a sporting smile. Unless it was something to do with the laxative.

QUICK AS THEY COME

'Fitzy,' said Sexy Suzie with a sigh, 'you may be a good hooker, but you're a lousy lover.'

Replied Fitzy, with a look of dismay, 'How can you tell after only ten seconds?'

HALF MONTY

A Province breker called Monty
Decided to tackle ou Jonty
He leapt over the stump
But mistimed his jump
And Jonty yelled 'NO BALLS' quite promptly.

RISE AND FALL

Percy Monty was asked to appear as a nude model for a statue called 'The Full Monty', to be placed outside Newlands Rugby Stadium. The fee was good, and Percy agreed. There was just one condition: his assets had to be covered by a fig-leaf. A very big fig-leaf, but a fig-leaf nonetheless.

The life-size statue was completed and placed outside Newlands. Two old maids were looking at the statue one Saturday afternoon. One wanted to move on, but the other stood transfixed to the spot, gazing at Percy in all his glory.

'Come on Sarah,' said her friend. 'What are you waiting for – Christmas?'

'No,' said Sarah. 'Autumn.'

NOG 'N MOF

The legendary Springbok lock, Frik du Preez, was travelling on a plane to England with the Springbok team. Sitting next to him was that doyen of Afrikaans rugby commentators, Gerhard Viviers.

After a while Frik, who was known for his practical jokes, turned to Gerhard and said in a very serious tone: 'Ou Gerrie, did you know that there's a moffie amongst our teammates?'

'You're joking,' said Gerhard.

'No genuine,' said Frik. He left it at that, turned to Mof Myburgh on his other side, and started telling him the same story. Gerhard saw that Frik was being very serious about the matter, and couldn't contain his curiosity any longer. He leaned over to Frik, whispering: 'Ou Frikkie, who's the moffie, hey?'

Frik put his mouth close to Gerhard's ear and whispered in a husky voice, 'Kiss me and I'll tell you.'

GOEIE MORROW

Op 'n grênd rugby banket in London was oom Boy in gesprek met die toekomstige koning van Engeland. Hy vra toe aan oom Boy: 'When are you lads returning to South Africa?'

'I dunno,' sê oom Boy, 'but I fink it is tomorrow or ormorrow.'

RABIE-SPELER

Mof Myburgh was another rugby player who had a battle with the English language. During his oral examination to qualify as a policeman he was asked by the examiner, 'What is rabies?'

Mof answered, 'Rabies is Jewish priests and you treat them wif respect.'

SOMMER SO

Just before heading back home after a tour of the British Isles, a TV reporter asked Mof: 'So, Mr Myburgh, how did you find London?'

Mof: 'Well the aeroplane just landed and there it was!'

MIND YOUR OWN BUSINESS

During a tour of England Mof had to say grace at a fancy rugby dinner. He mumbled a few inaudible phrases in

English, said 'amen' and sat down. Frik du Preez leaned over to Mof and said, 'I didn't hear a word you said.'

To which Mof replied, 'I wasn't talking to you.'

FAIRY TALE

During his policing career Mof caught two youngsters shoplifting, but they fervently denied the offence, speaking loudly and constantly interrupting one other. This went on for some time, until the frustrated Mof shouted: 'Sharrup! Don't speak so twice together, speak once upon a time!'

SOAP ON A ROPE

The legendary Springbok Boy Louw, who also had something of a problem with the English language, once walked into a shop in New Zealand and said to the assistant, 'I'd like some soap, please.'

'Certainly,' said the assistant, 'do you want it scented?'

To which oom Boy replied, 'No thanks, I'll sommer take it along.'

JUST THE TICKET

Little Schucks pitches up at a packed Ellis Park for a test between the All Blacks and the Boks, and seats himself on a prime seat where a ticket costs R300. The man sitting next to him asks, 'Where did you get the ticket, Schucks?'

Shucks says, 'I got it from my daddy.'

The man says, 'Really? That's very kind of him. So where is your daddy?'

And Shucks says, 'He's looking for his ticket.'

DOCTOR'S APPOINTMENT

Schucks asks his boss if he can have the afternoon off. 'I've urgently got to see my doctor,' he explains, with a look of desperation on his face.

'Well, all right, then,' says his boss, as a rare flicker of compassion crosses his features.

'I hope everything's okay, hey Schucks.'

But Schucks is already out of the door.

Later that afternoon, Schucks's boss is watching TV while pretending to attend to urgent business in the office. During a lull in the game – Blue Bulls versus the All Blacks at Loftus – the camera focuses on a familiar-looking face in the stands. It's Schucks.

Next day at the office, the boss comes down on Schucks like a pack of pitbulls.

'You blerrie liar! I saw you in the stands at Loftus! I thought you told me you had to go and see your doctor, man!'

'But I did,' says Schucks. 'My doctor is Uli Schmidt.'

FULL MONTY

Taking a break from the rigours of training and international rugby, a bunch of Amabokkebokke are sitting down to a meal at the Nando's outlet in Earl's Court, London. The proud South African expatriate manager brings a huge peri-peri chicken to the table. He starts carving it with ceremonial flair.

'This is for our two great props, Ollie and Garvey,' says the manager, as breaks the chicken breast in two.

He moves on to the drumsticks. 'And this is for the finest pair of legs in the Bok side, our two centres, Pieter Muller and Andre Snyman.' He hands them each a leg.

Then he breaks off the wings and says, 'This is for our two magnificent flying wings,' and he hands Pieter Rossouw and Stephan Terreblanche each a hot Nando's wing.

Moving on, the manager starts pulling at the chicken's rear. 'And finally, for our fullback, Percy Montgomery ...'

And Percy yells, 'Burger and chips, please!'

SIEK VAN VLIEG

'n Klein outjie sit op die vliegtuig langs ou Os. Dis gure weer, en die vliegtuig ruk en skud laat dit 'n naarheid is. Die kleintjie voel hier kom 'n ding en skiet 'n vet kat reg op ou Os se skoot. Os word wakker en sien die gemors in sy skoot. Die kleintjie kyk vreesbevange op na die grote Os en vra, 'Voel oom Os nou beter?'

SMALL PACKAGES

Ou Ollie dans rond in die stort na die Bokke die All Blacks gewen het: 'Check my, manne. Twee honderd en veertig pond se dinamiet.'

'Ja,' sê Joost, 'en net 'n kwartduim lontjie.'

RUGBY LESSON

Doing his bit for Sarfu's Rugby Development Programme, the coach took his all-white rugby team to a remote part of KwaZulu-Natal. The Minister of Sport came along for the ride.

In a small village tucked away in a distant valley, the coach was amazed to discover a multi-talented athlete who could run, kick, pass and juggle a coconut with the style and prowess of a professional.

'Man, this guy is brilliant,' said the coach, picking up a rugby ball and calling the young man over.

'Now then,' said the coach, 'This thing is BALL. You see BALL? Not ROUND BALL for soccer, EGG BALL for rugby.' He pointed at the goalposts saying: 'That – goal. GOAL! That goal-line. GOAL-LINE! You put BALL over GOAL-LINE, or kick ball over THAT. That is cross-bar. CROSS-BAR!'

The young man listened in silence, pursing his lips and nodding politely. Then he said, in a perfect Oxford English accent: 'Why, thank you very much for the advice, coach. I'm sure it will all come in very handy when I return to Oxford after the holidays. I'm a flyhalf in the First XV.'

The coach's face turned as red as a baboon's arse, and the Minister of Sport glared at him in fury. As the Minister opened his mouth to unleash a stream of invective, the coach butted in: 'I wasn't talking to him, Mr. Minister! I was talking to you.'

OLLIE SE TOLLIE

Joost and Ollie landed up in the same hotel room during a tour of New Zealand. 'Shame, poor Joost,' said Gary, going through the sleeping arrangements. 'He won't close an eye tonight because ou Ollie snores worse than an old bulldog.'

Next morning at breakfast Gary tapped his team-mate on the shoulder: 'So Joost, did ou Ollie's snoring keep you awake last night?'

'Not on your life,' said Joost. 'Just before he put out the light I put my hand on his thigh, kissed him on the cheek and said in a sexy voice: "Lekker slaap, my Ollie Tollie." So he stayed awake all night to watch me.'

LOOSE FORWARD

The Springbok prop was paging through a medical textbook, when an item of pertinent information caught his eye. Apparently, there are more than 200 sexual positions. So he went and asked the team captain where he could apply for one of them.

WHITE LINE FEVER

It's the Monday after the big World Cup celebrations. This oke lands up in court on a charge of public drunkenness. Sergeant Hoekie Bruintjes is in the witness box.

'We found the accused at three o' clock in the morning in the middle of Adderley Street, jou honour, with his pants on his ankles in a squatting position and singing "Hie' kommie Bokke".'

'Surely that doesn't mean he was drunk, officer,' the magistrate remarks.

'Maybe not, jou honour, but then why was he trying to roll up the white line?'

THOR LOSER

Thor, the god of thunder, was chatting to his chommie, Zeus, about the curious ways of the mortals down below.

'Take these Springboks, for instance,' thundered Thor. 'Just because they win a couple of test matches, they think they're invincible. I'd like to go down there and show them what "invincible" really means.'

'Well, why don't you?' asked Zeus. 'They're playing the British Lions this very Saturday.'

Good idea, thinks Thor. On the big day, he dons his Lions' jersey and takes his place on the field at Ellis Park. The ref blows the whistle, and into the game they go. That night, Thor reports back to Zeus.

'What a game!' he says. 'You should have seen me showing those Bokke who's boss. First thing I did, I charged down the line and thundered into Gary Teichman like a …'

'Who's Gary Teichman?' interrupted Zeus.

'You don't know who Gary Teichman is? Don't worry. I don't think he knows, either, after what I did to him today.'

'And what was that?'

'I butted him on the head, bit his ear, and kicked him in the nuts a couple of times,' boasted Thor. 'And then, for good measure, I kicked him in the nuts again. I think he knew it was me, because he kept using my Afrikaans name … "Nou wie de bliksem het my weer gedonner?"'

Thor chuckled loudly to himself as he recalled the look of befuddlement and agony on the Bok captain's face. But Zeus didn't seem amused.

'What's the matter?' asked Thor.

'The matter is that you have abused your power,' said Zeus. 'You should go back to earth right now and apologise to that poor mortal.'

Thor thought about it for a while, and finally agreed that he may have been a little too robust in his methods. So he popped back down to earth, found Gary at home in Durban, and said, 'Greetings. I am Thor.'

To which Gary said: 'YOU'RE Thor? Man, my balls are tho thor I can't even pith!'

ANC

ITCHY ELBOW

Two Springbok rugby players were travelling on a plane. Sitting between them was a prominent ANC politician. For some reason, he kept scratching his elbow, a habit that soon began irritating the two burly Bokke.

When the politician left his seat to go to the loo, the one rugby player turned to the other and said, 'What is it with this oke? I wish he'd stop scratching his elbow.'

'Ja,' said the other guy, 'I'm sure it's piles.'

'Piles? How can it be piles?'

'You know what these ANC okes are like,' explained his team-mate. 'They never can tell their arse from their elbow.'

LEKKER EET

Waaraan is Nelson Mandela se goeie gesondheid op 80 toe te skryf?

'n Lewenslange dieet van vitamines A en C.

KOPSEER

Hierdie ANC kandidaat is besig om stemme te werf vir sy party in Boksburg toe daar 'n ou teen 'n hengse spoed op 'n fiets verbykom. Hy vang 'n draai, maar misgis hom met die skerpte daarvan, tref die randsteen en tref die aarde met 'n moewiese slag.

Die ANC kandidaat is baie besorg, hardloop nader, en vra, 'Het jy seergekry? Moet ek jou hospitaal toe neem?'

Die ou sê, 'Nee, dis okei, dankie.' Die ANC kandidaat besluit om die geleentheid aan te gryp. 'Luister ou pêl,' sê hy, 'ek is die nuwe ANC kandidaat hier in Boksburg. Jy sal dit nie dalk oorweeg om vir my te stem nie?'

Die ander ou sê, 'Dis gaaf van jou. Maar ek het op my gat geval, nie op my kop nie.'

PIKSWART

Die SAL-vlieënier sit een aand lank en staar deur die voorruit van die Boeing.

'Wat staar jy so na buite?' wil sy mede-vlieënier weet.

'Ek sien die ANC', se die Kaptein.

'Die ANC?'

'Ja. Dis nag.'

ANIMAL KINGDOM

DUCK DOWN

These two ducks go to Sun City for their honeymoon. They're in their hotel room, marvelling at the softness of the duck-down duvet, when the lady duck whispers, 'Did you remember to bring the condoms?'

'Whoops,' says the male duck. Thinking quickly, he calls room service and asks them to deliver a pack of condoms. Minutes later, there's a knock at the door.

'Would you like me to put these on your bill?' asks the room service guy.

'What do you think I look like?' yells the duck, 'some kind of pervert?'

AIRLINE FOOD

Two elderly vultures, having had enough of life in the African jungle, decide to emigrate to Australia. At the

South African Airways check-in counter, the ground hostess notices that they're carrying two dead honey-badgers.

'Do you wish to check the badgers through as baggage?' asks the ground hostess.

'No thanks,' say the vultures. 'They're carrion.'

POPCORN

Die ou wil graag hê sy mak eend moet *The Lion King* sien. So stap hy een aand by die flieks in, eend onder die arm. Die bestuurder van die teater sê, 'Sorry meneer, ons laat ongelukkig nie mak eende toe nie.'

Die ou is vasbeslote, stap die gents binne en prop die eend hier voor by sy broek in.

Hy sit nog so lekker en fliek kyk toe die eend half benoud raak, en hy wikkel sy kop hier deur die ou se gulp uit vir so bietjie vars lug. Die dame langsaan ruk omtrent haar nek af van skok, pomp haar man in die ribbes en sê, 'Die ou langs my se dinges steek uit.'

Haar man is verdiep in die fliek en sê, 'Ag, ignoreer dit.'

'Ignoreer dit?' sê die vrou. 'Hy's besig om my blerrie popcorn op te vreet!'

BEAR NECESSITIES

It's a sunny morning in the Big Forest. The Bear family is just waking up. Baby Bear goes downstairs and sits in his small chair at the table. He looks into his small bowl. It's empty. 'Who's been eating my porridge?!' he squeaks.

Daddy Bear arrives at the table and sits in his big chair. He looks into his big bowl. It's empty. 'Who's been eating my porridge?!' he roars.

Mummy Bear puts her head through the serving hatch from the kitchen and screams, 'For goodness sake, how many times do we have to go through this? I haven't made the damn porridge yet!!'

LION KING

A lion wakes up in the Kruger Park one morning, feeling pretty damn pleased with himself. And why not? After all, he's the King of the Jungle. He decides to make sure that the other animals haven't forgotten.

He sneaks up to a vervet monkey and roars: 'Who's the King of the Jungle?' The monkey drops his nuts in fright. (Turns out he'd been gathering nuts to feed his kids.) 'Y-y-y-you are, oh Great and Noble Beast,' stammers the petrified primate.

The lion smirks to himself and roars off. He pounces on a lone zebra.

'Who is the King of the Jungle?' he asks. The zebra turns completely white with fright. 'You are, oh Mighty Monarch of the Bushveld,' trembles the quaking equine. The lion's on a roll. He sees an elephant snacking on a baobab tree.

'Hey!' shouts the lion, 'who is the King of the Jungle?'

The elephant turns around, drops the tree, wraps his trunk around the lion, smacks him against a rock, bounces him up and down, and sends him flying several metres into the air.

The lion picks himself up, dusts himself off, and snarls from a safe distance: 'Man, just because you don't know the answer, doesn't mean you have to get so pissed off.'

SKANDAAL

Tierwyfie staan vorentoe gebuk by die gat en water suip, en bobbejaan sien sy kans. Hy kom stilletjies van agter af gryp tierwyfie waar sy nie deur bobbejaan se kind gegryp wil wees nie. Sy brul soos sy gil, spring orent, gryp agter vas, en sien hoe bobbejaanmannetjie teen 270 k.p.u. om 'n bos verdwyn. Sy raak mal van woede, en sit bobbejaan agterna teen 'n stink spoed.

Die plaashuis lê voor, sy vat 'n woeste draai om die hoek by die kombuis, en sien 'n bebrilde man met bene gevou op die stoep koerant sit en lees. Dis bobbejaan.

Hy't geweet hy sou nooit voor tierwyfie kon wegkom nie, toe gryp hy die boer se bril en sy koerant. Tierwyfie kyk hom, en kyyyyk hom. Bobbejaan worry vreeslik en sê na 'n lang stilte, 'Juffrou tier, soek jy dalk na 'n bobbejaan wat jou onsedelik betas het?'

Tierwyfie se oë word groot. 'Moenie vir my sê dis klaar in die koerant nie!'

SHIP OF THE DESERT

The baby camel has reached that stage that every baby camel goes through. The 'asking-a-blerrie-lot-of-irritating-questions' stage.

'Mom,' he begins, 'why do I have such long eyelashes?'

'Because they shield your eyes from the dust of the desert,' says Mom.

'And why do I have such big feet?' asks the baby camel, looking down at his big feet.

'So that you won't sink down in the desert sand.'

'And why do I have this big hump on my back?'

'That's so you can store a large quantity of water and survive for months in the blazing desert,' says mum.

'Well, Mommy,' says the baby camel, 'then what the bliksem am I doing in the zoo?'

GOLDFISH

Two goldfish are in a tank.

The one says to the other, 'Do you know how to drive this thing?'

ADD IT UP

The waters had subsided. The Ark was on top of the mountain. The animals had made their way to dry land. Noah was wandering around, checking his inventory, when he came across a pair of snakes who were basking in the mellow morning sunshine.

'You're still here?' said Noah.

'We're still here,' said the snakes.

'You didn't hear the voice of the Lord, saying all the animals must go forth and multiply?'

'We heard,' said the snakes. 'But we can't.'

'You can't? What do you mean you can't?'

'We can't go forth and multiply.'

'Why not?' thundered Noah.

'Because we're ADDERS,' said the snakes.

PROMISES, PROMISES

The dung beetle was in his element, as the farmer had just bought ten new cows. He decided to visit his little dung-beetle chommie next door and tell him the good news.

'Man, there are so many cows now, I just laze around the farm the whole day and grab a handful of dung whenever I want to. It's a dung-beetle's dream. And how are things with you?' he asked his friend.

'Terrible, absolutely terrible,' said the other beetle. 'My farmer has just sold all his cows and bought a tractor. It goes around the farm the whole day long saying POEF-POEF-POEF. I can't live on promises, you know!'

ANIMALS IN BARS

SLOW DRINKER

The bartender is locking up for the night, when he hears the doorbell ring. He opens the door, but he can't see anyone there. Then he hears a voice at his feet. He looks down to see a snail sitting on the doorstep.

'What do you want?' asks the bartender. 'I'd like a drink,' says the snail.

'Sorry, we're closed,' says the bartender, 'and anyway, we don't serve snails.'

The snail pleads with the barman to change his mind. 'Please,' he says, 'just one drink! Is it too much trouble to serve me with just one drink? That's all I'm asking! Just one little drink!'

The bartender has had enough. He isn't going to stand around all night arguing with a snail.

He boots the snail across the carpark, and he slams the door. Exactly one year later, the bartender is locking up for the night, when he hears the doorbell ring. He opens the door. It's the snail.

'Can I help you?' asks the bartender.

And the snail says, 'What did you do that for, hey?'

WHITE HORSE

This white horse goes into a bar to order a dop. The barman says, 'That's incredible! Do you know we actually have a drink named after you?'

And the white horse says, 'Really? You have a drink named Eric?'

PUT IT ON MY BILL

A duck goes into a bar and asks the bartender, 'Got any fish?'

The bartender says, 'No. This is a bar and we don't sell fish.'

So the duck leaves.

Next day, the duck goes back to the bar and asks, 'Got any fish?'

The bartender says, 'I told you yesterday. This is a bar and we don't sell fish.'

The following day, the duck returns and asks, 'Got any fish?'

The bartender loses it. He grabs the duck by the throat, and screams, 'I TOLD YOU ONCE, I TOLD YOU TWICE. THIS IS A BAR. WE DON'T SELL FISH! IF YOU ASK JUST ONE MORE TIME, I'M GONNA NAIL YOUR *@#& WEBBED

FEET TO THE FLOOR, YOU STUPID DUCK!'

The next day, the duck goes back to the bar and asks, 'Got any nails?'

The bartender sighs and says, 'No, we don't have any nails.'

The duck says, 'Good. Got any fish?'

GETTING PLASTERED

This duck waddles into a bar, like ducks tend to do when they're thirsty. 'Gimme a beer,' says the duck.

The barman looks down at him in amazement. 'You're a duck!' he says.

'So? You don't serve ducks?'

'Of course we do,' says the barman. 'It's just that we don't get many ... um, ducks in here. Especially ducks that can talk.'

'So I'm a duck and I can talk,' says the duck. 'Big deal. Gimme a beer.'

The barman pulls a frothy, slides it across the counter, and says, 'What are you doing in town, if you don't mind me asking?'

'I'm working at that building site across the road,' says the duck. 'I'm on site for a couple of weeks, so you'll see me in here for an ale every lunchtime.'

'Great,' says the barman.

And the duck waddles back to work.

A couple of days later, the circus pulls into town. The barman calls the circus-owner.

'Have I got a great new act for your show,' he says.

Next day, the duck waddles in for his usual pint.

'You know,' says the barman, 'you really should think about getting into the circus.'

'Really?'

'Yes. You could make a lot of money. I can fix it up for you easily.'

'You could?'

'Sure.'

The duck takes a long, slow sip of ale. 'Let me get this straight,' he says. 'You're talking about a circus – that's one of those places with a big tent made out of canvas, right?'

'Right.'

'And a pole in the middle?'

'Yep,' says the barman. 'If you're interested, I could get you a job there as soon as tomorrow. I've already spoken to the circus-owner, and he's hugely keen.'

'Uh-huh,' says the duck, looking a little puzzled. 'Just tell me one thing. Why the heck would this guy want to hire a plasterer?'

MAMBA OF THE BAR

A snake walks into a bar and … well, okay, a snake slithers into a bar and orders a double Scotch on the rocks.

The bartender says, 'Sorry, I'm afraid I can't serve you.'

The snake says, 'Why the heck not?'

And the barman says, 'Because you can't hold your liquor.'

ARMY

BACK TO THE FRONT

The Major-General pays a visit to the troops in the field hospital. He goes up to one private and says, 'What's your problem, soldier?'

'Chronic syphilis, sir.'

'What treatment are you getting?'

'Five minutes with the wire brush each day.'

'What's your ambition?'

'To get back to the front, sir.'

'Good man,' says the Major-General.

He goes to the next bed.

'What's your problem, soldier?'

'Chronic piles, sir.'

'What treatment are you getting?'

'Five minutes with the wire brush each day.'

'What's your ambition?'

'To get back to the front, sir.'

'Good man,' says the Major-General.

He goes to the next bed. 'What's your problem, soldier?'

'Chronic gum disease, sir.'

'What treatment are you getting?'

'Five minutes with the wire brush each day.'

'What's your ambition?'

'To get the wire brush before the other two, sir!'

PASS UIT

Die ou moet army toe gaan terwyl sy vrou so sewe maande verwagtend is.

'Wanneer ons kind gebore is,' sê hy, 'moet my in hemelsnaam tog nie bel nie. Al ons telefoonoproepe word vir veiligheidsdoeleindes gemonitor, en as die manne hoor ek is pa, moet ek vir almal in die basis 'n dop koop, en daarvoor het ek tog nie die geld nie. Stuur net 'n telegram met my oorle' oupa se van daarop – Van Tonder. Dan weet ek jy's oukei en die baby is oukei.'

'Oukei,' sê sy.

So twee maande later kom die telegram van sy vrou toe by die basis aan. Die troep pass uit toe hy lees: 'VAN TONDER VAN TONDER VAN TONDER. TWEE MET GEWERE EN EEN DAARSONDER.'

BATTLE-DRESS

'You should make an appearance at the frontline, Mein Führer,' said Hitler's 2iC towards the end of World War 2. 'It will mean a lot to the morale of our soldiers.'

'Bring me mein tunic,' said Hitler.

The valet clicked his heels together, shouted 'Heil!', and returned with a bright red tunic.

'I brought the red one, Mein Führer, because Napoleon used to wear red during battle so that nobody would see when he was bleeding.'

'In that case,' said Hitler, 'bring me mein brown trousers.'

AUSSIES

HEY BUOY

Mike is lying on a beach in Perth. He's looking out at the ocean, puzzlement written all over his face. 'What are those black things there deep in the water?' he asks an Aussie passer-by.

The Aussie follows his gaze. 'Those? They're called buoys. We use them to hold up the shark nets.'

'Hell,' retorts Mike. 'You'd never get away with that in South Africa.'

SHARE AND SHARE ALIKE

This Aussie is walking down a country road in New Zealand, when he happens to glance over the fence and see a farmer having his way with a sheep.

The Aussie is quite taken aback by this, so he climbs the fence and walks over to the farmer. He taps him on the shoulder and says, 'You know mate, back home, we shear those!'

The New Zealander looks frantically around and says, 'I'm not bloody sharing this with no one!'

I LUV SHEILA

How can you tell an Aussie intellectual apart from all the other Aussies?

He's the one with fewer spelling mistakes on his tattoos.

BATHTIME

Did you hear about the Aussie who disposed of his wife in an acid bath?

Poor bloke. He lost his left arm trying to pull out the plug.

BIG FIVE

On a recent visit to the land of the Amabokkebokke, the Wallabies were treated to a double-decker-bus tour of the Kruger National Park.

Those down below whooped with joy whenever they saw one of the Big Five, and burst into tears whenever they saw a springbok. But there wasn't a sound coming from those sitting upstairs. The coach got worried and went upstairs to check things out. He found the Aussies gripping their seats with white knuckles.

'It's all right for you guys sitting down below,' said the Wallaby front-row, 'you've got a driver!'

DON'T DRINK THE WATER

Later in the day, the same bus stopped at the Sabie River, and a few Wallabies wandered off and went for a swim. They were back in no time, shouting their heads off after having confronted a hippo in the river.

'Nothing to worry about,' said the tour guide. 'The hippo is more frightened of you than you are of him.'

'In that case,' said the little scrumhalf, 'the water in that river is not fit to drink.'

SHEEP AT THE PRICE

That night the Aussies were taken on a tour of Hillbrow. They were sitting in a pub when a boeremeisie of the night approached them.

'Do you speak English?' asked one of the Aussies.

'Only a little,' said the boeremeisie.

'How much?' asked the Aussie.
'R200,' said the meisie.

KNITWITS

After much experimentation and research, Australian farmers have discovered a brand-new use for sheep.
Wool!

AUSSIE KWALIFIKASIE

Van besluit hy's Gautvol vir Gauteng en emigreer Australië toe. Hy kom by die immigrasiekantoor en moet 'n klomp vrae beantwoord.

'Het jy 'n kriminele rekord?' vra die immigrasiebeampte.

'Wat?!' vra Van verbaas. 'Moenie vir my sê dis nog steeds 'n vereiste om Australië te mag binnekom nie.'

BULL BY THE HORNS

Shortly after oom PW had met with Nelson for the first time back in '86, oom Frik Ras, a cattle farmer from Upington, started worrying about the prospect of an ANC takeover. Just in case, he decided to take his family to Australia and look around for a cattle farm.

Oom Frik spent weeks looking for his ideal farm, and finally found one that seemed to fit the bill, about 80 miles north of Sydney. Next day, while oom Frik was being shown around the farm by the estate agent, his nine-year-old daughter, Elsie, wandered off into the veld.

Suddenly a huge bull snorted behind Elsie, who was wearing a bright red dress. Elsie was terrified, and started running like she'd never run before, shrieking her head off. Oom Frik wasted no time. He tore down that farm road at 140 kays an hour, bailed over a two-metre fence without even touching it, and charged towards the bull.

Right then, a journalist from the *Sydney Morning Herald* happened to be passing by. He immediately stopped his car, grabbed his camera and began clicking away.

What he then witnessed was the most amazing feat of courage he had seen in his entire journalistic career. Oom Frik caught up with the bull, grabbed the charging creature by its tail, pulled himself onto its back, grabbed hold of its horns, and with the power of a Hercules, twisted the bull's neck around.

The bull died instantly, crashing to the ground centimetres short of the hysterical Elsie. The journalist was amazed. He rushed over to oom Frik, grabbed his hand and shook it wildly saying, 'What a hero you are, mate! I've never seen anything more courageous in my entire life! You're going to be in every major newspaper in Australia!'

He paused for a while, taking a closer look at this rugged, unshaven man from the Kalahari. 'You're not Australian, are you mate?'

'No', said the proud yet humble oom Frik, 'I'm a Souf African.'

The next morning the story was on the front page of every major Australian newspaper: 'SOUTH AFRICAN BASTARD KILLS LITTLE GIRL'S PET'.

LONG HAUL

The Aussie truck-driver, desperate to earn a little extra boozing money, pops into the employment agency early one morning.

'No worries, mate,' says the guy behind the counter. 'Got an urgent job, just come in. Long-distance delivery. Right up your alley.'

The Aussie brushes a fly from his unshaven face. 'What's the load, mate?'

'Bowling-balls.'

'Bowling-balls!'

'Said it was right up your alley, didn't I?'

The truck-driver doesn't laugh. He grabs the papers, signs on the line, and heads off to fill his truck with bowling-balls. It's a long haul – all the way from Adelaide in the southwest to the port of Darwin in the northeast.

Somewhere beyond the middle of nowhere, the truck-driver sees two Aborigines standing at the roadside. They've got a broken-down motorbike between them. The truck-driver brings his mammoth vehicle to a slow, grinding halt.

'Wanna lift?' he asks. The Aborigines are only too happy to accept. Because it's against regulations to pick up hitch-hikers, the truck-driver tells the guys they're going to have to hop in the back, with the bowling-balls. No worries, mate.

A couple of hundred kilometres down the road, the truck-driver pulls into a transport café. Regulations again: a policeman wants to inspect the load.

'Where are you heading, mate?' asks the cop.

'Darwin,' answers the driver.

The cop goes around to the back of the truck, opens the doors, and shuts them with a look of horror on his face. He rushes around to the driver's cab.

'Listen, mate,' he tells the truck-driver, 'you'd better bloody get moving to Darwin, and I mean right away!'

'How come?'

'Because two of your bloody eggs have hatched, and one of them's already stolen a bike!'

ANIMAL FARM

The Bokke are in Perth for the Tri-Nations. Looking for something a little more exciting to do than stare at the traffic from the balcony of his hotel, Joost rents a car and goes for a drive in the Aussie countryside.

Towards dusk, the car has a blow-out. Because this is an Aussie rental car, there's no spare wheel, leaving Joost with no option but to trek up to the farmhouse on the hill. It's the home of Big Merv, a fanatical Wallabies supporter.

He takes one look at Joost and says: 'I know who you are, mate. You're one of them Bokke. You're welcome to spend the night … in the barn with the other animals.' And then he slams the door in Joost's face.

Joost shrugs his shoulders, thanks Big Merv for his hospitality, and goes off to sleep in the barn. Next morning, Joost is up with the chickens. And the cows, and the sheep, and the pigs. He knocks on Big Merv's door. Merv looks like he's been up drinking all night.

'You won't believe this, Merv,' says Joost, 'but your animals can talk!'

'Pull the other one, mate,' says Merv, clutching his head in agony.

'No, I'm serious!' says Joost. 'Your cow Sissy ran out of milk two weeks ago and hasn't produced any milk since, right?'

'How the hell do you know that?' says Merv.

'Sissy told me so herself, I swear. And listen to this: your prize pig, Shane, was nearly run over by your mother-in-law last Wednesday, right?'

Merve is amazed. 'There's no other way you could have known these things,' he says. 'What are you, some kind of a ...'

'Oh, and by the way, your sheep Mitzi ...'

Merv sobers up immediately. 'Don't you believe a word that Mitzi tells you,' he says, 'she's a damn liar!'

AWB

RAINBOW NATION

Two AWB members, conspicuously clad in khaki, board an SAA plane from Johannesburg to Port Elizabeth. One takes the window seat, the other sits in the middle.

Just as the plane is about to take off, a harassed-looking black executive squeezes his way past the air hostess and plonks himself down on the aisle seat. He kicks off his shoes, wiggles his toes, and prepares to settle in. The plane takes to the air.

'Man, I'm thirsty,' says the AWB guy next to the window. 'I think I'm going to get up and fetch myself a Coke.'

The black guy hears this. 'Don't worry,' he says. 'Let me get it for you.'

While he is gone, the AWB guy picks up the black guy's shoe and spits into it. The black guy returns with the Coke. The other AWB guy says: 'That looks good. I'm going to get up and fetch myself one too.'

The black guy says, 'No problem,' and he goes off to fetch another Coke. While he is gone, the AWB guy picks up the other shoe and spits in it. The black guy returns with the Coke.

A couple of hours later, the plane is about to touch down. The black guy slides his feet into his shoes. Immediately, he can tell what's been happening.

He turns to the AWB guys. 'How much longer?' he asks. 'How much longer must this go on? This hatred between our peoples … this animosity … this spitting in shoes and pissing in Cokes?'

BUNGEEEEE!

Some manne of ET have hatched
A plan that can hardly be matched
Their members all want to
start teaching Umkhonto
To bungee-jump … no strings attached!

CRY-BABY

ET was having a dop with his 2iC in the Ventersdorp bar. The 2iC said, 'This blerrie New South Africa is causing me sleepless night, I don't close a damn eye.'

'No, I sleep like a baby,' said ET.

'Really?'

'Ja, I wake up every three hours crying after I've crapped my pants.'

ET – THE SEQUEL

Remember the whole ET and Jani saga?

It could have been a movie starring ET, the Extra Terra Testicle who relied on his AWBasic Instinct and went Dirty Dancing before Sleeping with the Enemy in a Room with a View when he took out his Dick Tracey which was no Lethal Weapon but barely a Naked Gun $2\frac{1}{2}$ inches in Fried Green Underpants.

BASEBALL BAT

Hierdie ou ry af in die hoofstraat van Ventersdorp en sien hoe 'n AWB vir Vusi ongenadiglik oor die kop takel met 'n knuppel. Hy slaan onmiddellik remme aan, hardloop na sy 'boot', haal 'n baseball bat uit en stap haastig nader.

Toe takel hulle eers vir Vusi.

WAVE GOODBYE

Overlooking the sea from his hotel room in Durbs, ET turned to his sidekick and said, 'Sien jy daai klomp swartes in die see?'

'Ja,' said his sidekick. 'Wat van hulle?'

'Ek gee hulle nog tien minute dan't hulle al die branders gebreek,' said ET.

BACHELORS

LAY-BYE

This smooth young Romeo walks into the jewellery store one Saturday morning. Hanging onto his arm, not to mention his every word, is the most beautiful blonde you've ever seen.

'Choose any ring you want, my sweetheart,' whispers Romeo. She chooses the ring she wants. Without blinking an eyelid, Romeo whips out his chequebook and writes out a cheque for R50 000. The jeweller's eyes light up like diamonds.

'Why, thank you, sir,' he says. 'I hope you will understand that I will have to keep the ring in the safe until the cheque is cleared on Monday morning.' Romeo understands.

First thing Tuesday morning, he's back in the shop. 'Oh, it's you, sir,' says the jeweller, this time sounding not so friendly. 'I'm terribly sorry to tell you that your cheque bounced.'

'No problem,' shrugs Romeo. 'I just popped by to thank you for the best weekend I've ever had.'

TOUGH CALL

Luigi, a ladies' man all his life, decides the time has come to settle down. Trouble is, he can't figure out which of his three devoted girlfriends he should marry.

After thinking long and hard about it, he decides to solve his dilemma in the old-fashioned way. With money. He'll give each of the ladies a sum of R20 000, to spend at their own discretion. Then he'll sit back and see what happens.

The first girlfriend, a blonde, goes out and gets a total makeover with her windfall. New clothes, new hairdo, manicure, pedicure, the works. She tells Luigi, 'I spent the money so I could look pretty for you because I love you so much.'

The second girlfriend, a brunette, goes on a wild shopping spree. New golf clubs, new television set, new stereo, the works. She tells Luigi, 'I bought these gifts for you with the money because I love you so much.'

The third girlfriend, a redhead, takes the R20 000 and invests it on the stock market. With careful planning and sound advice, she doubles her investment, returns the original sum to Luigi, and says, 'I am investing the rest of the money for our future because I love you so much.'

Luigi spends many agonising hours mulling over his decision. Finally, having weighed up all the permutations and possibilities, he goes out and marries the one with the biggest boobs.

GIVING HER THE EYE

A man who lived in a block of apartments thought it was raining. He put his head out the window to check. As he did so, a glass eye fell into his hand.

He looked up to see where it came from, and he saw a beautiful young woman looking down.

'Is this yours?' he asked.

'Yes,' she said. 'Would you mind bringing it up?'

The man agreed. The woman thanked him profusely, and invited him to stay for a drink. So he stayed for a drink. Then he stayed for dinner. Then, as he was about to leave, the woman said, 'I've had a wonderful evening. Would you like to stay the night?'

The man hesitated for half-a-second. 'Do you act like this with every man you meet?' he asked.

'No,' she replied. 'Only those who catch my eye.'

BABE MAGNET

Van is walking along the beach at Clifton, trying hard to pretend that he's not checking out the chicks. But the more he checks them out, the more concerned he gets that they're not checking him out. He goes to see his supersmooth pal, Luigi the lifeguard.

'Luigi,' he says, 'I just don't know what to do. How can I make those women on the beach take an interest in me?'

Luigi looks at Van. 'First thing you must do,' he says, 'is get rid of those stupid bathing-trunks.'

'What?' gasps Van. 'You want me to walk along the beach without anything on?'

'Don't be crazy,' says Luigi. 'I mean you must get yourself one of those itsy-bitsy little Speedo swimming-costumes. Then you walk up and down the beach. You'll see. Those babes will notice you.'

So Van gets himself the Speedo. He parades up and down Clifton. Not a single babe casts a single glance in his direction. He goes to see Luigi again. Luigi looks at him.

'Okay, I tell you what,' he says. 'You go to the greengrocer. You buy a big cucumber. You put it in your Speedo. Those girls will go crazy, or my name isn't Luigi.'

Van follows Luigi's advice. He returns a little later, shaking his head.

'It's just not working!' he says. Luigi looks at him.

'Okay,' he says. 'I've got one more suggestion. Why don't you try moving the cucumber to the front of your swimming-costume?'

NET GOEIE VRIENDE

Koos en Sannie het baie lank vas uitgegaan, so omtrent 18 jaar lank. Sannie het al die jare lank gehoop Koos gaan haar vra om te trou, maar dit het nooit gebeur nie.

Eendag sit die tweetjies op 'n Sondagmiddag buite Bloemfontein en kyk hoe die Gauteng karre die stad binnekom, toe Sannie al haar moed bymekaar skraap en sê, 'Koos, moet ek en jy nie maar daaraan dink om te trou nie.'

Daar was 'n lang stilte, toe sê Koos, 'Sannie, wie sal nou in ons twee belangstel?'

BAAS LOUIS

FERTILISER KING

Louis Luyt is on his way to a charity rugby match at Vredefort stadium, when he spots these two little boys constructing a building out of cow's dung. Louis stops, looks on with fascination, and asks: 'What's this thing you laaities are building?'

'We're building Ellis Park,' says the first kid.

'That's very interesting,' says Louis. 'But what about me?'

And the second kid says, 'Sorry, meneer, but we don't have enough to build you.'

BLAME IT ON THE IRISH

Louis Luyt and Muleleki George were having a heavy argument, as usual, during a meeting of the SARB.

'Okay, Muleleki, have it your way and go and tell the IRB you want to run South African rugby,' thundered Baas Louis at one point.

Muleleki immediately handed in his resignation.

'Why did Muleleki withdraw so suddenly?' asked an astonished Baas Louis.

'Because he thought the IRB was the B-side of the IRA,' explained an aide.

BIG BOSS

Louis goes to see his psychiatrist. 'What's up?' asks the doc, as Louis makes himself comfortable on a couple of couches.

'Ag, so many things,' says Louis. 'I just don't know where to start.'

'Well, why don't you start at the beginning,' suggests the shrink.

'Okay. In the beginning, I made heaven and earth …'

NO EXCUSES

A pollster is taking opinions outside the Union Buildings in Pretoria. He approaches four men waiting to cross the road. One is a Saudi, one is a Russian, one is a North Korean, and the other is Louis Luyt.

'Excuse me,' says the pollster, 'I would like your opinion on the current meat shortage.'

The Saudi replies, 'Excuse me, but what is a shortage?'

The Russian says, 'Excuse me, but what is meat?'

The North Korean answers, 'Excuse me, but what is an opinion?'

And Louis Luyt says, 'Excuse me, but what is "excuse me"?'

JUST AN IDEA

'Louis,' said Madiba, 'have you ever thought of doing something great for your country?'

'Like what?' asked Louis.

'Like emigrating,' suggested Madiba.

THE LAST STRAW

Louis gets stopped by a traffic cop. The cop can smell Louis has had a dop or two. 'Blow into this bag,' says the cop, producing his breathalyser.

'Not on your life,' says Louis. 'I suffer from emphysema, and one blow into that bag can cause my death.'

'No problem', says the cop, whipping an injection needle from his pocket. 'Then I'll sommer have to draw some blood.'

'Forget it!' says Louis. 'I'm a haemophiliac. One prick with that needle and I'll bleed myself to death.'

'Okay,' says the cop. He hands Louis a little bottle. 'Go and stand behind that tree and pee into this bottle.'

It's the last straw. Louis jumps out of his car, kicks the cop in the nuts and whacks him on the head with a fax machine. As he gets back into his car Louis says, 'Nobody, but nobody takes the piss out of Louis Luyt!'

LUYT LAGER

When Louis was still the King of Cow Dung he produced a beer called Luyt Lager. 'I won't touch that stuff,' said Mike, when Kallie offered him a can.

'Why not?' said Kallie, before knocking back a slurp.

'As hy akkies in sakke kan sit,' said Mike, 'kan hy pie-pie in blikke ôk sit.'

LOVE THY NEIGHBOUR

Vusi, a wealthy young stockbroker, bought a stand in a rich neighbourhood close to the Jo'burg Zoo. He checked out his neighbour Louis Luyt's beautiful abode, and decided his house should look exactly the same. And so he went to work on the mansion of his dreams.

One year later, Vusi was standing in his garden admiring his beautiful mansion, when Louis walked up to him.

'It's beautiful, Vusi,' he said. 'Congratulations.'

'Thanks Louis,' said Vusi. 'But you know what I really like about my house?

'What?' asked Louis.

'It's worth much more than yours.'

Louis frowned. 'What do you mean? As far as I can see our two houses are exactly the same.'

'That's true,' said Vusi, 'but when a prospective buyer asks me about my neighbours, I'll tell them I live next to the famous Luyts. When they ask you about your neighbours, you'll have to say you live next to Vusi.'

BAFANA BAFANA

OFF-SIDES

A beautiful woman called in a repairman to fix her television set. As it turned out, that wasn't the only thing he fixed. Just as he finished, the woman heard her husband's key in the lock.

'Hurry,' she said to the repairman, 'you'll have to hide! My husband is insanely jealous.'

There was no time to run out the back door, so the repairman hid inside the TV console. The husband came in and plopped down in his favourite chair to watch some football.

Inside the TV set, the repairman was all squashed up and getting hotter and hotter. Finally, he could stand it no longer.

He climbed out, marched across the room and out the front door. The husband looked at the TV set, looked at his wife, looked back at the set again and said, 'Bliksem. Now why the heck did the ref send that oke off the field?'

BAFANA BANANA

Die ou moes die aand werk toe Bafana Bafana in die eerste Wêreldbekerwedstryd teen Frankryk speel. Hy vermy die TV by die werk soos pes, sit pluisies in sy ore sodat hy nie kan hoor wat die score was nie, want sy vrou neem vir hom die game op en hy wil dit later die aand rustig voor die TV sit en kyk.

Hy kom by die huis, baie opgewonde, en sy vrou staan eenkant en stryk. Sy sê, 'Het jy gehoor wat Bafana Bafana ...'

Hy skree, 'Sharrup! Ek wil nie die score weet nie, ek wil self kyk.'

Sy sê, 'Oukei, ek sal jou niks sê nie.'

'Mooi,' sê hy, knak sy eerste Kasteel en trek die peanuts nader.

Net toe die game begin sê sy, 'Wat ek jou wel kan sê is jy gaan boggerôl goals sien nie.'

HOEZET MY BRA

What's the female version of Bafana Bafana?
Brafana Brafana

LADUUUUUUMA!

Wat's regtig fout met Bafana Bafana?
Hulle het nie 'n doel in die lewe nie.

IT'S A TOSS-UP

The Big Game was about to get underway in front of a packed FNB Stadium. Vusi, the ref, asked Fish for a 50c piece to toss for ends. 'Okay,' said Fish, holding out his hand, 'but only if you give me your watch for security.'

OUT OF SEASON

'Fred', said the ardent Bafana Bafana supporter's wife, 'I read in the newspaper that a man in Germiston swapped his wife for a season ticket to all of Bafana's games. Would you do a thing like that?'

'Hell no,' growled Fred, 'the season's half over.'

BALLS-UP

Vusi's goal in life was to become a sports announcer on the top-rated TV show, Mabaleng. He put in his application, went for an interview, and was overjoyed to receive an answer in the affirmative. On the Big Day, Vusi took his place in the studio, adjusted his tie, and nervously awaited the go-ahead from the floor manager.

'Hello, and welcome to Mabaleng,' said Vusi with a big smile. 'Today we'll be crossing live to one of the biggest sporting events of the year ... the Facup at Wembley Stadium.'

At the commercial break, the producer approached Vusi, patted him on the back, and said, 'You're doing great, Vuz. Just great. But please try and remember ... it's the F.A. Cup. Okay? The F.A. Cup.

HOME TEAM

Two ardent Bafana Bafana manne were talking about the coming Saturday's match against Nigeria.

'I'd love to go,' said the one oke, 'but my wife just won't let me.'

'Listen,' said his mate, 'you must show your wife who's boss around the house, man! Next Saturday afternoon you just take your hat, say "Goodbye" and you walk out the door. If she gives you any lip, you just pull her over your lap, lift her dress and spank her on her arse a few times. She'll never give you problems again.'

The following Monday his chommie said, 'What happened? Why weren't you at the game?'

'No man,' replied the chommie, 'I did exactly what you said. I took my hat, I said goodbye, she gave me lip. So I pulled her over my lap and lifted her dress. And then I thought, "Ag, Bafana's going to win anyway."'

BICYCLES

LIGHT SENTENCE

Koos from Kensington and Frik from Brits had just landed up in choekie in the bad old RSA. Sitting in their whites-only prison cell, Koos asked Frik, 'So why are you here, China?'

'Armed robbery,' said Frik.

'What did you get?'

'Ten months,' shrugged Frik. 'The judge said it would have been 15 if I hadn't been armed with a water-pistol. And you?'

'Ag, I'm in for rape,' said Koos.

'What did you get?'

'One year. Judge said it would have been two if the chick had been white.'

At this point Vusi from Tembisa was brought into the cell opposite the two. The door clanged shut, and Koos shouted across the great divide: 'Hei boy, how long you in for?'

'Six years,' said Vusi.

'Bliksem! How many people did you kill?'

'I didn't kill anybody,' said Vusi. 'I rode my bicycle without a light.'

'Jislaaik!' exclaimed Frik. 'And for that, you got six whole years?'

'Ag, it could have been worse,' replied Vusi. 'Judge said it would have been seven years if it had been during the night.'

DIS HOM!

Die dominee van Tweefontein preek die oggend oor die Tien Gebooie laat die miesies en die biesies bewe. Hy sê op 'n kol 'Jy mag nie steel nie', en skielik spring die dorp se posbode uit die gemeente op en skree, 'Dis hom!' Die dominee raak stil, frons, maar dreun dan weer voort: 'Jy mag nie jou naaste se vrou begeer nie.'

Weer spring dieselfde kêrel op en skree, 'Dis hom!' Die dominee trek op daai stadium maar by 'In die vierde plek,' maar skip toe sommer na 'In die laaste plek...'

Na die diens stap hy na die posbode en hy vra, 'Broer, vir wat spring jy toe nou so op en skree toe ek oor steel praat?'

'Nee, Dominee,' sê die posbode, 'ek het maar net gedink aan my bicycle wat gesteel is.'

'En toe ek praat oor jou naaste se vrou begeer, hoekom spring jy toe weer op?'

'Toe onthou ek waar ek my bicycle vergeet het, Dominee.'

BLONDES

HAPPY SNAP

These two Scandinavian blondes are having their picture taken for a sizzling hot fashion spread. The photographer, a particularly meticulous type, seems to be taking ages behind the lens.

'Vhy he ees taking zo lo-o-o-o-ong?' asks Helga.

'I sink he has got to fokus,' says Olga.

'No!' insists Helga. 'You go tell him to take picture first, and maybe fokus after.'

FAMILY AFFAIR

The blonde goes to see her lawyer. 'I want to divorce my husband,' she says.

'On what grounds?'

'Infidelity. I don't think he's the father of my child.'

BLONDE JOKES

Why can't you tell a knock-knock joke to a blonde?
Because as soon as you start, she runs to answer the door.

How do you drown a blonde?
Put a scratch-'n-sniff sticker on the bottom of a swimming pool.

What do you call 10 blondes lined up in a row?
A wind tunnel.

Why should you keep a blonde on the job seven days a week?
So you don't have to retrain her every Monday.

What did the blonde say when she found out she was pregnant?
I hope it's mine!

How can you tell if a blonde has been using your lawn mower?
The green 'Welcome' mat is ripped all to shreds.

What did the blonde's mom say before she left for a date?
'If you're not in bed by 10, come home!'

Die dosent vra die blond om 'n sin te maak met 'bo my vuurmaakplek'.
Die blond sê, 'My rok is so kort, dit hang net bo my vuurmaakplek.'

Why did the blonde climb the glass wall?
To see what was on the other side.

If a blonde and a brunette fell out of an aeroplane, who would land first?
The brunette. The blonde would have to stop and ask for directions.

Why don't blondes like pickles?
  They keep getting their head stuck in the jar.

Why aren't there any blonde pharmacists?
  They can't figure out how to get those little bottles into the typewriter.

Baas: Hoekom spel jy Philipolis met 'n 'F'?
Blonde: Want die tikmasjien se 'V' is stukkend.

Gehoor van die blond wat gedink het Sherlock Holmes is 'n behuisingskema?

What does a blonde say first thing in the morning?
  'Are all you guys on the same team?'

What do you call four blondes at a four-way stop?
  Eternity.

Did you hear about the blonde's postcard?
  It said, 'Having a great time. Where am I?'

What did the four blondes have in common?
  Nothing they could think of.

What goes 'VROOOM SCREECH! VROOOM SCREECH! VROOOM SCREECH!'
  A blonde at a flashing red light.

How does a blonde haemophiliac cure herself?
  With acupuncture.

Why does a blonde eat beans on Saturday?
  So she can take a bubble bath on Sunday.

Did you hear about the blonde who had a hysterectomy so she'd stop having grandchildren?

Did you hear about the blonde who was two hours late getting home because the escalator got stuck?

Hoekom het die blond vierkantige tieties?
Sy't vergeet om die tissue uit die boks te haal.

Did you hear about the blonde who lost her mind?
She worked in a brothel for six years before she found out the other girls got paid.

Why don't blondes like to make Kool-Aid?
They can't fit 500 mℓ of water in the little package.

What do you do when a blonde throws a grenade at you?
Pull the pin and throw it back.

Why does a blonde have fur on the hem of her dress?
To keep her neck warm.

Two blondes were walking along and came upon some tracks. One blonde said, 'Those look like impala tracks.' The other said, 'No, they look more like buffalo tracks'.
They were still arguing when the train hit them.

What did the blonde call her pet zebra?
Spot.

Did you hear about the blonde conservationist?
She used to rescue lobsters from their fishtanks and release them back into the woods.

This blonde goes to the doctor and says, 'Doc, I've got a terrible problem. Every time I sneeze, I get an orgasm.'
The doc says, 'Are you taking anything for it?'
And the blonde says, 'Yes. Snuff.'

Wat het die blond gesê toe sy onder die koei wakker word?
'Is julle vier manne nog steeds hier?'

Why don't blondes breast-feed their babies?
 Because it hurts too much when they boil their nipples.

What goes brunette, blonde, brunette, blonde …?
 A blonde doing cartwheels.

Why did the blonde leave a coat-hanger on the back-seat of her car?
 In case she locked her keys inside.

Wat noem jy 'n brunette met 'n blond aan weerskante van haar?
 'n Tolk.

Wat het die blondine gesê toe sy eendag sien hoe 'n vrag kitsgras by haar buurman afgelaai word?
 'As ek eendag ryk is gaan ek ook my gras wegstuur om gesny te word.'

MIRROR MIRROR

Two blondes are walking down the street. One blonde finds a little mirror. She looks in it, and looks in it again. With puzzlement written all over her face, she turns to her friend and says, 'I just know I've seen this face before!'

 'Give it to me,' says the other blonde. She looks in the mirror and says, 'Of course you have, silly! It's me!'

SMART BLONDES

Two blondes walk into a pub, sit at the bar and order two drinks. They raise their glasses in a raucous toast: 'Fifty-one days!'

 They glug their drinks, hug each other, and order another round. Again, they clink their glasses: 'Fifty-one days!'

 By the fourth round, the barman is getting a little curious. 'Pardon me, ladies,' he says, 'but what exactly are you celebrating? Why do you keep drinking a toast to fifty-one days?'

And the first blonde looks at him and says, 'You'll never believe it. The two of us managed to complete an entire jigsaw puzzle in only fifty-one days!'

'Fifty-one days?' echoes the barman, 'What's so good about that?'

And the second blonde gives him a really mean look and replies, 'It said 2 to 4 years on the box!'

UNAWARES

The doctor had just completed his full medical check-up on Soozee. 'All right,' he said, leaving the room, 'you can get dressed now.' But Soozee was missing a crucial item of clothing. She searched and searched, and when the doctor returned, she was still searching and searching.

'Whoops,' said the doctor to the totally naked Soozee, 'Looks like I caught you unawares.' Soozee put her hands on her hips and glared at the doc.

'Well, give them back to me,' she said. 'I've been looking all over the blerrie place for them!'

ITSY BITSY

Soosee van Welkom was beeldskoon. Agtien en absoluut beeldskoon. Maar sy was blond. Haar ma se droom was dat Soosee 'n internasionale model moes word. Sy't 'n stel foto's van Soosee na elke modelagentskap in Gauteng gestuur, en op 'n dag, siedaar, 'n vooraanstaande modelagentskap in Rosebank laat weet hulle wil vir Soosee sien.

So sit Soosee toe sak en pak af na Egoli. Die modelfotograaf was verbysterd oor haar skoonheid. 'Soosee,' het hy gesê, 'gaan solank na die kleedkamer en trek vir my daardie klein kledingstukkie aan wat op die rak lê. So 'n klein pienketjie, jy kan hom nie mis nie. Dan wag jy tot ek jou roep en dan neem ons 'n stel foto's vir jou portefeulje.'

Soosee kry toe die kledingstukkie in die kleedkamer. Dit was 'n G-string, maar sjoe, hy's klein. So 'n skrapse kledingstuk het Soosee nog nooit gesien nie, en sy probeer toe die affêretjie aantrek. Dit gaan maar sukkel-sukkel, en uiteindelik het sy hom aan, maar agterstevoor – stertriempie aan die voorkant en voorkant op die boudjies.

Later roep die fotograaf haar. Soosee skuifel-skuifel die ateljee binne, want die storie sit maar bra ongemaklik. Die fotograaf staan gereed agter sy kamera, swart doek oor die kop en se vir Soosee, 'Poseer.'

Soosee sê, 'Ja, nogal.'

NATURAL DISASTER

Three women are about to be executed. One is a brunette, one is a redhead, the other's a blonde. The brunette is first in line. 'Got any last requests?' asks the guard. The brunette shakes her head.

The guard shouts, 'Ready ... Aim ...' And suddenly the brunette yells, 'EARTHQUAKE!'

In the ensuing confusion, the brunette runs off. So they bring out the redhead. 'Got any last requests?' asks the guard. The redhead shakes her red head. The guard shouts, 'Ready ... Aim ...' And suddenly the redhead yells, 'TORNADO!'

In the ensuing confusion, she runs off. Now it's the blonde's turn. She's been watching closely, and she's worked out exactly what to do.

'Got any last requests?' asks the guard. The blonde shakes her mane. 'Ready ... Aim ...' And the blonde yells, 'FIRE!'

TUNNEL VISION

Shame, man. This blonde is crossing the road when she's sent flying by a fast-moving Fiat Uno.

'Didn't you see it coming?' asks the ambulance guy, as the driver of the small car looks on with concern.

'No, I saw it perfectly!' insists the blonde, 'but I thought it was a big car further away.'

GO PLAY IN THE TRAFFIC

The brunette is standing next to a busy road chanting, '75,75,75,75 ...'

Along comes a blonde. 'That looks like fun,' she says. 'Can I try?'

'Sure,' says the brunette, and the blonde begins shouting, '75! 75! 75! 75!'

'You know,' says the brunette, 'it's actually a lot more fun if you stand in the middle of the road.'

'Okay!' says the blonde, and she stands in the middle of the road, shouting '75,75,75,75 ...'

VROOOOOOM! Along comes a ZX3. KA-DOEFFFFFF! The blonde goes flying into the air.

And the brunette carries on chanting, '76,76,76,76 ...'

BOERE

WINDPOMP

Oom Louw sit op die voorstoep van sy pragtige ou plaashuis, Stukkieshalte, diep in die Vrystaat. Dis skemer. Dis droog. Dis morbied. Dis soos die ANC – dis nag.

Oom Louw is moedeloos en motherless. Hier het hy en sy geliefde Sêra de grootste deel van hulle lang lewe saam deurgebring. Net hier, en nêrens anders nie. Ja, die twee oues van dae het kwalik oor 48 jaar heen verder as die grense van Stukkieshalte beweeg.

En nou is die balju pas daar weg, want teen die einde van die maand moet hy en Tant Sêra die gesogte ou familieplaas ontruim as gevolg van opgehoopte skuld in 'n vrot Suid-Afrikaanse ekonomie. Daar's nog net een windpomp wat werk, en oor 'n maand sal alles wat nog leef en beef op Stukkieshalte op 'n bankrotveiling opgeveil word.

Die Klippies praat geruime tyd al hard met oom Louw. En vanaand weer. Soos hy die prop van die derde bottel Klippies met die palm van sy regterhand af spin, sit Tant Sêra en pink nog 'n traan weg. Sy's diep besorg. Dis nie net hulle geliefde plaas wat verval het nie, dis ook haar dierbare ou man.

Maar intussen het daar 'n wonderwerk gebeur waarvan die twee oues nie bewus is nie. 'n Skatryk neef wat in Australië woon het van oom Louw se smart verneem, en het besluit om sy oom uit sy diep finansiële penarie te red en al sy skuld af te los. Hy probeer oom Louw al weke lank met die goeie nuus skakel, maar die telefoon is 'n maand gelede reeds afgesny.

Nou's hy terug in Suid-Afrika, en baie vroeg die volgende oggend klim hy in 'n helikopter en sit die stuk van Lanseria af na Stukkieshalte om die goeie nuus aan oom Louw oor te dra.

Oom Louw sit tienuur die oggend nog steeds op die voorstoep, en trek die volgende kas Klippies nader. Tant Sêra maak pap in die kombuis. Skielik hoor oom Louw 'n gedreun in die verte: Doef-doef-doef-doef.

Die helikopter verskyn van agter 'n rantjie, doerrr verrr. Oom Louw sit regop, hy kyk, en hy kyk weer. Die helikopter dreun nader, doef-doef-doef. Oom Louw sit vasgenael, sy kakebeen hang, sy oë is wyd gesper. Die bottel Klippies val met 'n slag aan skerwe uit sy regterhand. Dis toe dat oom Louw vir tant Sêra gil, 'Ou vrou! O lieven Herentjie tog, ou vrou! Kom kyk! Daar f****f onse laaste windpomp ook!'

GROOTPENS

Koos was maar 'n lelike ou met 'n groot pens. Sy bynaam was Trombose want sy trom het oor sy bose gehang.

Hy gaan hou vakansie, en uit die duisende girls op Durban se strand kyk nie eens een vaagweg in sy rigting nie. Koos bekla sy lot by Piet en Piet stel toe 'n ding voor.

'Luister Koos,' sê hy, 'vat 'n aartappel, dan slip jy hom hier voor by jou koshie in. Dit betaal partykeer om te advertise, dan sien jy hoe mal gaan die cherries oor jou.'

Koos maak die volgende dag so, die aartappel is in die koshie, en die girls op die strand gil – nie van plesier nie, maar van skok. Soos Koos tussen hulle rondloop gee hulle hom een kyk, spring op en hol gillend weg.

Piet hoor die gille en storm nader. Koos is baie down en sê, 'Aag Piet, die ding werk nie man. Die girls vang nou 'n nog groter gly in my.'

Piet check Koos so 'n rukkie uit, en stap naderhand na sy agterkant.

'G'n wonder nie Koos,' sê hy. 'Jy moes die aartappel voor in jou broek gedruk het.'

LEKKER VARS

Die ou antie stap Komatie-slaghuis binne en sê, 'Ek soek lekker vars boerewors.'

Paul sê, 'Antie, ons wors is mos altyd lekker vars.'

Die antie sê, 'Man, ek soek hom so vars, die wors moet nog eintlik so aan die boer hang.'

BOOBS

SIZE COUNTS

This young woman goes to see her doctor. There's something she's just got to get off her chest.

'Doctor,' she says, 'It's my chest. It's so flat that no man will take a second look at me.'

The doctor takes a look. She's right.

'Okay,' says the doctor, 'I'm going to prescribe a simple series of exercise for you. All you have to do is stand upright, with your arms in a horizontal position. Now bend your arms so that they're right in front of your chest. Now, quickly push your elbows backwards, while saying to yourself, "I must, I must increase my bust." If you do this exercise every 15 minutes for two months, you should find that your breasts will grow larger.'

The woman agrees to give it a try. Later in the day, she's standing at the bus-stop. She looks at her watch and realises it's been 15 minutes since she last did her exercises. She gets her arms in position, swings her elbows back and forth, and repeats to herself: 'I must, I must increase my bust ...'

As she finishes, she feels a tap on her shoulder. She turns around to see a nerdish-looking man wearing bifocals. He looks at her and says, 'Excuse me, Miss, but could you tell me the time?'

'Sure,' she says. 'It's exactly ten past three.'

The nerd looks alarmed. 'Oh no! It's time!'

And he begins hopping up and down on the spot, repeating to himself: 'Hickory, dickory, dock ...'

TWO FOR THE MONEY

A guy goes over to his buddy's house. He rings the bell. His buddy's wife answers

'Hi,' says the guy, 'is Tony home?'

'No,' she says, 'he's just popped down to the shop on the corner.'

'Mind if I wait?'

'No problem. Come inside.'

So the guy goes inside. He's sitting there on the couch, sipping his tea and making small talk, when the talk suddenly turns big.

'You know, Suzie,' he says. 'You've got the most beautiful pair of breasts I've ever seen.'

Suzie doesn't know whether she should smack the guy in the face, or just smile and say thank you. Instead, she says, 'How would you know? You've never even seen them.'

'Ja, I know,' says the guy, 'and that's why I was thinking ... I'd give you a hundred bucks if you'd just let me see one.' Suzie thinks about this for a second. What the heck. She opens her robe and reveals one breast.

The guy promptly puts a R100 note down on the table.

There is silence for a while. Then the guy says, 'I'll give you another R100 if you let me see the other one.'

Suzie shrugs. she's getting used to this. She opens her robe again.

The guy puts another R100 on the table.

'Look,' he says, 'I really can't wait much longer. Tell Tony I was around, okay?' And off he goes.

A few minutes later, Tony walks into the house.

'That crazy friend of yours just came over,' Suzie tells him.

'He did? Well, did he drop of the R200 he owes me?'

HOW LOW CAN YOU GO?

What does a 75-year-old woman have between her breasts that a 25-year-old woman doesn't?

A belly-button.

MOOI SO

Van sien hierdie wel-bedeelde meisie op die strand en sê, 'Jy't die mooiste twee goedjies wat ek nog ooit gesien het.'

Sy sê, 'Hoe weet jy dit?'

Van sê, 'Ek het hulle getel.'

MILK RUN

A pretty young woman entered the doctor's clinic with a baby in her arms.

'I'm worried about the baby,' she told the doc. 'He seems undernourished.'

The doc examined the baby thoroughly, but couldn't find anything wrong.

'How do you feed him?' asked the doc, 'bottle or breast?'

'He's breast-fed,' replied the woman.

'Then I'd better check you too,' said the doc.

The young lady took off her blouse, and stood in front of the doc feeling rather embarrassed. He weighed each breast lightly in his hand, and gave the nipples a gentle squeeze.

'Hmmm,' he said. 'The problem is you're not producing any milk.'

'I know,' said the woman. 'That's because I'm the baby's aunt. But it was nice meeting you.'

DOEF-KADOEF

Hoekom het Dolly Parton met twee blou oë wakker geword?

Sy't die vorige aand sonder 'n bra tougespring.

NIKS VIR NIKS

'n Ou kyk hoe sy vrou haar nuwe bra voor die spieël aanpas.

'Hoekom bodder jy nog met 'n bra? Jy't niks om daarin te sit nie,' sê hy.

'Luister,' sê sy, 'ek moan nie as jy gaan onderbroeke koop nie.'

GEEN BRA

'Jy lyk pragtig,' sê Frik op 'n uithangfunksie vir sy vrou. 'As ek jy is sal ek altyd sonder 'n bra rondloop.'

'Baie dankie,' sê Serah, 'maar hoe weet jy ek dra nie 'n bra nie?'

'Want daar's geen plooie in jou gesig nie,' sê Gert.

BOXING

WHO'S THERE?

The boxer is having a hard time in the ring. He's being hammered with left hooks, right hooks, uppercuts and jabs to the head. It's only the bell that saves him from being knocked to the canvas.

'You're doing fantastic,' says his trainer. 'He hasn't laid a finger on you.'

'Then you must check out the ref,' says the fighter, ''cause somebody's donnering the shit out of me.'

BOXING CLEVER

Back in the days when they were still donnering and getting donnered in the ring, Mike and Kallie had to undergo regular psychiatric testing to determine the effect on their intellectual facilities.

Mike, not even being able to spell 'intellekshual', always worried himself sick over these tests. On one such occasion, he pleaded with Kallie to go in to see the shrink first. 'Okay,' said Kallie. 'I've got nothing to worry about.'

The test began. 'Mr Knoetze,' said the shrink, 'if you put your left hand over your left eye, what would you be?'

'I would be partly blind,' said Kallie.

'And if you put your right hand over your right eye, what would you be?'

'Also partly blind.'

'Now let's say you put your left hand over your left eye, and your right hand over your right eye, what would you be then?'

'Completely blind, sir.'

'Very good, Mr Knoetze. You may go now. Would you ask Mr Schutte to come in, please?'

Outside the door, Mike was a nervous wreck. 'Quick man, Kallie,' he said, 'give me the answers!'

'Relax,' said Kallie. 'It's a walk in the park. All you need to know is … partly blind, partly blind and completely blind.'

Muttering the answers to himself, Mike nodded a greeting to the psychiatrist and took his place on the couch.

'All right, Mr Schutte,' said the shrink. 'Let's say I cut off your left ear. What would you be then?'

'Partly blind,' answered Mike, quick as a flash.

'And if I cut off your right ear, what would you be then?'

'Partly blind,' repeated Mike.

'Now let's say I cut off both your ears,' said the shrink. 'What would you be then?'

'Completely blind,' said Mike.

'Hmmm,' said the shrink, making a note on his clipboard. 'Very interesting. Tell me, Mr Schutte, how do you arrive at that conclusion?'

'I would be completely blind, sir, because by that time my hat would have fallen over my ears!'

ALL CHANGE

'How far is the change room from the ring?' says the fighter to his trainer.

'Don't worry,' says the trainer. 'You won't be walking back.'

BROTHELS

BIG SPENDER

It's payday. Mike decides to paint the town red. He knocks on the door of the escort agency. Suddenly, he's face to face with the most beautiful woman he's ever seen in his life.

'Er, hullo,' says Mike. 'What can I get for five rand?'

'You can go and play with yourself,' says the luscious blonde, as she slams the door in his face.

Half an hour later, Mike knocks on the door again.

'What now?' asks the woman.

And Mike says, 'I've just come to pay you.'

BEAT IT

Sign on door of brothel: 'Beat it – we're closed!'

BIRTHDAY TREAT

This old toppie shuffles into a house of ill repute and tells the madam that he would like a young woman for the night.

The madam goois him a puzzled look and asks, 'Just how old are you, Oomie?'

'I'm 98 years old today,' boasts the old man.

'Ninety-eight!' exclaims the madam. 'Forget it, granddad – you've had it!'

'Oh,' he says, 'how much do I owe you then?'

BUMPER STICKERS

Viagra is a cock-up.

It's as bad as you think, and they are out to get you.

If you don't like the news, go out and make some.

All I want to do is massage your back – TRUST me.

Beauty is in the eye of the beer holder.

Sorry, I don't date outside my species.

It's lonely at the top, but you eat better.

Cover me … I'm changing lanes.

Friends don't let friends drive naked.

Support wildlife, throw a party!

If it's too loud, you're too old.

Wink, I'll do the rest!

The worst day of fishing is better than the best day at work.

Orgasm donor.

So many pedestrians, so little time.

Lead me not into temptation. I can find it myself!

Real women don't have hot flushes, they have power surges.

Forget the Joneses, I keep up with the Simpsons.

Do you think you could drive any better with that cellphone stuck up your arse?

I took an IQ test and the results were negative.

I don't care who you are, what you are driving, or where you would rather be.

I need someone really bad. Are you really bad?

I used to live in the real world, then I got evicted.

My other wife is beautiful.

Okay, who stopped the payment on my reality check?

Few women admit their age, few man act it!

I'm as confused as a baby in a topless bar.

I don't suffer from insanity. I enjoy every minute of it!

Learn from your parents' mistakes. Use birth control!

Hard work pays off in the long run. Laziness pays off now!

All I need is some peace and quiet. If I got a piece I'd be quiet!

Life is a banquet ... So eat me!

Are you going to come quietly, or do I have to use earplugs?

I fart to make you smell better.

Are you wearing a condom?

Which came first? The woman or the department store?

A kiss is an upper persuasion for lower invasion.

I don't have a License to Kill. I have a learner's permit.

Help! Daddy farted, and we can't get out!

To all you virgins out there ... thanks for nothing!

I have seen the evidence. I want different evidence!

According to my calculations, the problem doesn't exist.

There is one in every crowd, and somehow they always find me.

Horn not working, watch for hand signals.

I love animals. They taste great!

Eagles soar, but a weasel never gets sucked into a jet engine.

I brake for hallucinations.

Come closer and tell me about it.

A bartender is just a pharmacist with a limited inventory.

Reality? That's where the pizza delivery guy comes from.

I'm out of bed and dressed. What more do you want?

If you can read this, you're not from Bloemfontein.

Warning to hijackers: I drive with a maltese poodle on my lap.

Baby on board. Unless I left it on the roof.

Don't drink and drive. Walk and get mugged!

I don't have a hands-free kit. I just like talking to myself.

There is a light at the end of the SA tunnel, but somebody stole it.

I don't do drugs. I just lie back and let drugs do me.

If you don't like my driving, wait till you see my parking.

If women are from Venus, and men are from Mars, then homosexuals must be from Uranus.

Blow your horn if you're using Viagra.

BUSHMEN

HERE IS THE WEATHER

A film crew is on location deep in the Kalahari Desert. One day, an old Bushman comes up to the director and says, 'Tomorrow rain.' The director points at the blazing sun, snorts with laughter, and sends the Bushman on his way. Tomorrow comes. It rains.

Probably just coincidence, thinks the director. Then the Bushman appears again, and tells the guy: 'Tomorrow windstorm.' This time, the director doesn't laugh. He cancels the next day's shooting. Just as well: the day dawns with the biggest windstorm the Kalahari has seen in years.

The director is convinced. He tells his production assistant to hire the Bushman immediately. Weeks go by, and the Bushman's predictions prove to be unerringly accurate. Then, one day, on the eve of a crucial scene, the Bushman doesn't turn up on set.

The director sends for him. 'I'm shooting a big scene tomorrow,' he says. 'I'm depending on you. What's the weather going to be like?'

The Bushman shrugs. 'Don't know,' he says. 'What!' thunders the director, 'what do you mean you don't know?'

'Very sorry,' says the Bushman. 'Radio broken.'

COLLATERAL

The old Bushman sets out from his home in the deep Kalahari to see a man about a loan. After leaving his bow and arrows with the security guard, the Bushman is ushered into the bank manager's office.

'I need a loan of R500,' says the Bushman.

The bank manager smiles condescendingly. 'And what are you going to do with that much money?'

'I want to take paintings to the city and sell them.'

'What have got for collateral?' asks the bank manager.

'I do not know this collateral,' says the Bushman.

The bank manager explains, 'It's something of value that would cover the coast of the loan. Do you have any vehicles, for instance?'

The Bushman says: 'Yes. Donkey cart.'

The bank manager smiles. Then shakes his head. 'How about livestock?'

'I have a horse.'

'How old is it?'

'I don't know. It has no teeth.'

Finally, the bank manager decides to take the risk. He pushes a loan application form across the desk. The Bushman signs his name with an 'X', mostly because X is his name. He gets the money, and off he goes. A few weeks later, he's back in the bank manager's office.

He pulls a wad of bills from his pouch. 'I pay you back,' he says. The bank manager's eyes boggle.

'What are you planning to do with the rest of the money?' he asks. 'Put it in a hole in the trunk of a tree,' the Bushman says.

'Why don't you deposit it in my bank?'

'I don't know this deposit.'

'Well,' says the bank manager, leaning back in his upholstered leather chair, 'you put the money in our bank and we take care of it for you. When you want to use it, you can withdraw it.'

The old Bushman leans across the desk. 'What have you got for collateral?'

BIG CLUB

Setting out to bag a world record elephant trophy, the big-game hunter spends three weeks in the heart of the Kalahari. Armed with the latest high-tech equipment, he drives through the desert for hundreds of kilometres in his powerful Jeep Cherokee. But he doesn't see a single elephant.

Then, as he rounds a corner on the last day of his expedition, he sees one. It's the biggest elephant he's ever encountered in his hunting career, but unfortunately, it's already morsdood, lying there in the middle of the road. Sitting on the elephant's head is a tiny little Bushman, armed with nothing but a spear.

The big-game hunter gets out of his Cherokee. 'Man,' he asks the Bushman, 'what the hell happened to this elephant?'

'Me kill him big elephant,' says the Bushman.

'What equipment did you use?'

'Me use my club,' says the Bushman.

'Your club!?' says the incredulous American. 'How can you kill an elephant of that size with a club? Must be one helluva big club.'

'Yes,' says the Bushman, 'my club has five hundred members.'

BUTHELEZI

LET THEM EAT CAKE

The lady who is preparing tea and biscuits for the Parliamentary session stops an ANC MP on his way to have a P.

'Has Minister Buthelezi finished his speech yet?' she asks.

And the MP replies: 'He finished about half an hour ago but he hasn't stopped.'

ETCETERA ETCETERA ETCETERA

Minister Buthelezi was gaaning aan with one of his long political speeches in the Town Hall of Ulundi. Oom Frik went outside for a smoke break when oom Kallie approached him.

Oom Kallie: 'What's Gatsha talking about today?'

Oom Frik: 'He didn't say.'

WHAT DAY IS IT?

The Minister was just about midway through one of his long, boring speeches, when he noticed his audience shuffling around impatiently.

'I don't want to bore you with a long speech,' he said, 'but in fact I'm not wearing a watch.'

'Look behind you on the wall,' shouted an oke from the audience, 'there's a calendar.'

VELDWAGTER

Gatsha se veewagter-broer het maande op sy plaas iewers in KwaZulu-Natal in die veld deurgebring om beeste op te pas, en net so nou en dan is daar vir hom kosvoorraad gebring deur ouboet Gatsha. Tydens so 'n gebeurtenis het die gesprek nie einde nie.

'Ek sien djy het vir my kos gabreng?' sê die broer.

'Ja, ek het vir jou kos gebring,' sê Gatsha.

'Djy't vor my die lekkar kos gabreng?'

'Ja Bafana, baie lekker kos.'

'Mmmmm. Wanneer djy breng weer vor my die lekker kos?'

'So oor drie weke, Bafana.'

'Darie kos ok hy gaan die lekkar kos wees soos die een?'

'Au, net die beste Bafana, net die heel beste.'

En so aan. Gatsha sien sy boetie is, soos hy, amper hongerder vir kommunikeer as wat hy altyd is, en besluit om bietjie langer te kuier. 'Sê vir my Bafana,' vra hy, 'wat doen jy die hele dag hierso in die veld?'

'Ek denk.'

'Wat dink jy?

'Ek denk die beeste.'

'Ja?'

'En ek denk die gras.'

Lang stilte.

'En wat dink jy nog?'

'Ek denk die reën.' Hy kyk op in die lug.

'Nou ek denk die groot voël.'

'Ja?'

'Dan ek denk weer die gras ... nou ek denk die meerkat.'

'Ja?'

'Nou darie groot voël hy gryp darie meerkat ... Darie

meerkat hy skree en skree toe darie groot voël met hom vlieg. Nou ek denk darie meerkat … hy hou fôkol van vlieg.'

CANNIBALS

A LITTLE TOO MUCH SALT

Mike and Kallie, on safari in deepest, darkest Africa, are captured by a tribe of previously undiscovered cannibals.

The cannibals tie Mike and Kallie up and march them by assegai-point to the nearest village. There, Mike and Kallie are ceremoniously stripped of their safari suits and dumped into a huge potjie full of water. The potjie goes on top of a fire. The fire is lit. As the smoke begins to rise, Mike begins chuckling softly to himself.

Then he begins laughing, louder and louder.

'What's so funny?' asks Kallie. 'We're about to be boiled alive! These okes are going to eat us! How can you possibly find anything to laugh about at a time like this?'

Mike just smiles at Kallie and says: 'Shhhh, man. I just peed in the soup!'

CLOWNING AROUND

Two cannibals are chewing on a clown. The one says to the other, 'Does this taste funny to you?'

HULLO MA

Die mensvreter en sy seun stap deur die bos en kom op 'n beeldskone meisie in 'n tanga af. Die seun sê, 'Pa, kom ons slag haar.'

'Not 'n dêm,' antwoord die pa, 'kom ons vat haar huis toe en slag vir ma.'

YUCK

Two cannibals are sitting by a fire. The first says, 'You know, I really hate my mother-in-law.'

The second says, 'So, try the potatoes.'

CARS & TRUCKS

DON'T FLOOD THE ENGINE

Meisie comes home from her shopping expedition, looking somewhat bedraggled and bedonnerd.

'Okkie,' she says, 'you're going to have to go and fix the car.'

'The car?' says Okkie, 'what's wrong with the car?'

'There's water on the carburettor.'

Okkie gets ready to leave. 'So where is the car, Meisie?'

'In the Vaal River,' she says.

TALKING BULL

The city slicker is winding down a quiet country road when his car splutters to a halt near a field filled with cows. The driver gets out, slams the door, and peers under the bonnet, devoid of any notion of what he's supposed to be peering at. One of the cows comes over to the fence.

'I believe it's your radiator,' says the cow. The city slicker almost jumps out of his jeans. He runs to the nearest farmhouse and knocks on the door.

'A cow just gave me advice about my car!' he shouts, waving frantically in the direction of the field. The farmer gives the driver a slow and curious look.

'Would that be the cow with the two big black spots?'

'Yes!' says the city slicker, 'That's the one!' The farmer pulls on his pipe and nods slowly to himself.

'That's Ethel,' he says. 'I wouldn't pay any attention to her. She doesn't know the first damn thing about cars!'

FULL CLEARANCE

Mike and Kallie, long-distance truckers, are sharing the wheel on a journey from Jo'burg to Beaufort West. After many hours on the road, they find themselves at an overpass.

The sign reads: 'Clearance – 2,4 metres'. Mike gets out and measures the truck. It's 2,6 metres high. He gets back into the cab.

'Any cops around?' asks Kallie.

'No,' says Mike.

'Okay, then … let's go for it!'

LEKKER MOTOR

Hoe laat jy 'n draadkar olie lek?

Sit vir hom 'n Alpha badge op.

TUG-A-BUG

Mike is walking down the road when he sees two Volkswagen Beetles with their bumpers locked. They've just had a prang, and the owners of the vehicles are having great difficulty prising them apart.

'I've got an idea,' says Mike. 'Why don't you throw a bucket of water over them?'

GLASOOG

Die ou het 'n glasoog, en sit al vyf jaar tevergeefs en wag vir 'n oogoorplanting.

Een rustige dag sit hy in 'n pub in Knysna, toe 'n ou met 'n hengse motorfiets skielik deur die deur bars teen 160 k.p.u. Hy ry met 'n moewiese slag teen die kroegtoonbank vas, trek soos 'n vrot vel oor die toonbank, en land met sy kop tussen die honderde drankbottels op die rak. Hy slaat soos 'n os agteroor en land met 'n slag op die toonbank.

Teen daardie tyd is daar niemand meer in daai kroeg nie, want in Suid-Afrika hang jy nie rond as mense met motorfietse in kroeë ingejaag kom nie. Die enigste een wat bly sit is ons ou met die glasoog. En vir 'n goeie rede. Hy soek 'n oog.

Hy kyk vinnig rond of niemand hom sien nie, vat die lepel uit die ysbak en skep blitsig vir hom een van die oë uit die oogbank uit. Sien, as jy kan bloed kry by die bloedbank, reken hy, kan jy 'n oog by die oogbank ook kry. Hy pop sy glasoog uit, sit vinnig die nuwe oog in, en hy's fort.

Twee pragtige siende blou oë en so drie maande later, begin hierdie ou worry. Sê nou maar net daai ou in die kroeg was nie dood nie, en hier sit hy vandag met die arme ou se oog. Dit begin hom te ry, nag en dag, so erg dat hy naderhand met sy predikant gaan praat, en dié raai hom uiteindelik aan om terug te gaan en eerstehands te gaan uitvind of die arme ou toe werklik dood is of nie. Hy kry die kroegman op 'n Dinsdagoggend net na 11 alleen in die kroeg.

'Sê my meneer,' vra hy, 'daai ou wat so 'n ruk gelede hier met sy motorbike by die kroeg ingejaag het ...'

'Ja?' sê die kroegman.

'Is daai ou toe dood?'

'Morsdood,' sê die kroegman. 'Sjym, hy't al die pad van die Kaap af gekom om vir sy meisie hier in Knysna te kom kuier, en toe eindig dit toe so.'

'Sjym,' sê die ou vir die kroegman, en 'dankie tog' vir homself.

'Daar's net een probleem met daai ou,' sê die kroegman.

'Ja?' vra die ou, skielik weer bekommerd.

'Hierdie dorp van Knysna gis nou al maande lank oor daai ou,' sê die kroegman.

'Waaroor nogal?' vra die ou, nou nog meer bekommerd.

Die kroegman staar lank voor hom uit voor hy sê:

'Die ding wat die mense so puzzle, is hoe daai ou sy motorbike al die pad van die Kaap af kon ry met twee glasoë ...'

CELLPHONES

IT'S FOR YOU

Mike, Jimmy and Kallie were having a couple of dops in the pub when a phone rang.

''Scuse me, manne,' said Kallie. He put his thumb into his ear and spoke into the end of his little finger. Mike and Jimmy were impressed, so Kallie explained, 'I had a silicon chip put into my thumb and another one into my little finger. Now I don't have to carry a cellphone around the whole day.'

A month later the threesome met in the same pub. A phone rang, and Jimmy started talking away without even using any fingers.

'Heng ou Jimmy,' said Mike, 'how'd you do that?'

'Aag it's easy,' said Jimmy. 'I had a silicon chip inserted in my ear and another in my tooth. Now I don't even need to lift a hand when I'm taking a call.'

Suddenly, Mike grabbed his tummy, made growling noises and complained of heavy cramps in his stomach. He pulled down his pants and bent forward, with his bum in the air and his hands on the pub counter.

'What's the matter?' asked the concerned Jimmy and Kallie.

'Ag, I'm just gonna receive a fax,' said Mike.

CHICKENS

WHAT CAME FIRST?

A chicken and an egg are lying in bed. The egg is frowning and looking annoyed, and the chicken is smoking a cigarette with a big smile on its face.

The egg says, 'Well, I guess we answered that question.'

DAILY CHICKEN

After months of negotiation, pleading, and schlepping back and forth across the ocean, the managing director of South Africa's largest poultry supplier finally manages to arrange an audience with the Pope. The guy is ushered into an office in the Vatican, and is told to wait. The Pope arrives, raising his hand in greeting and benediction.

The chicken guy dispenses with the small talk and gets right down to business.

'Your Holiness,' he says, 'I'd like to make a proposition. I represent the biggest supplier of frozen chickens in the southern hemisphere. My company has interests in the chicken business all around the world. If you could issue an edict changing the words of the Lord's Prayer from "Give us this day our daily bread" to "Give us this day our daily chicken", my company will be prepared to donate $500 million to the Church.'

The Pope is aghast. 'That is impossible!' he says. 'The Prayer is the Word of the Lord and can never be changed.'

'I understand that,' says the chicken man. 'And that's why I am prepared to donate $1 billion to the Church if you will issue an edict changing the words of the Lord's Prayer from "Give us this day our daily bread" to "Give us this day our daily chicken".'

The Pope is still aghast. The chicken man ups his offer to $5 billion. Then $10 billion. The Pope shakes his head, and shakes his head again. Then he says, 'I will have to discuss this with my Cardinals.'

The next day, the Pope meets with his Cardinals. 'I've got good news and bad news,' he says. 'The good news is that the Church has come into $10 billion.'

The Cardinals raise their eyebrows and silently nod their approval. Then they look expectantly at the Pope.

'The bad news is that we have lost the Wonderbread account.'

PIK PIK

Winnie visited Madiba one day to talk about maintenance.

When she left, Madiba suddenly heard a heng of a racket amongst the chickens in the backyard. He rushed out, and to his utmost disbelief, saw Winnie wringing one chicken's neck after the other.

'What the devil are you doing, Winnie?' enquired the shocked Madiba.

Throwing the last chicken head over her shoulder, Winnie shouted, 'They're part of the old system. They walk around the yard all day shouting, "Pik Pik Pik de Kleeeerk!"'

PECK PECK

What goes peck, peck, peck, boom?

A chicken in a mine field.

HOME COOKING

'This chicken has a funny taste,' complained Mike to Nellie.

'Ja, well it was burnt,' said Nellie, 'so I sommer put some Vaseline on it.'

CHINESE

NICE JOB

It's the gold rush in Jo'burg. Men from all over the world have come to find their fortune. A mine owner, cigar clamped between his teeth, is hiring new workers.

A solidly built German steps up and says, 'I can pick gold faster than any man alive.' The owner hires him on the spot. A hugely muscled Russian wanders up and says, 'I can load gold faster than any man alive.' The owner can't believe his luck. He hires the Russian too.

Then a weedy little Chinese oke walks up and asks for a job. The owner is about to turn him away when he has a second thought. 'Wait,' he says. 'If these two men are as good as they say they are, I won't need any more muscle. I'll put you in charge of supplies.'

The next day, the owner goes to check on his new workers. Sure enough, the German is picking gold at an unbelievable rate, while the Russian is loading it as fast as the other workers can haul it out. The owner looks around. He can't find the Chinese oke anywhere.

He walks around the mine, getting more and more irritated. Suddenly, as he rounds a dark corner, the little Chinese oke jumps out from behind a bush and yells, 'SUPPLIES!'

CHINESE TAKE-AWAY

A Chinese couple are lying in bed. The husband says, 'I want a 69.'

His wife says, 'Why you want beef and broccoli now?'

ACQUIRED TASTE

Always eager to try out a new taste sensation, Mike books a table and a couple of chairs at the Chinese restaurant down the road. Midway through his not-very-satisfying meal, Mike yells at the manager: 'This chicken is bloody rubbery, man!'

'Ah, thank you velly much,' beams the manager.

FOREIGN EXCHANGE

The Chinese businessman goes to see his bank manager about the mysterious two per cent drop in the interest rate on his current account.

'Fluctuations,' says the bank manager.

'And fluck you Aflikaners too!' says the Chinese guy, storming off in a huff.

HOWZIT CHINA

I've got four kids. My wife wants a fifth, but I told her to forget about it. It's not that I've got anything against kids

– it's just that I read somewhere that every fifth baby born in the world is Chinese.

SORE TOOTH

This Chinese oke calls his dentist to make an appointment for a check-up.

'Two-thirty okay?' asks the receptionist.

'Yes, tooth hurty okay,' says the Chinese guy. 'What time can I come in for a check-up?'

CONDOMS

EMERGENCY

Van phones his doctor and yells down the line, 'Doctor, come quick – my son has just swallowed a condom!' The doctor rushes over, but when he gets there, Van says, 'Ag, don't worry, I found another one.'

SHY BUY

Did you hear about the oke who walked into the crowded shop and asked for a packet of condoms?

He was too embarrassed to ask for a Bles Bridges tape.

ONE FOR LUCK

I walked into a pharmacy the other day and saw this snooty old lady behind the counter.

'Miss,' I said, 'could you give me three condoms, please.'

She gave me a filthy look and said, 'Don't you 'Miss' me!'

I said, 'Sorry, make it four.'

DUMB AND DUMBER

Jimmy discovers a pencil in his wife's handbag. He tells Kallie and Mike, 'Check what I found in my wife's handbag.

I dunno what she wants to do with it, because she can't even write.'

'That's nothing', says Kallie. 'I discovered a book in my wife's handbag, and she can't even read.'

'Well, just wait till you hear what I found in my wife's handbag,' says Mike.

'What?' ask his Chinas.

'A packet of condoms. And the dom blerrie woman doesn't even have a tollie.'

CUT-OFF DATE

Struggling to cope with eight screaming kids, Mrs and Mrs Luigi went to see their doctor about family planning. The doc advised Luigi to wear a condom in future. Three months later, Mrs Luigi was pregnant again.

'You didn't listen to me, Luigi,' said the doc. 'You're not wearing the condom.'

'I swear I never take it off-a once!' said Luigi. 'But every morning I gotta pee so I cutt-a off the end.'

HOU VAS

Mike koop 'n pakkie kondome en die dame in die apteek sê, 'Dis R11.50 met tax.'

'Vergeet die tax,' sê Mike, 'ek sal hom sommer met 'n lyntjie vasmaak.'

TAP-TAP-TAP

Leon, sy vrou en hulle sewe kinders staan by die busstop en wag vir die bus, toe 'n ou omie met 'n kierie daar aankom. Die omie het 'n bewe-probleem, en soos hy staan en wag 'tap-tap-tap' sy kierie teen die randsteen. Dis baie irriterend, en Leon en sy vrou kyk, maar sê niks.

Die bus stop en daar's maar min plek op daai bus. 'Klim julle maar op', sê Leon vir sy vrou en kinders sonder om eers aan die ou omie te dink, 'ek sal wag vir die volgende bus.'

Vrou en kinders is fort in die bus, en hier begin daai 'tap-tap-tap' van die kierie weer. Nou kan Leon dit nie meer hou nie en sê vir die oom, 'Wil oom nie daaraan dink om 'n stukkie rubber aan die einde van oom se kierie te sit nie?'

Die ou oom sê blitsig, 'Ou seun, as jy daaraan gedink het om 'n stukkie rubber aan jou kierie te sit sou ons twee nou op daai bus gewees het.'

IT'S A WRAP

Every week, Mike would wander into his local pharmacy and order two dozen boxes of condoms. As the weeks went by, the pharmacist could contain his curiosity no longer.

'Man,' he said, leaning across the counter, 'you must have the stamina of a bull. Talk about getting lucky! How do you use that many condoms a week?'

Mike looked confused. 'No man,' he told the pharmacist, 'they're not for me, they're for Suzie.'

'Suzie?' said the pharmacist, 'who's Suzie?'

'She's my Rottweiler,' said Mike. Now the pharmacist was REALLY curious.

'Why on earth would you want condoms for your Rottweiler?'

'Don't be stupid, man,' said Mike. 'I feed her the things and she poops in these lekker neat little plastic bags.'

OPREG

'n Opregte Namibiese boereseun loop by die apteek in en sê vir die apteker, 'A can Doom, please.'

Die apteker vra, 'For flying insects or for crawling insects?'

Die boereseun sê, 'No, just for normal sex.'

CORRUPTION

CHEAP VOTE

On the big day of democracy's dawning in the new South Africa, Van steps into the ballot booth, casts his vote, and slips the little piece of paper into the box. Back in the fresh air, he complains to his pal: 'This has to be the most corrupt election I've ever voted in.'

'What makes you say that?' says his pal.

'Well, the one candidate offered me R10 to vote for him,' says Van, 'and the other candidate offered me R5.'

'So what did you do?'

'I decided to vote for the oke who offered me R5, because he's only half as corrupt as the other oke.'

AFTER YOU

The trial of the allegedly corrupt government official was in full swing, when the prosecutor began attacking a defence witness.

'Isn't it true,' said the prosecutor, 'that you accepted a sum of R50 000 to compromise this case?'

The witness stared out of the window. The prosecutor said, 'I repeat, isn't it true that you accepted a sum of R50 000 to compromise this case?' The witness carried on staring out of the window.

Finally, the judge leaned over and said, 'Answer the question, please.' With a jolt, the startled witness stopped staring out of the window.

'Oh! I'm sorry, Your Honour,' he said. 'I thought the prosecutor was talking to you.'

BRIBERY EN CORRUPTION

'Die nuwe SA is darem lekker korrup,' sê Van vir sy ander pêl.

'Hoe so?' vra die pêl.

'Ek stap Saterdag daar by die rugby op Ellispark in sonder om te betaal,' sê Van.

'Nou wat's so korrup daaraan?' vra sy pêl.

'Nee,' sê Van, 'ek moes die donder met R100 bribe.'

TRY A CASE

Van is about to appear in court on a charge of bribery and corruption. His drinking pal offers him a few words of advice: 'If you want to get off, just send the judge a case of whisky.'

Van likes the idea. He mentions it to his attorney. His attorney hits the roof.

'You'll do no such thing!' he says. 'This judge is as straight as an arrow. Don't even think about it. You're in enough trouble as it is.'

Van goes to court. To the amazement of almost everybody concerned, he wins the case.

'See?' says his attorney. 'Thank goodness you didn't send the judge that case of whisky.'

'Oh but I did,' says Van. 'I just put the other party's name on the card.'

COURTS

MERCY OF THE COURT

Definition of justice, South African style: You murder your parents, and the court lets you off because you're an orphan.

@#^& *%!, YOUR HONOUR!

Because he somehow never got around to paying his admission-of-guilt fine, Van was forced to take a day off work to appear in court on a minor traffic charge. Van grew increasingly irritable as he sat waiting for his case to be heard.

Finally, late in the afternoon, he found himself standing before the judge. 'Court adjourned,' said the judge, banging his gavel on the bench. 'You will return to this courtroom at 9 a.m. tomorrow.'

Van couldn't believe his ears. 'What for?' he snapped at the judge.

His honour, equally stressed-out by a long and tiresome day of dispensing justice, roared at the defendant: 'Fifty Rand, contempt of court. That's why!'

Van stuck his hand into his pocket and pulled out his wallet.

'That's all right,' said the judge. 'You don't have to pay now.'

To which Van replied, 'I'm just seeing if I have enough for two more words.'

KICK-OFF

Van is up in court on a charge of kicking Vusi in the stomach. He pleads not guilty, arguing that there was no malicious intent. The judge is incredulous.

'How in the world can you possibly say that you delivered this terrific kick in the stomach without intending to do so?'

'Well,' replies Van, 'The oke just turned around too blerrie quick, that's all.'

TAKEN FOR A RIDE

Vusi is in court to answer a charge of stealing a brand-new BMW. He pleads not guilty.

After several hours of intense argument by his hotshot lawyer, Vusi is allowed to go free. Later that day, he is back in court, knocking urgently on the magistrate's door.

'Your Honour,' says Vusi, when His Honour answers, 'I want you to issue a warrant of arrest for that crooked lawyer of mine.'

'Why?' asks the magistrate. 'He won your case for you.

Why would you want to have him arrested?'

'Well, Your Honour,' explains Vusi, 'I didn't have the money to pay him his fee, so he went and took the car I stole.'

HAMERKOP

Die ou is op vir moord. Hy't sy vrou doodgeslaan met 'n hamer. Hy pleit onskuldig, en 'n vrot ou skree uit die gehoor, 'Voetsek jou %&&**!!!'

Die ou raak stil. Die regter raak kwaad. Maar vir eers sê hy niks.

'Waar het u die hamer gekry?' vra die aanklaer.

Die beskuldigde sê, 'Die hamer was in my in toolbox.' Die vrot ou skree, 'Jou ouma se ***%$^!!'

Nou's die regter kwaad. 'Approach the bench,' sê hy vir die vrot ou.

'Ek beboet jou R3 000 vir minagting van die hof. Wat's jou saak met jou gevloekery van die beskuldigde?'

'Hy's 'n d**s,' sê die vrot ou.

'Nog R2 000,' sê die regter. 'Ek wil weet hoekom vloek jy die beskuldigde so?'

'Meneer,' sê die vrot ou, 'ek bly al ses jaar langs die kak, en elke keer as ek sy hamer wil leen sê hy hy het nie een nie.'

VAT SO

Koos was in die hof omdat hy Vusi Dlamini aangerand het nadat hy sy motorradio gesteel het.

'Hoe hard het jy die verweerder geslaan, Mnr Van der Merwe?' wou die aanklaer weet.

'Nie baie hard nie, u Edele.'

'Wel, wys my presies hoe hard.'

Die volgende oomblik storm Koos op Vusi in die getuiebank af, pluk hom regoor die bank, gee hom twee geweldige opstoppers, gryp hom aan die kraag, slinger hom op die vloer neer en skop sewe van sy tande uit.

Toe sê Koos, 'U Edele, dit was omtrent een agste van hoe hard ek hom werklik geslaan het.'

DO YOU SWEAR TO TELL THE TRUTH?

Die regter vra vir Gatiep, 'Het jy enige iets te sê ter versagting?'

Gatiep: 'Fôkol.'

Die regter leun vorentoe, en vra vir die klerk, 'Wat het hy gesê?' Die klerk sê, 'Hy't "fôkol" gesê, u Edele.'

'Snaaks,' sê die regter. 'Ek kon sweer ek sien sy lippe beweeg.'

CROSS PATCH

'Have you ever been cross-examined before?' asked the judge.

'Yes, Your Honour,' said Mike. 'I'm a married man.'

YOU LAUGHING AT ME?

A lady who was seven months pregnant boarded a train at Roodepoort Station. She took her seat, pulled a paperback from her handbag, and began reading. But from the corner of her eye, she could see that the young man in the opposite seat was smiling at her.

She smiled back at him very briefly, and then she carried on reading. He kept on smiling. She began feeling a little uncomfortable about his unsolicited attention, so she quietly got up and moved to another seat.

But from the corner of her eye, she noticed that the young man was still staring at her. He wasn't smiling anymore; he was giggling. She glared at him and moved to another seat. This time, the guy burst out laughing.

She moved again. The guy doubled over in his seat, unable to contain his hysterical chuckling and chortling. So the woman took him to court on a charge of *crimen injuria*.

The magistrate asked the young man to state his case. Why had he persisted in such unseemly behaviour towards an innocent woman in an advanced stage of pregnancy?

'Your Honour,' began the accused, 'When the lady in question sat down the first time, there was a poster above her head advertising a new movie release. It read: "Coming soon: *Twins*". I started giggling.

'Then she moved, and seated herself under an advertisement which read: "Sloan's Liniment removes swelling". I couldn't help but chuckle. She moved yet again, and this time landed under an advertisement featuring a rugby player promoting an underarm deodorant. It said: "Percy's stick will do the trick".

'I tried to suppress my laughter, but it was impossible. And when she moved for the fourth time and landed up underneath an advertisement which read: "Dunlop Rubber would have prevented this accident", I'm afraid I just totally lost it, Your Honour.'

The oke got off scott-free.

NIKS

'Wat het jy gekry?' vra 'n ou gevangene op Robbeneiland vir 'n nuwe een.

'Ses jaar,' sê die nuwe ou.

'Wat het jy gedoen?'

'Niks.'

'Dis snaaks. Vir niks kry jy gewoonlik drie jaar.'

UP AND ABOUT

'Is this the first time you've been up before me?' the judge asked Gatiep.

'I dunno djou Honour,' replied the accused. 'What time do you get up?'

COWBOYS & INDIANS

OLD COWBOY

The old cowboy, dressed in a cowboy shirt, hat, jeans, spurs and chaps, bursts through the saloon doors, sits down at the bar, and orders a drink. Soon, a pretty young woman sits down next to him.

'Are you a real cowboy?' she asks.

'We-e-e-ell,' replies the old cowhand, 'I've spent my whole life on the ranch herding cows, breaking horses, and mending fences ... so I reckon I am.'

He sips his bourbon. She sips her martini. He turns to her and says, 'And what about you, Miss?'

She sighs, stirs her drink, replies, 'Well, I've never been on a ranch so I'm not a cowboy. Not a cowgirl, either. But I sure as hell am a lesbian. Spend my whole day just thinking about women. Soon as I get up in the morning, I think of women. When I eat, shower, watch TV. Everything I do seems to make me think of women.'

She finishes her drink, bids the old cowboy farewell, and heads out of the bar.

The cowboy orders another drink. Soon, a couple sit down next to him. The woman asks: 'Are you a real cowboy?'

To which he replies: 'Hell, I always thought I was, but I just found out that I'm a lesbian.'

HONEST INJUN

On an old Indian reservation, alongside a small university in the mid-western states of America, there lives an old Indian who has never forgotten a single thing he has said, heard, seen or done in his life. Sounds unlikely?

That's what the cocky young student thought when his pals told him about the old Indian over a couple of beers one night. 'Well, why don't we go check it out?' suggests one of the students. Great idea.

They hop into a car and head on over to the reservation. There they find the old Indian, sitting cross-legged at the side of the road. They stop the car. The old man looks up at them, smiles, and says: 'How.' They stammer 'How', and then they just stand there, unsure of what to do next.

Finally, the cocky young student says, 'Excuse me, old man, but can I ask you a question?'

'Sure,' replies the old man.

'Is it true that you never ever forget anything?'

'Yes it is,' replies the old man.

'All right, then. What did you have for breakfast the first Tuesday after your 14th birthday?'

'Eggs!' says the old man, without hesitation.

The cocky young student isn't impressed.

'This is bull,' he says to his buddies. 'Either this guy always has eggs for breakfast, or he's just plain lying. Come on, lets get out of here.'

The years flash by. The cocky young student graduates, gets a job, raises a family, climbs up the corporate ladder, retires, and settles down. One day, he's on his way back to his Alma Mater for a reunion, when he drives by the entrance to the Indian reservation. Something compels him to drive inside.

Who does he see sitting by the side of the road? Yep. The old Indian. He looks up and smiles. The once-cocky, once-young student nods his head respectfully and says, 'How.'

'Scrambled!' replies the old man.

THE MAN WITH NO HORSE

A mean-looking cowboy rides into town. He hitches up his horse and walks into the saloon. He slams down his money, demands a beer, knocks it back, wipes his lips, and walks out.

Two seconds later, he's back inside, swing-doors rattling behind him.

'All right,' he snarls, casting his gaze around the room. 'Someone in here has stolen my horse.'

Silence. Blank looks. The cowboy continues: 'If my horse ain't back out there in exactly one minute from now, I'm going to have to do what I did in Dodge City.'

Silence. Finally, an old-timer says, 'And what did you do in Dodge City?'

The cowboy gives the room a long, mean look. Then he says, 'I walked!'

LAATLAMMETJIE

This Red Indian kid goes to see his mother in the tepee one day. He's got something on his mind.

'Mother,' he says, 'why is my bigger brother named Mighty Storm?'

'Because he was conceived during a mighty storm,' replies his mother.

'And why is my sister named Cornflower?'

'Because your father and I were in a cornfield when she was conceived,' says Mum.

'And what about my other sister, Moonchild?'

'Ah, well, we were watching the moon landing when she was conceived,' says Mum, smiling at the memory.

Then she puts her hand on her young son's shoulder, and looks him in the eye.

'Tell me, Broken Rubber, why are you so curious?'

SITTING BULL

The Indian chief was sitting in the tepee, groaning softly to himself. The problem: chronic constipation. The chief called for one of his top warriors, and sent him on an urgent mission to the medicine man.

'Big chief, no shit,' said the warrior. The medicine man gave him a tablet.

'Give this to chief,' he said. 'He'll be fine tomorrow.' The chief took the tablet. He wasn't fine. So the warrior went back to the medicine man.

'Big chief, no shit,' he reported.

'Give chief two tablets,' said the medicine man. 'He'll be much better in the morning.' But the chief wasn't much better in the morning. The warrior went back. 'Big chief, no shit,' he said.

By now, the medicine man was getting a little tired of the daily ritual.

'Here,' he said. 'Tell chief to take whole bottle of tablets. If he still isn't better, come and see me again.' So the chief took the whole bottle. The next morning, the warrior stood in the medicine man's tepee again.

'Yes?' said the medicine man. The warrior shrugged his shoulders and replied: 'Big shit, no chief.'

CRIME WAVE

PANTS UP

I'm telling you, these Gauteng skelms are getting cleverer by the day. The other day they stole an oke's pants off his arse and hung weights on his suspenders so he wouldn't notice it was gone.

TIGHT FIT

Man, this crime wave in South Africa is really getting bad.

If you go into the shop to buy a pair of stockings, the first thing they do is ask you for your head size.

SHRINKAGE

Vusi finally cracks an appointment to see his psychiatrist in Sandton. 'Doc,' he says, 'you've got to help me. Everywhere I go, I find myself overcome by this terrible urge to steal things.'

The doc nods his head, and scrawls out a prescription. 'Try these tablets for the next two weeks,' he says. 'And if they don't work, get me a video recorder and a colour TV.'

CRIME SURVEY

Carrying a clipboard in his hand, Vusi goes up to this oke in the parking lot at Sandton City.

'Excuse me, sir,' says Vusi, 'I'm doing a survey on self-defence. Would you know how to defend yourself against a sudden armed attack?' The oke shakes his head: 'No, I'm afraid not.'

'Good,' says Vusi. 'Hand over your car-keys!'

WATCH OUT

Vusi sidles up to Koos outside the supermarket.

'Pssst,' he whispers. 'You wanna buy a watch?'

'Let's have a look at it,' says Koos.

'Shhh,' says Vusi, finger on his lips. 'The guy next to you is wearing it.'

CRIME DOESN'T PAY

Maybe it's time we tried the Scottish solution to the crime problem. They put an end to criminal activity overnight by erecting the following sign above their jailhouses:

ANYBODY CONVICTED AND PUT IN JAIL WILL HAVE TO PAY FOR HIS OWN BOARDING AND LODGING.

BIG BEETLE

This oke is walking down the street in Johannesburg, when a two-metre tall beetle pops up, pulls out a knife, and stabs him twenty times. Then the beetle bliksems the daylights out of him, and steals his watch, wallet, and car-keys.

The oke staggers to the nearest hospital and tells the nurse what happened. 'Oh, don't worry too much about it,' says the nurse. 'It's just a nasty bug that's been going around.'

THE BARGAIN

A shoplifter was caught red-handed trying to steal a watch from an exclusive jewellery store. 'Listen,' said the shoplifter, 'I know you don't want any trouble either. What do you say I just buy the watch and we forget about this?'

The manager agreed and wrote up the sales slip. The crook looked at the slip and said, 'This is a little more than I intended to spend. Can you show me something less expensive?'

SOMEBODY'S WATCHING YOU

Vusi breaks into a house in the suburbs late one night. Lekker, he thinks to himself. Nobody's home. He tiptoes into the lounge and has a good look around. Nice place. Then, just as he's sizing up the big-screen colour TV with the Home Theatre sound-system, he hears a voice from out of the darkness.

'Jesus is watching you.'

He spins around in fear. No-one there. Must be his imagination. He shrugs, sighs with relief, and carries on looking. That voice again. 'Jesus is watching you.' Vusi's heart skips a beat. He freezes in his tracks, but all he can hear is silence. So he moves slowly forward again.

'Jesus is watching you.' Now Vusi has had enough. He switches on the light, looks carefully around, and in the corner he sees ... a big birdcage. With a parrot inside. Vusi bursts out laughing.

'Was that you who said Jesus is watching me?' he asks the parrot. 'Yes,' says the parrot. 'So what's your name?' asks Vusi. The parrot answers: 'Clarence.'

'Clarence!' roars Vusi, 'What kind of idiot named you Clarence?'

And the parrot says, 'The same idiot who named the Rottweiler Jesus.'

BANZAI!

Mr Yamaguchi, one of Japan's leading businessmen and investors, flies into South Africa on a fact-finding visit. One of the first facts he finds is that the crime rate in the country is among the highest in the world. So he calls an executive protection agency and says, 'I want the best bodyguard you have.'

The boss of the agency invites Mr Yamaguchi to come and around and make the selection himself. Soon, Mr Yamaguchi is sitting in a room in a plush office-block in Sandton. The boss of the agency walks in with a small glass jar in his hand. He opens the lid of the jar, and out flies a fly. BANZAI!

A Samurai warrior bursts through the door, unsheathes his sword, and slices the air in a blur of shiny metal. The fly falls to the ground, neatly sliced in half.

'Very good,' says Mr Yamaguchi. 'I'll take this man.'

'Wait,' says the agency boss. 'There are still two more men we'd like to show you.'

Another fly is unleashed. BANZAI! In leaps another Samurai swordsman. He wields his weapon with the skill of a master. The fly falls to the ground, neatly sliced in four.

'Even better,' says Mr Yamaguchi. 'I'll take this man.'

'Please wait,' says the agency boss again. 'We would like you to see the final candidate before you make up your mind.'

BANZAI! The third Samurai swordsman shows his mettle. This time, the fly falls to the floor, stays there for a second, and then starts walking around in a daze.

'What's going on?' asks Mr Yamaguchi. 'The fly is still alive!'

'Ah yes,' says the Samurai warrior, putting his sword back in its sheath, 'but he'll never make love again!'

STICK 'EM UP

Vusi was patiently waiting his turn in the lunchtime bank queue. Suddenly, he drew his weapon and shouted through his balaclava: 'This is a balls-up!'

'I think you mean a hold-up,' said the teller, who was getting used to this kind of thing.

'No,' insisted Vusi, 'it's a balls-up 'cause I forgot the bullets.'

COMMUNICATION BREAKDOWN

In a major breakthrough for the forces of law and order, Vusi is arrested on suspicion of having robbed a bank. As Constable Van prepares to cuff the suspect, Vusi starts rattling away in Zulu. Unfortunately, Van can't understand a word. Fortunately, Gammat happens to be walking past at that very moment.

'Can I help?' he says. 'I speak Zulu fluently.'

'Thank you,' says Constable Van. 'Ask this man whether he robbed the bank.'

Gammat translates. Vusi answers. Gammat translates again. 'Yes, he said he did rob the bank.'

'Ask him where are the others that helped him.'

Gammat translates. 'He says the others drove away in a stolen car. He doesn't have a clue where they went.'

'Where are the weapons they used?' asks the policeman.

Vusi translates. 'He says the weapons were all taken by the gangsters who escaped in the car.'

'Okay, ask him what they did with the money they stole.'

Gammat rattles off in Zulu again.

Vusi replies in Zulu, 'The money is buried at my uncle's house at 64 Rakanga Street in Soweto.'

Gammat schemes for a while, and then he tells Constable Van: 'He says you're a dom f****n Boer, and he wouldn't tell you even if he knew.'

FAIR SWAP

Vusi and his wife were leaving Pick 'n Pay with a pram. Mrs Vusi looked inside the pram and screamed: 'Vusi! It's the wrong child!'

'Shhh,' said Vusi. 'It's a better pram.'

SOUND OF SIRENS

(To be sung to the tune of 'Sounds of Silence'.)

Hello darkness my old friend
You've come to rob me once again
I hear your footsteps softly creeping
Through my house as I lie sleeping
And the brick you used to smash my window pane
Still remains
within the sounds of sirens

(Sound effects of alarm siren)

In restless streets I walked alone
They stole my car I can't get home
'Neath the halo of a street lamp
They grabbed my wallet by the Autobank
When I was stabbed by a gangster net links van die
Telkompaal
It split my skull
I heard the sounds of sirens

(Sound effects of police siren)

And in the naked light I saw
just one konstabel not one more
he shouted, 'Freeze! this is the law speaking!'
they broke his kakebeen without listening
people running loose 'cause they been released on bail
no place in jail
amidst the sounds of sirens

(Sound effects of mixture of sirens)

Why they do it I don't know
violence like a cancer grows
Hear my words that I might teach you
Take my TV and my radio

But a life is a sacred thing my broer
It's given once …
Don't let it echo … (gunshot followed by shriek)
… into silence

And in the naked light I saw
A shadow move across my door
I waited quietly and I klapped him once
It was the outjie from Armed Response
'Ag sorry,' I said as he fell down on his head
My face was red
reflected in the sounds of sirens …

YOUR GRACE

Alan Boesak was on the run from his oppressors, when he hopped a high fence and found himself in the middle of the Kruger National Park.

Suddenly he heard a tremendous roar. He froze as he saw a lion appearing from behind a bush.

Alan fell to his knees, and started praying like he never prayed before. When he opened his eyes, he saw to his astonishment that the lion was also on his knees in prayer.

'It's miracle!' said the former priest. 'A miracle!'

'Shut up,' said the lion, 'can't you see I'm saying grace?'

CROCODILES

CROC SUIT

Mike and Jimmy visit the crocodile farm at Sun City. Mike sees this beautiful croc-skin handbag in the curio shop and decides to buy it for his cherry. He walks over to the attendant and asks, 'How much for that handbag?'

'Five hundred and fifty rand,' says the attendant.

'You're blerrie mal in jou kop man,' says Mike as they leave the shop.

Later, wandering around the farm, Mike and Jimmy see a blue-suited cleaner who has just been swallowed by a massive croc. The cleaner's legs are sticking out; the rest of him is sticking in.

'Hell ou Jimmy,' says Mike, 'if that lady wanted five hundred and fifty for that handbag, can you imagine what that oke must have paid for that sleeping bag.'

JUST FOR SPORT

Madiba is doing a nationwide helicopter tour of out-of-the-way farms and settlements. Somewhere over the Limpopo River, he sees two men in a motor boat, towing a black man on skies.

He instructs the pilot to swoop a little lower, and he pulls out his loud-hailer.

'Hello, how are you,' shouts Madiba. 'I just want to congratulate you on striving so hard to improve race relations in our country. Mooi so, boere.'

Down in the boat, ET looks puzzled as he turns to oom Jaap.

'Man, that Madiba isn't such a bad oke,' says ET. 'But he knows boggerall about crocodile hunting.'

DARKEST AFRICA

ON YOUR BIKE

The tribe was getting some English lessons from the professor.

'Tree, monkey, bush, river,' he said, pointing out the different objects to the tribe.

Suddenly they came across a nude couple making love behind a bush. 'What's that?' asked the chief.

The embarrassed Prof. thought for a second and said, 'Bike.'

The chief took his spear and drove it into the man's arse.

'My bike,' he said.

VINKEL EN KOLJANDER

Die ou stap die pub binne – lang ponytail, stukkiesbaard, dik letsels van die tienerpuisies. Hy't iemand saam met hom – lang ponytail, stukkiesbaard, dik letsels van die tienerpuisies. Hulle is soos Vinkel en Koljander. Enigste verskil is, die een is ses voet vyf duim lank, en die ander net twintig duim. Die barman vra, 'Wat sal dit wees?'

Die grote sê beleefd, 'Twee Kastele, asseblief.'

Die kleintjie ontplof van woede en gil in 'n skril stemmetjie, 'Jy kan mos sien ons is Kasteel-manne! Hoekom vra jy nog!?'

Die barman frons en skink. Hy vra, 'Waar kom julle vandaan?'

'Ons is grootwildjagters,' sê die grote. 'Kom nou net doer uit Midde-Afrika.'

Die kleintjie gaan weer gal-af, 'Enige poepol kan sien ons is grootwildjagters! Skink nog 'n Kasteel en hou op stront praat!'

Die barman loop 'n paar draaie, en keer later terug, lekker nuuskierig oor die vreemde spektakel. Hy vra versigtig, 'Wat het julle manne geskiet?'

Die grote sê, ''n Paar leeus, drie luiperds, twee olifante.'

Die kleintjie is nou lekker gatvol, en gil harder as ooit, 'Lyk ons soos blerrie moffies, huh?! Dink jy ons skiet f****n tarentale?!'

Die barman los hulle 'n lang ruk uit, maar sy nuuskierig-heid dwing hom vir oulaas terug.

'Waar presies het julle manne in Afrika gejag?'

Die grote sê vriendelik, 'Ons was in Botswana, Kenia, Zaïre, Zimbabwe en eee ...' Hy kyk af na die kleintjie langs hom, en vra, 'Ouboet, wat's daai plek nou weer waar jy vir die toordokter gesê het sy ma se m**r?'

DENTISTS

HOES!

Tolla se hy sal nooit 'n tandarts word nie.

'Hoekom nie?,' vra ek.

'Nee,' sê Tolla, 'ek sit nou annerdag in die wagkamer en die tandarts se deur is op so 'n skrefie oop. Daar's 'n oulike stuk in die stoel, en soos daai tandarts sy naald regkry vir die inspuiting, gryp sy hom hier van onder, amper soos die army-dokter die troepe gegryp het om te hoes, net 'n bietjie duideliker. "Wat maak jy, juffrou?!" vra daai dokter met 'n gil. Toe sê die stuk met 'n groot smile, "Ons gaan mekaar nie seermaak nie dokter, gaan ons?"'

TANDPYN

Oom Frik gaan uiteindelik tandarts toe nadat hy die afspraak maande lank uitgestel het. 'Ek is skuitbang, Dok,' sê oom Frik. 'Ek kan nie pyn verdra nie.'

'Moenie worry nie,' sê die tandarts nadat hy Oom Frik se mond deeglik ondersoek het. 'Net 'n stopseltjie hier en daar, twee ou vrottetjies vinnig trek en so 'n bietjie kanaalwerk, en siedaar, als is klaar.'

Oom Frik hop met een vinnige hop uit die tandarts se stoel, gryp sy hoed en sê, 'Cheers, Dok.'

Die tandarts sê, 'Oom Frik, luister. Doen my 'n guns en bel net gou hierdie een pasiënt van my. Hy sal jou vertel ek is 'n pynlose tandarts.'

Oom Frik maak toe maar so, en bel die tandarts se pasiënt.

'Jy ken my nie,' sê hy vir die ou aan die ander kant, 'maar ek en jy het dieselfde tandarts. Hy sê my hy't aan jou bek gewerk en jy's niks gevoel nie. Issit so?'

'Kom ek stel dit so,' sê 'n growwe stem aan die ander kant. 'Ek is 'n haasvanger van beroep. Ek vang hase in strikke. Nou annerdag was ek weer in die veld toe ek skielik 'n groot nood ontwikkel. Ek gaan sit toe agter 'n bos, laat sak my broek op my enkels en …'

'Luister,' val Oom Frik hom in die rede, 'ek wil weet van jou tanne …'

'Ek kom daarby,' sê die haasvanger kortaf. 'Ek was net op pad om my ding te doen, toe ek per ongeluk met my linkervoet die haasstrik trigger presies daar waar ek hom die vorige week gestel het. Daai staalkake klap met 'n hengse slag vas om my knaters. Ek los 'n hengse gil en ek spring in die lug op, toe ek skielik herinner word dat my strik met 'n kort stukkie ketting vasgeanker is aan 'n staalpen in die grond.

'Om nou jou vraag te antwoord: dit was die eerste keer ná ek by daai tannedokter was dat my tanne nie gepyn het nie.'

DIETING

BEER-BOEP

What's a balanced diet?
A Castle in each hand.

WEIGHT-WATCHER

Suzy goes to see the doc about her love-life. She's not getting enough. The doc asks her to strip. He notes that she's just a little on the hefty side.

'Why don't you diet?' he says.

She looks down.

'Really? What colour do you suggest?' she asks.

MAERMAAK

Daar is 'n wonderlike nuwe maermaakmetode ontdek. Die dokter verwyder al jou bene uit jou liggaam. Behalwe dat jy nou baie minder weeg, lyk jy sommer baie meer ontspanne.

FATSO

'You're overweight,' said the doctor to Schucks.

'I want a second opinion.'

'Okay, you're ugly as well.'

DIVORCE

KITCHEN-SINK DRAMA

Koos bumps into Piet at the pub. 'Hey, Piet,' he says, 'how are things going with you and your wife?'

'Ag no fine,' says Piet, 'We're getting divorced.'

'You're getting divorced! How come?'

'Man, I just can't take any more of her filthy, disgusting habits,' says Piet.

'What do you mean?'

'Well, this morning I went to take a leak in the sink, only to find that it was full of dirty dishes.'

TRY AGAIN

Here's one for the ladies. What's the difference between rugby and your ex-husband?

In rugby, you get three points for kicking the ball between the uprights.

JUKSKEI

Meeste mans oor 40 speel jukskei. Eers jeuk hulle, en dan skei hulle.

MAINTENANCE MAN

The magistrate in Divorce Court B bangs his gavel on the desk and glares at Van der Merwe.

'After due consideration,' declares His Honour, 'I have decided to give your wife the sum of R2 750 per week.'

'Thanks, Your Honour,' says Van der Merwe. 'I'll try to send her a few bucks myself every now and again.'

COCKTAILS

A woman meets a man at a cocktail party. They make small talk for a while. He fetches her a drink. Their eyes lock for a split second longer than decorum allows.

'You know,' she says, 'you look just like my third husband.'

'How many times have you been married?' asks the man.

'Twice,' replies the lady.

THE GIFT THAT KEEPS ON GIVING

The yuppie and his wife were having a raging argument about nothing in particular.

'You just don't care anymore!' yelled the wife.

'You're just upset,' pooh-poohed the yuppie. 'Why don't I buy you something to make you feel better?'

'Like what?' she yelled again.

'How about a trip to Europe?'

'No!'

'What about a new Jaguar?'

'No!'

'Well, what do you want, then?' he asked.

'I want a divorce!'

The yuppie thought about it for a moment.

'Actually,' he said, 'I wasn't planning on spending that much.'

AL UITGEPUT

'Op watter gronde wil u van Mnr van der Merwe skei,' vra Van se vrou se prokureur.

'Op grond van gesondheid en uitputting,' sê Mev Van.

'Hoe bedoel mevrou dan nou, mevrou?' vra die prokureur.

'Ek is siek en sat vir die klein wetter,' sê sy.

JUST LIKE OLD TIMES

An oke meets up with his ex-wife at a party. After a few dops, he puts his arm around her and suggests they go to bed.

'Over my dead body,' she snarls at him.

He downs his drink and says, 'I see you haven't changed.'

DOCTORS

EATING DISORDER

Mike Schutte walks into the doctor's surgery one day. He's got a cucumber up his nose, a carrot in his left ear, and a banana in his right ear.

'What's the matter with me, doc?' asks Mike.

And the doc looks up and says, 'Ag, Mike, you're just not eating properly.'

PLUMB CRAZY

A pipe bursts in a doctor's house. He calls a plumber. The plumber arrives, unpacks his tools, tightens a few washers here, loosens a few widgets there, and knocks on the pipe a few times with his monkey-wrench. Then he hands the doctor a bill for R750. The doctor almost faints.

'This is ridiculous,' he says. 'I don't even make this much as a doctor!'

I know,' says the plumber. 'Neither did I when I was a doctor.'

YOU MUST BE CHOKING

Schucks phones the doctor late one night. 'Doc,' he says, 'I've just swallowed a chicken bone!'

'Are you choking?' asks the doctor.

'No,' says Schucks, 'I'm blerrie serious.'

DRONKLAP

Tolla se dokter ondersoek hom en sê uiteindelik, 'Ou Tolla jong, dit lyk vir my maar sleg, ou pêl. Ek dink dis van te veel drink.'

'Dis oukei, Dok,' sê Tolla, 'ek sal terugkom as jy nugter is.'

NO PAIN

Wearing a bandage around his head, Mike goes to see his doctor.

'So what does the X-ray of my head show, hey doc?'

The doctor holds the X-ray up to the light. 'Ag, nothing,' he says.

SNYKUNS

Drie snydokters sit en praat oor hulle sny-eskapades.

'Ek het vanmore 'n Jap gedoen,' sê die eerste dokter. 'Dis ongelooflik. Al sy dele is gelabel en gekleur kodifiseer. Dit was die mees kliniese en maklikste snywerk wat ek ooit gedoen het.'

Die tweede snydokter sê, 'My Duitser van vanoggend lyk soos die binnekant van 'n BMW. Elke part is genommer, gechrome en het 'n stamp op. Ek kon sy pankreas amper geblinddoek verwyder.'

Nou's dit Dr Koos se beurt. 'Ek is seker,' sê Koos, 'my operasie van vanoggend was die heel maklikste ooit.'

'Wie't jy nogal gesny?' vra die ander twee.

''n Politikus. Ek het gevind hy't net twee bewegende parte, sy mond en sy anus. Albei doen presies dieselfe werk: niemand sal agterkom as jy hulle omruil nie.'

BEDSIDE MANNER

The doctor and his wife were having a roaring argument at breakfast. 'You aren't so good in bed either!' shouted the doc as he stormed off to work. Midway through the day, he began to feel remorseful about his outburst. He phoned home. After many rings, his wife picked up the phone.

'What took you so long to answer?' asked the doc.

'I was in bed.'

'What were you doing in bed this late?'

'Getting a second opinion.'

DOKTER DOKTER

Twee bejaarde dokters sit in die park en gesels toe daar 'n ou oom aangestap kom. Sy kniekoppe is styf teen mekaar gedruk, en sy hande is na binnetoe in vuiste geklem.

'Kom ons kyk of jy nog reg kan diagnoseer,' sê die een dokter. 'Wat dink jy is fout met daai ou?'

Die ander ou dokter het die omie stip bestudeer vir 'n paar oomblikke en sê toe, 'Artritis, geen twyfel nie. Wat sê jy?'

Die ander dokter kyk mooi na die ou oom en sê na 'n rukkie, 'Serebrale verlamming. Ek's bereid om te wed daarop.'

Net toe hulle die ou oom self wil vra, skuifel hy na hulle toe en sê, 'Weet julle dalk waar's die k*khuis?'

LOOK ON THE BRIGHT SIDE

With a worried look on his face, the doctor steps out of the surgery and says to the woman waiting in the corridor, 'I don't like the look of your husband.'

'Neither do I,' she says, 'but he's good with the kids.'

NEANDERTHAL MAN

'Doctor,' says Mike, 'when I came out of my room this morning, I couldn't walk upright.'

'No wonder,' replied Doc. 'You've got your fly buttoned to your waistcoat.'

MONSTER

Mike gaan dokter toe. Die dokter gee hom 'n botteltjie en sê, 'Piepie vir ons 'n monster, asseblief.'

Mike sê, 'Oukei, dan k*k jy vir ons 'n krokodil.'

SAY 'AAAAAAAAAAA!'

Oom Frans Stroebel word gehijack, kom lewendig anderkant uit maar as gevolg van die traumatiese ervaring verloor hy sy stem. G'n dokter kan hom help nie, tot hy op 'n dag by Dr. Van uitkom. Dié het hom deeglik ondersoek, niks fout gevind nie, en uiteindelik sy eie onortodokse stemherwinningsmetode op die proef gestel.

'Trek af jou broek en buk vooroor met jou hande op my lessenaar,' sê Dr Van. Oom Frans is desperaat en sal enige iets doen.

So staan hy daar broek op die enkels gebuk oor die lessenaar.

Dr Van neem die vensterstok met die haak aan die punt, vat so drie tree se aanloop en druk hom met groot geweld van agter af in: 'Aaaaaaaaaaaaa!' gil oom Frans van pure pyn.

'Kom môre terug vir "B",' sê Dok Van.

EINA

A young woman goes to see her doctor, complaining of pain. 'Where does it hurt?' asks the doctor.

'It hurts all over,' says the woman.

'What do you mean, all over?' asks the doc. 'You'll have to be a little more specific.'

So the woman touches her right knee with her index finger. 'Ow,' she yells, 'that hurts.' Then she touches her left cheek and yells, 'Eina! That hurts, too.' Then she touches her right earlobe. 'Yeeow! Even THAT hurts,' she cries.

The doctor looks at her thoughtfully for a moment. Then he asks, 'Are you a natural blonde?'

'Why, yes,' says the woman.
'I thought so,' says the doc. 'You have a broken finger.'

DOCTOR DOCTOR

This volupto … voluptu … hell of a sexy blonde goes for her annual medical check-up. She's standing behind the screen in the doctor's room, dispensing with every item of clothing.

'Where should I throw my clothes, doctor?' she asks.
'Right there in the corner next to mine,' he says.

BED-WETTER

A woman writes to the doctor complaining about her son wetting his bed. The doctor writes back, saying it's quite normal. The woman writes back to the doctor: 'Well I don't think it's normal and neither does my son's wife.'

MEDICAL MATTER

At an international medical seminar, two surgeons are having a heated argument. The surgeon from New Delhi says, 'No man, I am telling you, it is WOOOMBAAA.'

The surgeon from Nairobi shakes his head and says, 'You are wrong, my friend. It is WHOOOOOMMMMM.'

Overhearing the conversation, a surgeon from London says, 'Excuse me for butting in chaps, but I do believe the word you are trying to say is WOMB.'

As he walks away, the Indian surgeon turns to his colleague and says, 'I bet you he has never even seen a hippopotamus, let alone heard one fart under water.'

INSTANT CURE

Van wakes up one day with a splitting headache. He swallows a couple of industrial-strength tablets. They don't help. So he goes to see his doctor. The doctor can't find anything wrong.

He says to Van: 'You know Van, whenever I feel this type of headache coming on, I go straight home and make passionate love to my wife. It really works for me. I strongly advise you to try it.'

Van returns after a week. He's looking like a new man. 'Doc,' he says, 'that was the best advice I ever got from any doctor. We bonked for hours on end, and wragtig, every time we're finished, weg is my kopseer!'

'I'm glad it worked for you, Van. Keep it up.'

'No, for sure, doc', says Van on his way out. 'I'm on my way to her right now.'

'Mooi,' says the doctor.

'Oh, and by the way, doc,' says Van, 'I just love those mirrors above your double bed.'

MAN OR MOUSE

A man swallowed a mouse while sleeping on the couch. His wife quickly called the doctor and said, 'Doctor, please hurry! My husband just swallowed a mouse and he's gagging and thrashing about.'

'I'll be right over,' said the doc. 'In the meantime, try waving a piece of cheese over your husband's mouth. It'll attract the mouse and help you get him out of there.'

When the doctor arrived, he saw the wife waving a piece of smoked herring over her husband's mouth.

'What are you doing?' said the doctor. 'I told you to use a piece of cheese, not herring.'

'I know,' said the woman. 'But I'm trying to get the cat out first.'

ANIMAL INSTINCT

Did you hear about the doctor who lost his license because he had an affair with one of his patients?

A pity, actually. He was one of the best veterinarians in the country.

MEDICAL TEST

What is the difference between a haematologist and a urologist?

A haematologist pricks your finger.

MOTHER'S MILK

Vusi, the medical student, is writing his final exam. He reads the first question: 'Name the three main advantages of mother's milk.' That's easy, thinks Vusi.

'One: It has all the healthful nutrients needed to sustain a baby. Two: It is inside the mother's body and therefore protected from germs and infections.'

Three? Vusi bites his lips, frowns, scratches his head. Ah! He scrawls the answer in perfect imitation of a real doctor's handwriting. 'It comes in such nice containers.'

ALARM BELLS

A worried-sounding Van phones his doctor. 'Doc,' he says, 'I've got this terrible problem. Every morning at exactly ten past five, I have a bowel movement.'

'That's not a problem,' the doc reassures him. 'A punctual bowel movement like that is actually a very healthy sign.'

'You don't understand, doc,' says Van. 'I only wake up at six o'clock.'

NOOD VIR BROOD

Die ou se seksdrang het opgepak, en hy gaan na 'n homeopaat-pêl van hom vir raad. Die homeopaat sê, 'Eet baie bruinbrood, dit sit die vonk terug in jou stronk.'

Hy gaan na die Griek om die hoek en sê, 'Gee my R200 se bruinbrode.'

Die Griek sê, 'R200 se bruinbrood? Ou pêl, voor jy dit opgeëet het, is dit kliphard.'

Die ou sê, 'Fyn, maak dit R400 s'n.'

YOU MUST BE JOKING

Four nurses worked for an arrogant, opinionated doctor who treated them like dirt. They decided to teach him a lesson by playing a series of practical jokes on him. At lunch in the hospital canteen, they gathered to discuss their progress.

'I stuffed cotton in his stethoscope so he couldn't hear,' said the first nurse.

'I let the mercury out of his thermometers and painted them all to read 106 degrees,' said the second nurse.

'I did even better than that,' said the third nurse. 'I poked holes in all of the condoms that he keeps in his desk drawer.'

The fourth nurse fainted.

WHOOPS

Did you hear about the clumsy surgeon who was performing a vasectomy?

He missed and got the sack.

DOGS

SPECIAL BREED

Mike was taking these two small dogs for a walk. A passing pedestrian paused and said, 'Nice dogs. Are they Jack Russels?'

'No,' said Mike. 'They're mine.'

CAT SCAN

Die vrou daag laat een koue Saterdagaand op by die veearts met haar lewelose Maltesie in haar arms. Sy's bitter bedroef, want 'n Rottweiler het haar hondjie aangeval.

'Dokter,' snik sy, 'maak tog vir my seker of hy heeltemaal dood is.'

Die veearts het die middag gholf gespeel en lank by putjie nommer 19 gedraai, so hy's lekker blink. Hy check die hondjie so en sê, 'Wag, laat ek gou 'n kat loop haal.'

Hy kom terug met die kat, sit dit op die hondjie, en laat die kat oor die hond loop. Geen reaksie van die hondjie nie. Die dokter sê, 'Mevrou, jou hond is so dood soos 'n mossie.' Hy gryp die hondjie aan sy stert, slinger hom in die kaggelvuur en sê, 'Dit sal R110 wees vir die konsultasie, R140 vir die kremasie en R250 vir die cat scan.'

ATTITUDE

On holiday in London, Mike pauses for a pint in a London pub. Then he pauses for a pee. He returns from the Gents to find that a dog has chewed his brand-new hat to pieces. Mike is furious. He approaches the dog's owner, a genuine, honest-to-goodness, salt-of-the-earth Cockney.

'Can you see what your mongrel did to my new hat?' barks Mike.

'Sure I can see mate,' says the Cockney. 'And how stupid of you to leave it lying on a chair right next to my dog.'

'Are you going to pay me the money to buy myself a new hat?' asks a very upset Mike.

'Screw you mate,' says the Cockney. 'And screw your hat too.'

'I don't like your attitude!' yells Mike, now ready to knock the oke's block off.

But the Cockney just shrugs.

'No, it's not my attitude, mate.' He points to his dog. 'It's YOUR bloody 'at 'e chewed!'

EVERY DOG HAS HIS DAY

Old Vusi from the Transkei walks into the pub with his dog. The barman says, 'Hey! No dogs allowed.'

The dog turns to Vusi and says, 'Bugger this oke, let's go someplace else.' The barman is amazed.

'Come back!' he says. 'Did I hear that dog talk?'

'Sure you did,' says Vusi. 'He's been talking for years.'

Vusi knocks back a few beers, while the barman has a long conversation with the dog. When Vusi gets up to go to the Gents, the barman leans across the counter and says to the mutt: 'My cousin runs a pub across the road. It would be great if you would go over and ask him for a beer. He'll get the shock of his life.'

The dog hesitates, but when the barman offers him R50, he snatches the money between his teeth, hops off the barstool and heads for the door.

Vusi comes back from the Gents. "Where's my dog?' he asks the barman. The barman tells him.

'What?! You fool! He's not a city dog! He'll get run over in the traffic!'

Vusi rushes out of the pub, and there, on the pavement, is Vusi's dog, enjoying the company of a good-looking poodle. The old man is shocked.

'I've never seen you do that before,' he says to the dog.

'I've never had the money before,' says the dog.

DRUNKS

4U2P

This oke in the pub brags that he can down 16 beers in no time, which he does. He gets up from his chair, swings from side to side, stumbles outside and opens his fly. A policeman spots him and says, 'Hey, you can't pee here.'

The oke says, 'I'm not gonna pee here. I'm gonna pee theeeeere.'

PROVE IT

This professional juggler is driving to his next performance, when he is ordered to pull over by the cops.

'What are all these knives doing in your car?' asks the officer in charge.

'They're part of my act,' says the oke behind the wheel. 'I'm a professional juggler.'

'Oh ja?' says the cop, knowingly nodding his head. 'Let's see you prove it.'

So the juggler starts tossing and juggling the knives.

A guy driving by sees this and says to his buddy, 'Boy, am I glad I quit drinking. Look at the test they're making you do now!'

FATHER KNOWS BEST

This oke who smells like a brewery takes his seat next to Father O'Reilly at the bus-stop. The oke's tie is stained, his face is smeared with bright red lipstick, and there's a half-jack of brandy sticking out of his pocket. The oke reaches into the rubbish-bin, pulls out a newspaper, and begins reading.

'Excuse me, Father,' slurs the oke after a few minutes. 'Would you by any chance be able to tell me what causes arthritis?'

Sensing an opportunity to spread the word on redemption, Father O'Reilly says, 'Sir, arthritis is caused by loose living, cheap women, too much alcohol and a contempt for your fellow man.'

'Well I'll be damned,' says the drunk.

'Indeed,' says the priest. But after a moment's thought, he begins to regret his harsh words of judgement. He turns to the drunk and says, 'Forgive me for coming on so strong to you, my good man. How long have you had arthritis?'

And the good man says, 'Oh, I don't have arthritis, Father. But it says here that the Pope does.'

FINE FARE

This seriously drunk oke somehow stumbles his way into the back seat of a taxi.

'Excuse me,' he manages to say to the driver. 'Do you

have room in the front seat for a pizza and six bottles of Castle?'

'Sure,' says the driver.

And the drunk leans over and throws up on the front seat.

DAYLIGHT ROBBERY

Seriously intoxicated, not to mention drunk out of his skull, this oke totters into the cop shop to report a stolen car. His own.

'Where did you leave it?' asks the constable on duty.

'It was right here on the end of my key,' says the drunk, producing his ignition key as proof. The constable isn't impressed.

'You should be ashamed of yourself, coming into the police station at this time of night in such a condition. Look at yourself, man. Even your fly is wide open.'

The drunk looks down.

'Oh no,' he says, 'they've stolen my girlfriend too!'

WRONG NUMBER

This oke falls through the church doors at one o' clock in the morning, sloshed out of his senses.

He finally stumbles into a confession booth, falls over and lands flat on his belly. He hears the priest's voice from the other side: 'Can I help?'

'Ja. Paash vir my die k*kpapier, assheblief.'

LEKKER GESUIP

Die ou tannie het die oom met 'n jong dingetjie in die bed betrap. Hulle is op pad dominee toe, toe 'n spietkop hulle in 'n snelstrik betrap. Die spietkop stap nader en sê, 'Besef u dat u teen 120 k.p.u. in 'n beboude gebied gery het?'

'Onmoontlik,' sê die ou oom, 'ek ry nooit vinniger as 60 nie.'

'Hy lieg,' chip die ou tannie in, 'hy's 'n spoedvraat en hy ry nooit stadiger as 130 nie.'

Die oom staar haar aan.

'Ek sien u dra nie u gordel nie,' sê die verkeersman terwyl hy die kaartjie uitskryf.

'Ek dra dit altyd, maar ek het dit net vinnig losgemaak om my beursie uit te haal,' sê die ou oom.

'Hy lieg soos 'n ketter,' sê die ou tannie weer. Hy dra dit nooit nie, al nag ek hom altyd om dit te dra.'

Die oom raak rooi van die woede en bars uit, 'Wat de hel gaan met jou aan, vrou?!'

Die spietkop vra, 'Mevrou, is u man altyd so aggressief?'

'Nee, nes hy gesuip is,' sê die ou tannie.

K*K EN BETAAL

Schucks stap die pub binne en sê vir die barman, 'Gee my 'n dubbel whiskey voor die k*k kom.'

Die barman skink 'n vinnige dubbel. Schucks gooi hom rats in sy keelgat af, slaan die glas op die toonbank neer en sê vir die barman, 'Gee my nog 'n dubbel, voor die k*k kom.'

Die barman stribbel nie teë nie, gooi 'n volgende dubbel, en Schucks sluk hom af met een teug. Hy sê, 'Nog 'n dubbel, voor die k*k kom.'

So gaan dit aan vir nog drie dubbels.

Die barman sit die tab op die toonbank neer en sê, 'Jy skuld my R64.'

'Hier kom die k*k nou,' sê Schucks.

BIG BOEP

The young woman looked at the roffie in the pub and said, 'If that stomach were on a woman, she would be pregnant.'

'It was,' said the roffie, 'and she is.'

TONGBRAND

'Brand jou tong ôk as jy so baie drink?' vra Kallie vir Mike.
'Ek weet nie, sê Mike, 'ek het hom nog nooit try light nie.'

MOTHERLESS

This oke comes home one night, motherless again. Gatvol again, his wife says, 'I'm sick and tired of your drinking! What will you do if you come home one night and find me in bed with another man?!'

'I'll break his walking stick and shoot his guide dog.'

IN THE DOGBOX

The same oke eventually lands up in the dogbox – literally. He spends night after night with Tamsin, the family's placid Bouvier.

'I'm living the life of a dog,' the oke tells his chommies in the pub. 'I ought to report her to the SPCA. I've got to eat from the same bowl as the blerrie mutt. It's inhuman. I should actually report my wife to the TRC.'

'Go home one night without drinking,' advises his best chommie, 'and see what happens.'

This he does. *Voilà!* His wife welcomes him with open arms, prepares him a wonderful dinner and makes passionate love to him that night.

Next day after work the oke rushes to the pub and shares his joy with his chommies. Before he knows what hit him, he's motherless once more. He gets home and his wife doesn't say a word. She just stands there on the doorstep, pointing at the dogbox and the Bouvier.

The oke gets the message. But as he climbs into the dogbox on all fours, Tamsin snarls, growls and starts attacking him viciously.

'Tamsin!' he says, 'what the?? ... eina! ... stoppit, you bitch ... ouch! What's got into you?!'

Tamsin grabs hold of his nuts, shakes them between her teeth and says, 'And where were you last night?'

ELEPHANTS

STARTING AT THE BOTTOM

Vusi goes to see his doctor, complaining about a recurring rash on his right arm.

'What work do you do?' asks the doc, as he takes a closer look at the affected area.

'I give enemas to elephants in the circus,' says Vusi.

The doctor is intrigued. 'So tell me, how do you give an elephant an enema?'

'Well,' says Vusi, 'you stick your arm up his behind and you … well, you know, you give him an enema.'

'Hmmm,' hmmms the doc. 'Look, Vusi,' he says, 'there's only one sure way you're going to get rid of this rash on your arm. Get yourself a new job.'

'What?' exclaims Vusi, 'and give up show business?'

EAT MY DUST

This mouse is walking through the jungle with his pal, the elephant.

'Wow!' says the mouse, looking over his shoulder, 'just check how much dust we leave behind!'

TRUNK CALL

What does an elephant use for a condom?
The MTN blimp.

JUMBO SIZE

What do you get if you cross an elephant with a prostitute?
A hooker who never forgets you and does it for peanuts.

FARMERS

COCK-A-DOODLE-DO

Derek Hanekom is visiting some farmers in the Free State, when he accidentally runs over a rooster. He drives over to the farm and comes across the farmer's wife.

'Look,' says the Minister, 'I'm terribly sorry, but I just ran over your rooster.'

'That wasn't just a rooster,' says the farmer's wife. 'That was Felix.'

Now the Minister really feels bad. That poor chicken was one of the family.

'I'd like to replace your rooster,' says the Minister.

'Please yourself,' says the farmer's wife. 'The hens are around the back.'

COCK AND BULL STORY

Two Free State boere are talking about Derek Hanekom, the Minister of Agriculture.

'I see the Minister says he is committed to serving the farmers,' says the first boer.

'Ja, I know,' says the second. 'Like the bulls serve the cow.'

NO SUCH LUCK

Farmer Van had three teenage daughters. Deeply concerned about their welfare in an often wayward world, he vetted their suitors with an eagle eye and a shotgun by his side.

One night, all three daughters were going out on dates. It was the first time this had happened, so Farmer Van had no option but to be even more vigilant than usual. The doorbell rang.

Farmer Van answered, shotgun at the ready. Not a threat, just a subtle reminder.

The boy at the door said, 'My name's Joe, I'm here for Flo. We're going to the show, is she ready to go?'

Farmer Van nodded, and the kids went on their way.

The doorbell rang again. Farmer Van answered. Another clean-cut boy stood waiting.

'My name's Eddie, I'm here for Betty, we're going to get spaghetti, is she ready?'

Farmer Van nodded, and the kids went on their way.

A little while later, the doorbell rang again. Farmer Van answered. The boy began: 'Hi, my name's Chuck …'

And Farmer Van shot him.

TOILET PAPER

Derek Hanekom is op besoek aan 'n paar boere in die Waterberg-distrik. Hy kom by 'n plaashuis aan en 'n outjie van so sewe maak die deur oop. 'Is jou pa hier?' vra Derek.

'Nee, Oom, hy's dorp toe.'

'Is jy seker?' vra Derek.

'Doodseker, Oom.'

'En jou ma?'

'Sy't my boetie by die skool gaan haal.'

'Is jy seker?'

Doodseker, Oom.'

'Bly hier enige ander mense?'

'Ja, Oom. My ouma.'

'Waar's sy?'

Sy sit daar buite op die long drop, Oom.'

'Is jy seker?'

'Doodseker, Oom, want sy's hier weg met die *Sunday Times* en ek weet sy kan nie Engels lees nie.'

PASOP VIR VARKE

Die Minister van Landbou se chauffeur, Vusi, ry per ongeluk 'n boer se vark morsdood buite Ventersdorp. Die Minister voel baie sleg, en ry na die boer se plaas toe. Hy klop aan die deur, die boer maak oop en die Minister sê:

'Middag meneer. Ons het ongelukkig een van u varke doodgery. Dit spyt my, maar ek sal u finansieel vergoed vir u verlies.'

Die boer vererg hom bloediglik, gryp die Minister aan sy broek se gat en boender hom by die voordeur uit, 'Jy sit nooit weer jou blerrie voete op my plaas nie!'

Nou voel die Minister se chauffeur baie sleg, want dit was mos hy wat die vark doodgery het. Terwyl hy die Minister se baadjie afstof sê hy, 'Sorry Meneer, dit was eintlik my skuld. Ek sal die saak met die boer gaan regstel.'

Hy's toe fort plaashuis toe, en hy bly 'n hele ruk weg. Later kom hy terug met handevol biltong, droëwors en 'n paar lekker steaks.

Die Minister kan sy oë nie glo nie en vra, 'Hoe de hel het jy dit reggekry, Vusi?'

'Ek weet self nie, Meneer,' sê Vusi. 'Ek het net vir hom gesê ek is die Minister van Landbou se chauffeur en ek het die vark doodgery.'

VARKBOERE

Koos het sleg tweede gekom tydens sy egskeiding, want die prokureur wat die saak tussen hom en vroulief moes skik, gaan staan toe en raak verlief op Koos se vrou. Koos was bitter, en ry een aand in dorp toe om sy sorrows te drown.

'Bliksemse vark. Dis wat hy is. Niks minder as 'n donnerse vark nie,' mompel Koos soos hy die een Klipdrift na die ander wegslaan. Die kroegman hoor Koos se gewraakte uitlatings, leun oor die kroegtoonbank en sê, 'U moet baie versigtig wees wat u in die kroeg sê, meneer.'

'Hoekom?' vra Koos, 'is hier 'n prokureur in die bar?'

'Nee,' sê die kroegman, 'hier's 'n paar varkboere.'

SOME THINGS YOU CAN'T EXPLAIN

Koos the farmer is sitting in the neighbourhood one-star, getting slowly but surely sloshed. His buddy walks in and says, 'Hey Koos, why are you sitting here on this beautiful day getting drunk all by yourself?'

'Ag,' sighs Koos, 'there are some things you just can't explain.'

'Try me,' says his chommie. 'What happened?'

'Well,' says Koos, ordering another shot of brandy 'n Coke, 'I was milking old Bessie this morning, and ...'

'Bessie's your cow?'

'Of course Bessie's my cow, man. What do you think? Anyway, just as I got the bucket almost full, Bessie took her left leg and kicked over the bucket.'

'Ag, that's not so bad.'

'Ja, but some things you just can't explain.'

'What do you mean?'

'Well, I took the cow's leg and tied it to the post on the left.'

'And then?'

'And then I sat back down and continued to milk her. Just as I got the bucket almost full again, she took her right leg and kicked over the bucket.'

'Again?'

'Ja. Some things you just can't explain.'

'Well, what did you do next?' asks the oke.

Van sighs. 'I took her right leg and tied it to the post on the right.'

'And then?'

'And then I sat back down and began milking her again. Just as I got the bucket almost full, the stupid cow knocked over the bucket with her tail.'

'Bliksem. So what did you do?'

'Ag, some things you just can't explain.'

Van knocks back his dop, and signals to the barman for another.

'You see, man, I didn't have any more rope, so I took off my belt and tied her tail to the rafter. In that moment, my pants fell down and my wife walked in. Ja, boet. Some things you just can't explain.'

BY THE BALLS

Oom Bull lost control of his bakkie and it landed up in a dam. He scrambled to the top of the bakkie and waited for someone to come and rescue him.

Two hours later a car stopped. It was his neighbour Frikkie Baardt. Just then another car stopped. It was his other neighbours, Sam and Suzie Ball. The Baardts pulled Oom Bull to safety, and as he stepped onto dry ground he said, 'Thank goodness you were here first. I would hate to be pulled out by the Balls.'

LET THEM EAT CAKE

Then there was the day that oom Frik and tant Mien invited their fancy new English neighbours, the Claphams, for tea. This was a very special occasion for the old Boere couple, as their cattle farm, 'Stukkiesrus', was situated in a very remote part of Botswana, and they seldom had the opportunity to socialise.

Tant Mien spring-cleaned her house for days on end, and took out her grandmother's finest china tea set for the occasion. The night before the big event, oom Frik and tant Mien were sitting on the stoep at sunset, looking at their beloved old Jersey cow, Milktart, lazily grazing away at their lawn.

'I'm baking her favourite tomorrow,' said tant Mien. 'I wonder whether there's another cow in the world who is so mad about a milktart as our Milktart.'

The couple sat there in total peace for another hour, before tant Mien spoke again.

'You know Frik,' she said, 'we are so richly blessed in our lives. Just imagine, tomorrow we meet some new people and if we click, we might even have visitors over for tea every nine months or so!'

Oom Frik just nodded and stared at the setting sun. Finally he said, 'Nag vrou,' and went to bed.

'Ag I'm going to sit up a little longer, Pappie,' said tant

Mien. 'I'm so excited about tomorrow, I just won't be able to sleep.'

Tant Mien sat on that stoep until the early hours of the morning. She milked Bessie just after sunrise, and began spring-cleaning her kitchen and woonkamer for the ninth time that week.

Finally the big grandfather clock struck 11, and the Claphams arrived in their Silver Cloud Rolls Royce. At first, it was a bit of a 'n stywe affêre, but gradually, the Claphams overcame their reserve and surrendered to tant Mien's traditional Boere hospitality. Tant Mien was elated that everything was going according to plan.

Then disaster struck. While tant Mien was carrying the milktart into the woonkamer, Milktart the cow caught a whiff of her favourite delicacy. She hopped on to the stoep and was in the woonkamer in no time. Mrs Clapham shrieked. Then Milktart emptied her massive bowels on tant Mien's Persian carpet. Mrs Clapham fainted.

Tant Mien's eyes were as wide as saucers. She pointed to the mess on the carpet and shouted, 'Kyk! O henetjie tog, kyk, kyk!!'

It was right at this point that a visibly upset Mr Clapham jumped up from his chair, grabbed his hat and dragged his wife to the front door shouting, 'If that is cake, we are certainly not staying for tea!'

FARTS

HAVING A GAS

After much procrastination, delay, and denial, Vusi finally plucks up the courage to go and see his doctor about an embarrassing complaint. Even then, he's too embarrassed to say a word. He doesn't need to.

'FFFFFARRRRT!' goes Vusi as he shifts uneasily in the chair. It's got nothing to do with the chair. 'FFFFARRRRT!' goes Vusi again. 'Excuse me,' says the shamefaced Vusi, rapidly followed by 'FFFFFARRRRT!'

It's the worst case of excessive flatulence the doctor's ever seen. Or heard.

'All right, Vusi,' he says, 'I want you to take off your trousers and lie face down on the couch.'

Vusi does as he is told. The doctor goes over to a closet and pulls out a long pole with a sharp spike at one end. Vusi looks over his shoulder, farts loudly, and screams: 'Aiiiyeee! What are you going to do with that thing?'

'Relax, Vusi,' says the doctor. 'I'm just going to open the window.'

SOUNDS OF SILENCE

Mike walks into the doctor's waiting-room. It's crowded. Suddenly, it's not crowded anymore. Mike gets to see the doctor straight away. He gets straight to the point.

'Doctor,' he says, 'I fart all the time. The strange thing is, they're soundless, and they have no odour. In fact, since I've been here, I've farted no less than twenty times. Excuse me, twenty-one. What can I do, doc?'

'Here's a prescription, Mike. Take these pills three times a day for seven days and come back and see me in a week.'

The next week, an upset Mike storms into the doc's office.

'Doctor,' he says, 'I don't know what was in those pills, but the problem is worse! I'm farting just as much, and they're still soundless, but now they smell terrible! What do you have to say for yourself?'

'Calm down, Mike,' says the doctor. 'Now that we've fixed your sinuses, we'll work on your hearing.'

KA-BOOMPH

A wise old man once advised his son that if he wanted to live a long life, the secret was to sprinkle a little gunpowder on his cornflakes every morning. The son did this religiously, and he lived to the age of 93. When he died, he left 14 children, 28 grandchildren, 35 great-grandchildren, and a three-metre hole in the wall of the crematorium.

BLAME IT ON WAGTER

The dominee is doing his rounds in the neighbourhood. He isn't feeling too lekker. That take-away curry he had for supper is beginning to backfire on him. Or maybe it's the baked bean stew he had for lunch.

Either way, he's doing his best to sit through his first visit without losing his dignity. Then a teeny little portion of it escapes. 'Pfrrrt,' says the dominee, although the sound doesn't come from his mouth. The dominee pretends not to notice.

'Wagter!' yells Mrs Botha, wagging a finger at the family dog, who is dozing peacefully under the dominee's chair.

Relieved that the dog has taken the blame, the dominee lets out another one. This time it sounds more like, 'PFFFRRRRTTT'.

'Wagter!' Mrs Botha yells again.

Thank goodness, thinks the dominee. One more and I'll feel fine. So he lets loose a really big one.

'PPPPPPFFFFFFFFRRRRRRRRRRRRRRRTTTTTTTTTTT!!!!'

'Wagter!!' shrieks Mrs Botha, 'get out from under that chair before the dominee craps on your head!

FASHION

TWO OF A KIND

Kallie bumps into Mike in the street one day. 'Eina,' says Mike, rubbing his head, 'why don't you watch where you're going, man?'

'Sorry, Mike,' says Kallie, 'I was too busy looking at your shoes.'

'What about them?' asks Mike.

'Well,' replies Kallie, 'the one is black and the other is white. They must be unique.'

'Ag, not really,' shrugs Mike. 'I've got another pair just like them at home.'

HOT PANTS

Mike and Kallie are strolling down the road, heading towards their usual destination. Nowhere in particular.

Mike turns to his pal and says, 'You know, Kallie, soon as I get home, I'm going to rip my wife's panties off.'

'And why's that, hey Mike?'

'Because this blerrie elastic is killing me.'

FINANCE

WELCOME HOME

Mrs Van's financial advisor is preparing a quote for an endowment policy.

'What is your husband's average income?' he asks.

'Oh,' she replies, 'about midnight.'

QUID PRO QUO

When a stray fork of summer lightning burns the family mansion to the ground, Mrs Gundelfinger calls the insurance broker on her cell. 'We had that house insured for five hundred thousand Rand,' she says. 'We want the money now.'

'Whoaaa!' says the broker. 'Just hold on a minute. It doesn't work quite like that. We'll have to ascertain the value of your house first, and then we'll provide you with a new one of comparable worth.'

Silence as Mrs Gundelfinger contemplates this information.

'In that case,' she says, 'I'd like to cancel the policy on my husband.'

BRANDWAGTER

'Ek gaan my kar teen brand verseker,' vertel Mike vir Kallie.

'Wat van diefstal?' sê Kallie.

'Nooit,' antwoord Mike. 'Wie sal nou 'n kar wat brand steel?'

HOME BUSINESS

This Jewish couple have been married for over 40 years. One day the husband comes home and tells his wife that he's going to climb to the top of the tallest building in the city.

'And then what?' asks his wife.

'And then I'm going to jump off,' says the husband.

When she asks him what he would want to do that for, he shows her the front page of the newspaper. The stock market has crashed, and he's lost every cent he'd invested in a couple of sure-fire stocks. The wife doesn't look too worried.

'I thought this might happen some day,' she says. 'And that's why, from the beginning of our marriage, I've been putting R20 aside every time we've had sex. Those savings have grown to over R100 000.'

'Oy vey,' sighs the husband.

'What's the matter?' asks the wife. 'You're not happy?'

'I'm happy!' says the husband. 'I'm just kicking myself because I didn't give you all of my business!'

HIGH ROLLER

Abie walks into the bank and says he wants to borrow R200 for six months. The bank manager asks if he has any collateral.

'Sure I've got collateral,' says Abie. 'My Rolls Royce is parked outside. You can keep it until the loan is paid off.'

Abie hands over the keys, and returns six months later to pay off the loan, plus R50 interest. The bank manager thanks him. Then he says, 'Excuse me, Mr Goldberg, but

I'm curious. Why should a man who drives a Rolls Royce need to borrow R200?'

'Ah,' says Abie, 'that's exactly the point. I had to go to Europe for six months. Where else would I be able to store a Rolls Royce for that long, and pay only R50?'

FISHING

HOOK, LINE, AND SINKER

Little Van and little Vusi are fishing down at the dam, right next to the sign that says 'No Fishing Without A Valid Licence'.

The fish are piling up on the bank, when suddenly, from out of the bushes, up pops a valid licence inspector. He's just about to conduct his official licence check, when little Vusi throws down his rod and runs like crazy. The inspector gives chase.

Several hundred metres later, little Vusi pauses to catch his breath, and the licence inspector nabs him by the scruff of the neck.

'Okay, kid,' he says, 'let me see your licence. And I mean NOW!'

Vusi reaches into his pocket and pulls out a valid fishing licence. The inspector inspects it. It's valid, all right. Flabbergasted, he hands the licence back to Vusi.

'What's the matter with you, boy? You don't have to run from me if you've got a valid fishing licence!' Vusi shrugs his shoulders. 'I know, sir. But my friend back there at the dam ...'

'Yes?'

'He doesn't have a licence.'

CATCH OF THE DAY

Koos and the sexy blonde were walking along the beach. Koos had his rod slung over his shoulder. His fishing rod, that is. Piet spotted him and shouted, 'Hey Koos, did you catch anything?' Koos looked at the blonde and said, 'Hell I hope not.'

HELSE GROOT VIS

Van die visserman gooi eendag sy lyn in, sy voet gly en hy val van die rotse af in 'n baie rowwe see. Tien minute later staan hy voor Petrus. Petrus kyk Van se boekie deur en sê, 'Jammer, ek kan jou nie inlaat nie. Hier's te veel leuens hier.'

Van sê, 'Hei ou pêl, wees bietjie genadig, man. Onthou, jy was ook op 'n kol 'n visterman.'

FLY-FISHING

Koos en Piet were sitting on the banks of the Vaal outside Vereeniging, preparing to fish.

'Het jy al ingegooi?' asked Piet.

'Nee', sê Koos, 'ek soek nog die glase.'

Two hours later and without a single bite – except for the bite of Klipdrift in the throat – Piet said, 'Did you know that a single butterfly can lay twenty thousand eggs a year?'

'Hell,' said Koos, 'can you imagine what a married one could lay.'

FISHY STORY

'I didn't see you in church last Sunday, Van,' says the dominee. 'I heard you were out playing rugby.'

Van is taken aback at the very thought of it.

'That's just not true, dominee,' he says. 'And I've got the fish to prove it!'

THE ONE THAT GOT AWAY

Little Mike bursts into the house, bawling his eyes out. 'What's the matter?' asks his ma, reaching down to wipe away the tears.

'Me and Daddy went fishing,' sobs little Mike, 'and Daddy hooked this really, really big fish. But just as he was reeling it in, the line broke and the fish got away.'

'Ag, shame,' tuts Ma. 'But you're a big boy now, and you really shouldn't be crying over something like that. You should have just laughed it off.'

And little Mike says, 'But that's exactly what I did, Mommy.'

INNIE VISKAS

Hy't vir sy vrou gelieg en gesê hy't die naweek gaan visvang, maar hy't 'n stoute een met sy sekretaresse gehad.

'Hoe was dit toe?' vra sy vrou toe hy by die huis kom.

'Nee dit was great,' sê hy, 'maar jy't vergeet om my skeergoed in te pak.'

'Ek het nie,' sê sy met 'n wrang glimlag, 'ek het dit in jou viskas gesit.'

THE MAN WHO GOT HIMSELF HOOKED

There was this oke, Johnny Baardt, who was the most dedicated angler this country had ever produced. Man, he loved his fishing. He spent hours and hours at the Vaal with his dad as a kid, and he had time for nothing else in his life. He became Northern Transvaal champ in the light angling division, went on to become a Springbok and represented his country in many an international contest, which he always won.

He never once went out for a beer with his chommies, and he never sought the attention of the fairer sex, which kept him a very content man.

Then one day it happened, out of the blue with no warning. Johnny got married. Now this lady Johnny got married to wasn't an ordinary woman. No, she was the ugliest lady who had ever set foot on the southern part of the African continent. Man, she was ugly. She had four blonde hairs ... hanging out of her left nostril.

She had a red head. No hair, just a red head. Her mouth looked like it should have a hook inside it, and everyone thought maybe that was why Johnny married her. And she was fat. At school her friends called her the Sterkfontein Dam 'cause she was 90 per cent full. If she stood up in church there were three seats empty.

Her dad was a strawberry farmer, and he'd make her play with her dolls in his strawberry fields to keep the birds away. In fact, the birds were so scared of her they used to return the seeds they stole the previous season.

One day Johnny was sitting on the banks of Harties, and his longtime angling chommie Assie Roux gathered up enough guts to ask the one question that was on everybody's lips.

'Johnny,' he said, 'you know that every single oke in the angling fraternity in this country was shocked out of their senses when you got married – you, the one oke in the world who lived only for one thing, and that was his angling. As I say, that was a terrible shock to all of us. But an even greater shock, Johnny, and please excuse me for asking this, but nobody will ever understand this one thing: why, my ou maat, why oh why did you marry such a terribly, devastatingly ugly woman?'

There was a long silence as Johnny carefully worked his piece of custard pap onto his hook. Then he spoke:

'I married her 'cause she's got worms.'

FLASHERS

A TEENY BIT

Flip the Flasher had recently had a most humiliating experience. A woman charged him in the Small Claims Court.

JUST A QUICKIE

Two ou tannies were sitting in the park when an oke in a raincoat flashed his pride and joy at them.

Two of the tannies had a stroke. The third was too slow.

STICK AROUND

Piet the flasher was a real lazy oke. He had a sign hanging on the last button of his overcoat: 'Next session 2 p.m.'

THIS SMALL

It was so cold in Cape Town the other day, that the local flasher on the Waterfront was found describing himself to a group of women.

OU TOPPIE

Two ou aunties were sitting in the park of the old age home when this ou omie approached them.

'How old do you think I am?' he asked the aunties.

'Take off your clothes and I'll tell you,' said the one auntie.

The ou oom obliged, and soon he was standing in front of them stark naked.

'Okay,' said the auntie. 'Now turn around.'

The ou oom did as he was told.

'Now bend forward,' said the old auntie, 'and wriggle your bum.' After a few minutes the auntie said, 'You're 81.'

'How did you know?' asked the ou oom.

'You told me yesterday,' said the auntie.

GAMBLING

ZAMA-ZAMA

A man rushes into his house and yells to his wife, 'Martha, pack up your things. I just won the Zama-Zama lottery!'

Martha replies, 'Shall I pack for warm weather or cold?'

The man responds, 'I don't care. Just so long as you're out of the house by noon!'

PICK A NUMBER

Suzie Finkelbaum, the vivaciously flirtatious divorcee, meets a to-die-for man at the roulette table at Sun City.

'What number should I play?' she asks him, false eyelashes all a-flutter.

'Why not play your age,' he suggests, with that James Bond kind of leer.

So Suzie puts R1 000 on number 34.

The wheel spins and spins in a blur of black and red and white.

The ball lands on 41.

And Suzie promptly passes out.

VOICE FROM THE DEEP

Van is strolling along the beach at Plett, when he suddenly hears a deep, booming voice: 'DIG!'

Van looks around. There's nobody there. He shrugs and moves on. Then he hears the voice again.

'I SAID, DIG!'

Van scratches his head. He looks around to see if anybody's watching. Nobody is. So he gets down in the sand and starts digging with his bare hands. A few centimetres down, he finds a small chest with a rusty lock.

The deep voice says: 'OPEN!'

Van doesn't need to be told twice. He finds a rock, smashes the lock, opens the chest. It's filled to the brim with glittering gold coins.

The deep voice says: 'CASINO!'

Van grits his teeth, hefts the chest onto his shoulders, and makes his way through the sand to his 4×4. Then he drives to the casino.

The deep voice says: 'ROULETTE!'

Van changes all the gold into a huge pile of roulette tokens. He wanders over to a table, where the players stare at him in disbelief. Van sits there with his stash, awaiting further instructions.

The deep voice says: 'TWENTY-SEVEN!'

Van takes the whole pile and drops it on 27.

The table falls quiet. The croupier throws the ball. It lands on 26.

The deep voice says: 'SHIT!'

GAMMAT, GATIEP & MERAAI

PUBLIC TRANSPORT

Gatiep: 'Hei Gammat, ek sê lend me fifty cents for the bus.'

Gammat: 'Sorry. I only got a five rand.'

Gatiep: 'That's okay, I'll take a taxi.'

SHOWBIZ

Gatiep brought in his snoek after four days of heavy fishing in Table Bay and Meraai was waiting for him at the harbour, looking her sexiest best.

Gatiep said, 'Hei Meraai, djy't dan nie unnerwear aan nie.'

'So?' asked Meraai. 'Dra djy ear plugs as djy na die Nico Malan toe gaan?'

BRAND IN DIE SAND

Gammat en Meraai lê op die strand en tan. Skielik sien Gammat hoe die sandvlooie vir Meraai begin takel. Hulle kies haastig koers na al die donker plekkies. Gammat spring op, hol teen 'n spoed na die strandkafee en gaan koop 'n blik Doom.

Hy's terug in 'n oogwink, en begin daai Doom op plekke spuit waar Meraai nie geweet het sy't plekke nie. Sy spring op en begin 'n riel dans soos die goed haar op daai plekke brand.

'Gammat!' skree sy, 'Is djy mal? Hoe spuit djy dan nou als dood wat djy vanaand nog wil gebruik?'

HEAVY LOAD

Gatiep stops his heavy-duty truck next to the road just outside Colesberg. He grabs a heavy-duty stick and hits it against the side of the truck, making a hell of a racket. Another truck driver sees the commotion, and pulls up alongside.

'Hey, Gatiep,' he shouts, 'what are you doing, man?'

Gatiep finally notices the other guy amidst all the commotion.

'Ag,' he says, 'This is a four-ton truck and I'm transporting eight tons of canaries. I'm doing this so that half of them can fly.'

DON'T BE SHELLFISH

Gammat goes out to sea, trawling fish for I&J. Four weeks later, he's back. Who does he see leaning against a lamp-post on the foreshore, but a lady of his casual acquaintance named Meraai. After a bit of haggling, they decide to get casually re-acquainted.

Six months later Gammat returns from the sea again. Sure enough, there's Meraai leaning against the lamp-post again. Only this time, she doesn't look too pleased to see Gammat.

'Nou vir wat lyk djy dan nou vandag soe bek-af?' he asks.

'Dis djy djou vark,' she snaps at him. 'Djy't my crabs gegee!'

'So, wat expect djy vir twenty bucks,' he shrugs. 'Prawns?'

HOLY WATER

When his faithful old tjorrie spluttered to a halt in the middle of the main road of Velddrift in the Western Cape, the local NG dominee got out and walked across to the Shell garage.

The attendant doffed his cap, listened to the dominee's tale of woe, and ran off to fetch a suitable container.

'Sorry, Dominee,' said the attendant, brandishing a battered old pee-pot, 'this is all I could find.'

The dominee smiled and said it would have to do. The attendant filled the pee-pot to the brim with petrol, and the dominee walked back to his car. As he poured the precious liquid into the fuel-tank, the dominee was spotted by Gatiep, staggering into the street from Western Cape Cellars.

'Ek sê, Dominee,' hailed Gatiep, waving his bottle of cheap wine in the air, 'wil djy nie sommer ook vir my hierdie Tassies in 'n KWV veranner nie?'

POUND SEATS

The headmaster calls Gatiep into his office. It's not his first offence.

'Where were you yesterday, boy?' roars the headmaster.

Gatiep cannot tell a lie.

'I went to the bioscope, sir,' he says.

'Well, come and see me after school today,' instructs the headmaster, 'and I'll give you a bioscope you won't easily forget.'

Just before the hometime bell rings, Gatiep grabs a few of his heftier schoolbooks and shoves them underneath his pants. Then he goes to get a bioscope he won't easily forget.

'Bend over,' says the headmaster. Gatiep obeys. A book falls onto the floor.

'And this? What's this doing under your pants?'

Gatiep says, 'Well you said we were going to have bioscope today, so I just booked my seat.'

TENGA

Gammat sit en check hierdie sexy cherrie op die strand.

'Hei Gatiep,' vra hy, 'dra sy 'n tenga, of issit net 'n geboortevlek?'

SOMETHING FISHY

These two okes are fishing on the foreshore in Cape Town. Not only are they fishing; they're actually catching fish. So many, in fact, that the one turns to the other and says, 'Ek sê, my pêl, we should sommer start our own fishing business, hey.'

And his pal says, 'Ja, but what should we call it, hey?'

And the fisherman says, 'I en Djy.'

HOT-WIRED

Gatiep and Gammat are sitting on their haunches outside a bank in Knysna when a lady with a very short dress falls into the queue for the auto teller.

Gammat, 'Hei Gatiep, ek sê, sal djy daai stuk vat as djy hom kan kry?

'Nei,' says Gammat. 'Check al daai varicose veins.'

'Djy bedoel daai spatare?' sê Gatiep. 'Djy moet mal wees!'

The lady overhears and turns around, 'Hei, ek sê screw djou en djou chommie too. Daai is nie spatare nie, daai is wiring vir my hotplate.'

BLACK AND BLUE

It was the morning after the Boks had beaten the Wallabies at Newlands. Gatiep was sitting down to breakfast, looking about as hale and hearty as a Wallaby.

His wife, Meraai, gave him a look that was cold enough to curdle bacon.

'Is djy dan nou weer lekka de donner in omlat ek vanmore drie-uur bietjie onner die weer van Newlands af gekom het?' asked Gatiep, clutching his aching head.

'Nei,' neighed Meraai.

'Nou is djy dan nou de donner in omlat ek by die huis ingeval het met 'n blou ogietjie?'

'Nei. Djy't hom nie gehad toe djy by die huis ingeval het nie.'

GAAN VLIEG

Meraai is aangekla van moord op haar man. Sy't hom op heterdaad met 'n jong dingetjie in die bed betrap, toe gryp sy hom en gooi hom deur die venster van hul woonstel.

Hy't sewe verdiepings ver getravel, en nou wil die regter weet waarom sy tot hierdie uiterste gegaan het.

'Wel djou honour,' sê sy, 'ek het gerieken dis 'n muskiet wat daar op die bed lê. En toe rieken ek as 'n muskiet kan stiek kan hy mos vlieg oek.'

OIL PAINTING

Gatiep and Gammat are sitting on a bus in Cape Town when this lady gets on with a face made up to kill: bloodshot red lips, seven layers of base and such massive eyelashes that she can barely keep her eyes open.

There's no vacant seats, so she stands, hanging onto the leather strap.

'Hei Gammat,' says Gatiep, 'why don't you offer the lady your seat?'

'Nei,' says Gammat, 'a painting's got to hang.'

THE ONE AND ONLY

Gammat word aangekla dat hy vir Meraai 'n bitch genoem het. Tydens kruisverhoor sê Gammat, 'Djy't da' boe oppie balcony gastaan, en ek da' onner innie straat.'

'Ja,' sê Meraai.

'Daar was mos baie anner mense by djou da' oppie balcony,' sê Gammat.

'Ja,' sê Meraai.

'Nou hoe wiet djy dan ek het met djou gapraat?'

'Omlat ek die enigste 'bitch' daar was,' sê Meraai.

SELLE OU STORIE

Die Regter kyk vir Gammat in die oog en sê: 'Dis die sesde jaar na mekaar dat jy in my hof in die beskuldigde-bank staan.'

'Djou honour,' sê Gammat, 'djy moenie vir my kom blame omlat jy nie promotion kan kry nie.'

GARDENING

GROW YOUR OWN

There's this blonde who loves to work in her vegetable garden. But no matter how hard she tries, no matter how much manure she uses, she just can't get her tomatoes to ripen. One day, peering over the wall, she notices her neighbour's tomatoes. They're big, red, ready-to-eat.

'How do you do it?' she asks the old man.

He's a little hesitant at first, but he finally admits, 'Twice each day, in the morning and in the evening, I expose myself in front of the tomatoes, and they turn red with embarrassment.'

The blonde decides to give it a try. Two weeks go by, and her neighbour calls to check on her progress.

'So,' he asks, 'any luck with your tomatoes?'

'No,' admits the blonde. 'But you should see the size of my cucumbers!'

GOLF

GOLFING GENIE

Two chommies are playing golf when one pulls out a cigar. He doesn't have a lighter on him, so he asks his pal to gooi him a light.

'Of course,' he says, and he reaches into his golf bag and pulls out a 12 inch Bic lighter.

'Wow!' says his friend, 'where'd you get that enormous lighter?'

'I got it from my genie.'

'You have a genie?'

'Ja, man, he's right here in my golf bag.' He opens his golf bag and out pops the genie.

The friend says, 'Listen, I'm a good friend of your master. Will you grant me one wish?'

'Yes I will,' the genie says. The friend asks for a million bucks. The genie hops back into the golf bag and leaves the friend standing there waiting for his million bucks. Suddenly, the sky begins to darken, and the sound of a million ducks flying overhead can be heard.

'I asked for a million bucks, not a million ducks!' yells the friend.

'Oh, I forgot to tell you,' replies his buddy, 'the genie is a little hard of hearing. Do you really think I asked him for a 12 inch Bic?'

FORE!

A guy is standing over his tee shot, looking up, looking down, measuring the distance, figuring the wind direction and speed. His partner says, 'What's taking so long?'

The first guy says, 'My wife is on the clubhouse porch, so I want to make a perfect shot.' His partner says, 'Forget it. You'll never hit her from here.'

MASTER OF THE GAME

On the day after his Master's victory, Tiger Woods tries to enter this very exclusive golf club. He is stopped at the gate by a security guard.

'Sorry, sir,' says the guard, 'but I am afraid this club does not allow black people to enter. If you'd like a game, however, there is a very good public course about a 3-wood down the road.'

Tiger can't believe what he's hearing. 'But I'm Tiger Woods!' he says.

The guard takes a closer look. He apologises profusely. 'I'm terribly sorry I did not recognise you, sir. In that case, the other course is an easy 5-iron down the road.'

CHEAP ROUND

Why are Scotsmen so good at golf?

They realise that the fewer times they hit the ball, the longer it will last.

HOWZIT CHINA

Mr Wong is in Johannesburg on a business trip from Beijing. His hosts decide to treat him to a round of golf at a luxury course in the northern suburbs. Mr Wong has never played the game before, but he soon picks up the basics.

Back home, Mrs Wong asks how the trip went.

'Great,' he says. 'Played most interesting game. Hit little white ball with long stick in large cow pasture. Name of game is "Oh shit".'

WATCH THE BUNNY

Asked about the phenomenal improvement in his golfing game, Mike modestly puts it down to his choice of equipment. Instead of a golf ball, he uses a rabbit. Sure, it's a lot more cumbersome to hit, but wherever it lands, it heads straight for the hole.

SURE SHOT

Two women are playing golf. One asks the other, 'Do you and your husband have mutual climax?'

'No,' answers her friend, lining up her shot. 'I think we have Mutual & Federal.'

SECRET FORMULA

This foursome of company directors has a standing date to play golf every Saturday. Sadly, one of the four is transferred to another city. Happily, his replacement is also an avid golfer. The remaining threesome invite him to fill the gap on Saturday.

'What time do you tee off?' asks the new player. 'At 9 a.m.,' comes the reply.

'I may be about ten minutes late,' says the new player. 'If I am, just wait for me.'

Saturday comes. The new guy is waiting on the green. They tee off, and the new guy whips his way to a spectacular victory. At the 19th hole, the original threesome ask if the new guy would play the next Saturday as well, to give them a chance to get their money back.

'What time do you tee off?' he asks. The three reply, 'Same as today. 9 a.m.' The new player says, 'I may be about ten minutes late. If I am, just wait for me.'

So Saturday comes again. There's the guy, ready and waiting. They tee off. This time, the new guy plays left-handed. He still whips the three, even more soundly.

At the 19th hole, the three say, 'Man, we've never seen anyone play as well as you. But tell us, how do you know from which side to play?'

The new guy says, 'It's very simple. When I get up on Saturday morning, if my wife is sleeping on her right side, I tee it up from the right. If she's sleeping on her left, I tee it up from the left.'

'And what is she is sleeping on her back?' ask the threesome.

'Well, then I'm ten minutes late!' says the new guy.

GOTCHA!

Schucks, the prime hacker, walks over to Ernie Els during a celebrity golfing day at Knysna.

'Ernie,' says Schucks, 'I bet you I can beat the crap out of you over eighteen holes.'

'Go play with yourself,' says Ernie.

'No,' says Schucks, 'I wanna play with you.'

'How much did you say?'

'Make it twenty thousand,' says Schucks.

'Are we talking dollars?'

'If that's what you want, sure.'

The club members hose themselves. They start laying their own bets on the side. This is going to be easy money.

Just before they tee off, Schucks turns to Ernie. 'There's just one condition,' he says. 'We play "Gotcha" on two holes.'

Ernie shrugs. 'Whatever you want, pal. You go first.'

Schucks tees off with a freshie, and Ernie falls over laughing.

Four hours later in the clubhouse, Ernie isn't laughing anymore. He's making out a $20 000 cheque to Schucks.

The club members are more than a little amazed. 'How the heck did this happen?' one of them asks Ernie.

'Man,' he says, 'I was teeing off at the first hole. I had just taken up my stance, legs spread nicely, head down, about to send that ball to Mars, when this blerrie oke sticks a hand through my legs from behind, grabs my balls, squeezes them, and shouts "Gotcha!"'

Ernie winces at the memory.

'Do you know what's it like trying to play seventeen holes of golf when you're waiting for that second Gotcha?'

DESERT ISLAND DREAM

This oke has been stranded on a desert island for ten years. One day, he sees something approaching. It's not a ship. It's a beautiful woman in a wetsuit. She swims to shore, walks slowly up the beach, and shakes out her long blonde hair.

She says to the guy, 'How long has it been since you've had a smoke?'

'I've been stranded on this island for ten years,' he says. 'I haven't had a smoke in all that time.'

The blonde unzips a pocket on the right sleeve of her wetsuit. She pulls out a pack of cigarettes. She lights one. The guy smokes it with a look of sheer bliss on his face.

'How long has it been since you've had a drink?' she asks.

'I've been stranded on this island for ten years,' says the guy. 'I haven't had a drink in all that time.' So she unzips a pocket on her left sleeve. Out comes a bottle of Scotch.

As the guy sips and savours the nectar of the gods, the blonde starts unzipping the front of her wetsuit. 'How long has it been since you've played around?' she asks.

His jaw drops. His eyes almost pop out of their sockets.

'Don't tell me you've got golf clubs in there!'

BALLS FOR SALE

This woman is cleaning out her attic, when she comes across a small shoebox she hasn't seen before. She opens it. Inside: three golf balls, and R500 in cash. There's only one golfer in the house, so she asks him when he gets home from work.

He breaks down under cross-examination. 'Every time I was unfaithful to you, darling, I put a golf ball in the box.'

For a while, there is a furious yelling match, but then she thinks to herself, 'Thirty years of marriage. Three golf balls. It's not the end of the world.'

She tells her husband she doesn't approve of his infidelity, but she is prepared to forgive him. They embrace. 'Just one more thing,' she says. 'What about that money in the shoebox?'

Finally, he is forced to come clean: 'Well, darling, every time I had collected a dozen balls, I would sell them.'

GOING APE

A man and his gorilla are sitting in the clubhouse. The club champion walks in. 'I'll bet you five hundred bucks my gorilla can play better golf than you,' says the man. The champ looks at the man. The champ looks at the gorilla.

'You're on,' he snorts. They wander off to the first tee. The first hole is a long par four over water. With supreme style and confidence, the champ hits a beautiful drive straight up the middle, over the water, within chipping distance from the green.

'Nice shot,' whistles the man. The gorilla tees up. He whacks the drive right onto the green, and into the hole. The champ looks on in disbelief. Just lucky, he thinks to himself. He picks up his ball and they head off to the next hole.

It's a beautiful par five, along the creek with a slight dogleg left. The gorilla tees up. Boom. The ball soars through the air, and comes to rest just centimetres from the pin. The champ shakes his head. He knows when he's beaten. He concedes the hole and the match, and the party retreats to the clubhouse.

'That gorilla of yours plays an amazing game,' admits the champ. 'I've never seen anyone drive the ball so far. But since he aced the first hole and I conceded the second, I was just wondering ... what's his putting like?'

'Oh,' says the man, pocketing his five hundred bucks, 'he putts exactly like he drives!'

BUSY BEE

Minutes after beginning her round, a young woman is stung by a bee. She goes back to the pro shop and asks the pro what she should do.

'Where were you stung?' he asks.

'Between the first and second hole,' she replies.

'Well,' says the pro, 'first of all, your feet are too far apart.'

LIKELY STORY

After an enjoyable 18 holes of the beautiful game, a man stops at a bar for a beer before heading home. He strikes up a conversation with a ravishing blonde. The beer turns into two beers. Then three. The small talk turns into big talk. Then a walk around the corner, and up the stairs into her apartment.

They make wild, passionate love for a couple of hours. Finally, he heads home. He doesn't feel good. It's not the booze; it's his conscience. He loves his wife, and is troubled by the thought of a spontaneous indiscretion ruining years of a good marriage. There's only one way to handle this. He's got to come clean.

'Darling,' he says, when his wife opens the door. 'I have a confession to make. After golf today, I stopped by the bar for a beer. I met a beautiful woman, went to her apartment, and made love to her for two hours. I'm sorry. I promise it won't ever happen again. I only hope you can find it in your heart to forgive me.'

His wife scowls. She looks at him with fire in her eyes. 'Don't lie to me, you miserable rat!' she yells. 'You played 36 holes, didn't you?'

PAR FOR THE COURSE

A golfer slouches into the clubhouse after a particularly bad round. 'Looks like you had a pretty rough day,' says the pro.

'You bet I did,' sighs the golfer. 'The best two balls I hit all day, was when I was coming out of the sand trap and stepped on the rake!'

SMACK ON TARGET

These two women are playing golf one sunny morning. The first tees off. It's not a bad drive. Unfortunately, there is a foursome of men standing directly in the flight path. The woman watches in horror as one of the guys doubles over in agony, clasping his hands at his crotch. The woman rushes over.

'I'm sorry, I'm sorry!' she says. She explains that she is

a physiotherapist by profession, and she'll do what she can to ease the pain.

'N-n-n-n-n-o,' stammers the man. 'I'll be fine. Really, I'll be ... aaaarghhh ... fine.'

He rolls onto the green, wincing and moaning. Ignoring his now-feeble protests, the woman kneels down beside him, and slowly massages the immediate area of injury. The man falls silent.

After a few minutes, the woman asks, 'Does that feel any better?'

The man looks up at her and says, 'Ja, it does feel pretty good, thanks ... but my thumb still hurts like hell!'

SPOT THE BALL

What's the difference between a golf ball and a woman's G-spot?

A guy will take 20 minutes to look for a golf ball.

DRIVE SAFELY

Mike Schutte and Gary Player are travelling in Gary's fancy new imported American limo. Gary presses a button. WHOOSH. The roof lifts off automatically. Mike is amazed. 'Hell, this is some car, hey ou Gary.'

'You ain't seen nothing yet,' says ou Gary. He pushes another button, and in a flash a tray with drinks slides out automatically between the two seats. Mike is even more amazed. He takes a swig from his beer when Gary pushes a third button. BOINGGG! A little microwave pops up from inside the cubby-hole with a freshly grilled Nando's chicken.

'Jislaaik!' says Mike, as he grabs a chicken leg and starts chomping away.

Gary stops at a traffic light. One of his golf tees falls from the dashboard and onto Mike's lap.

'What's this?' enquires Mike.

'Oh, that's a tee,' says Gary.

'What's a "tee"?'

'You put your balls on it when you drive,' explains the champ.

Mike checks out the tee in his hand. 'Bliksem ou Gary,' he says, 'these Americans think of everything when it comes to cars, hey.'

SLOW GAME

The golfer's wife is frantic. It's been hours since he went out to play his weekly round of golf. Two hours is okay. Three hours is pushing it. But eight hours?

She's about to call the police, when her husband walks through the door and collapses on the couch.

'What took you so long?' she yells. 'I've been frantic with worry!'

The husband catches his breath, and says, 'Let me tell you what happened. There we were at the fourth tee. Harry hits this magnificent drive. Then he keels over and dies on the spot. Heart attack.'

'Oh no!' says the wife. 'That's terrible!'

'You're darn right,' says the husband. 'All day long, it's been hit the ball, drag Harry, hit the ball, drag Harry ...'

NOT BAD

Mike is playing his way through a tournament in Durban. He's not doing badly. He's doing terribly. For 18 holes, his caddy has been chortling and snickering behind his back. Finally, Mike has had enough.

'Man, you must be the worst blerrie caddy in the world!' he yells at the oke.

And the caddy says, 'I don't think so, sir. That would be too much of a coincidence.'

SAND TRAP

An avid golfer is lining up on the 17th tee. All of a sudden, a naked woman comes running out of the woods. She sprints across the green and disappears into the woods on the opposite side. The golfer shrugs, shifts his feet, and bears down on the ball again. In the middle of his backswing, a guy in a white coat runs out of the woods.

'Excuse me,' he says. 'You didn't perhaps see a naked lady running past here?'

'Yes,' says the golfer, pointing into the woods. 'She went that-a-way.'

The guy in the white coat thanks him and runs off. The golfer gets back to business.

At the height of his swing, he's interrupted again. It's another guy in a white coat. But this one is carrying a big red bucket full of sand.

'Excuse me,' says the guy. 'You didn't perhaps see a man in a white coat passing this way, running after a naked lady?'

'Yes,' says the golfer, 'they went that-a-way.'

The guy says thanks, and prepares to dash off. But the golfer stops him. 'Would you mind telling me what's going on around here?' he says.

The guy explains. 'You see, we work at the sanatorium up there on the hill. Every now and again, this woman manages to escape. All she wants to do is get naked and make love.'

'Oh,' says the golfer. 'Well, what's the bucket of sand for?'

'The bucket of sand? That's my handicap,' says the guy in the white coat. 'You see, I caught her last time!'

TWO OF A KIND

Back from his round, Abie puts down his clubs with a sigh that says it all. Still, his loving wife, Dora, asks: 'So how was the game, Abie?'

'Not so good,' says Abie. 'I was hitting pretty well, but my eyesight's gotten so bad I couldn't see where the ball went.'

'But you're seventy-five years old, Abie!' says his wife.

'Why don't you take my brother Hymie along?'

'Hymie? But he's eighty-five, and he doesn't even play golf anymore,' counters Abie.

'So what?' says Dora. 'He's got perfect eyesight. He could watch your ball.'

Finally, Abie likes the idea. The next day, he tees off with Hymie looking on. Abie swings, and the ball disappears down the middle of the fairway.

'Do you see it?' asks Abie.

'Of course I see it,' says Hymie.

'So where is it?' demands Abie.

'I forget,' says Hymie.

HOLY HACKERS

A priest, a rabbi, and a minister of religion meet every Wednesday afternoon to play a round of golf. Although they're not the world's greatest golfers, they enjoy the company, the game, and the opportunity to spend a couple of hours away from the burdens of their congregations.

But one particular Wednesday, they find their enjoyment hampered by an annoyingly slow and cumbersome group of golfers up ahead. These guys are total hackers: they're hitting the balls into the rough on the left, they're hitting them into the rough on the right, and they're taking all day to get through the course.

Back at the clubhouse, the priest, the rabbi, and the minister go looking for the pro manager.

'What's going on?' they demand. 'How can you let these hackers ruin our game? They shouldn't even be allowed on the course.'

The pro manager is alarmed and profusely apologetic.

'I'm terribly sorry, gentlemen,' he says. 'I should have told you. That was a group of blind golfers. They were playing with sonar balls, so they had to try and listen to where the balls landed in order to be able to find them.'

Silence descends over the clergy as they absorb this information. Suddenly, the priest crosses himself, bows his head, and says, 'Lord, please forgive me for speaking ill of these people of your flock. I am ashamed at my sinning.'

The minister looks up to the heavens and says, 'Oh dear Lord, I am so sorry to have been so unkind and thoughtless about your children. Especially such specially challenged children as these. Please forgive my rush to judgement.'

And the rabbi looks at the pro manager and says, 'So? Why can't they play at night?'

CLOSE CALL

Mike, the serious hacker, is pleased as punch to be paired with one of the club's finest players. Mike hits first, swings awkwardly, and tops his drive.

Fishing for free advice, Mike earnestly inquires: 'Do you see anything I can correct?'

'I see you're standing too close to the ball,' says his partner. 'After you hit it.'

PLAY IT AS IT LAYS

It's the day after the wedding. The groom steps out of the bedroom, golf bag over his shoulder.

'Honey,' he says, 'I've got a confession to make. I'm a golf nut. You'll never see me on weekends during golf season.'

The bride nods her head understandingly. 'I've got a confession to make too, darling. I'm a hooker.'

'No big deal,' says the husband. 'Just keep your head down and your left arm straight.'

ON COURSE

The husband and wife, married for many years, are deep in meaningful conversation.

'Sweetheart,' he says, 'If I died tomorrow, would you remarry?'

'Well, I suppose so,' she shrugs. 'Eventually.'
'Would you and he sleep in the same bed as we do?'
'I suppose so,' she says.
'Would you make love to him?'
'I suppose I would, dear. We'd be married, after all.'
'And would you give him my golf clubs?'
'No,' says the wife. 'He's left-handed.'

SUBSTITUTE

Eager to play a round at the Randburg Golf Club, non-member Schucks rocks up with his golf-bag at the ready.
'Did you book a game?' asks the manager.
'No,' says Schucks. 'I didn't.'
'Sorry, we're full,' says the manager.
Schucks puts his golf-bag down and glares at the manager.
'If I were Ernie Els, would you allow me to play here today?'
'Of course we would,' says the manager.
'Well,' says Schucks, 'Ernie is playing in the American Open, so I'd like to take his place.'

MY BALL

Sign on Soweto golf course: 'Members will refrain from picking up balls until they have stopped rolling.'

@**!

Why did they call it golf?
Because the other four-letter words had already been taken.

THE ETHICS OF GOLF

Difficult golfing situation: What do you do when your opponent claims he has found his ball in the rough, and you know he's lying because you've got it in your pocket?

GOLF TROPHY

The blonde saw a few golf balls lying on her boss's desk.

'What's this?' she asked. The boss replied, 'Golf balls.'

The following Monday there was a golf ball on his desk again.

The blonde said, 'I see you've shot another golf.'

HONEST TO GOODNESS

A club official noticed Leon standing at least half a meter on the wrong side of the tee marker.

'Excuse me,' said the official, 'at this club we don't believe in cheating, or trying to gain advantage by driving from in front of the tee marker.'

'Neither do I,' said Leon, 'but this is my second shot.'

MOOI SKOOT

Die ou kry die volmaakte gelukhou op die gholfbaan. Hy gaan vier sy geluk in die klubhuis, en na sy derde dop lui sy selfoon. Dis sy vrou wat van die kraamsaal af skakel.

'Ons het pas die ouers van 'n drieling geword!' sê sy opgewonde.

'Mooi Mammie!' sê hy, 'byt net vas, ek ry nou van die klubhuis af.'

'Hoe't jy dit reggekry, my man?' vra sy moeg maar gelukkig.

'Dit was maar moeilik,' sê hy, 'hy't maar stadig ingerol, maar hel dit was lekker.'

PART EXCHANGE

Vier ouens speel al jarelank elke Woensdagmiddag golf. Daarna shower drie van hulle en gaan maak 'n paar doppe, maar die vierde ou maak altyd 'n vinnige kraak huis toe.

Na baie jare vra hulle die een ou hoekom hy nooit vir die stort en die dop wil bly nie.

'Om die eerlike waarheid te praat,' sê die ou, 'ek is maar swak bedeeld, en ek is baie skaam daaroor, dan gaan stort ek maar by die huis.'

'Werk dit?' vra een van die ander ouens.

'Natuurlik werk dit.'

'Wel wat sê jy daarvan om een wat werk te verruil vir een wat goed lyk in die shower?'

GUIDE-DOGS

NO DOGS ALLOWED

There's a guy with a Doberman Pinscher and a guy with a Chihuahua. The guy with the Doberman Pinscher says to the guy with the Chihuahua, 'Let's go over to that restaurant and get something to eat.'

The guy with the Chihuahua says, 'We can't go in there. We've got dogs with us.'

The guy with the Doberman Pinscher says, 'Just follow my lead.'

They walk over to the restaurant. The guy with the Doberman Pinscher puts on a pair of dark glasses, and he starts to walk in. A guy at the door says, 'Sorry, pal, no pets allowed.'

The guy with the Doberman Pinscher says, 'You don't understand. This is my seeing-eye dog.'

The guy at the door says, 'A Doberman Pinscher?' He says, 'Yes, we're using them now. They're very good.'

The guy at the door says, 'Come on in.'

The guy with the Chihuahua reckons, 'What the heck,' so he puts on a pair of dark glasses and starts to walk in.

The guy at the door says, 'Sorry, pal, no pets allowed.'

The guy with the Chihuahua says, 'You don't understand. This is my seeing-eye dog.'

The guy at the door says, 'A Chihuahua?'

The guy with the Chihuahua says, 'What! You mean they gave me a Chihuahua?'

SEEING-EYE DOG

This blind oke walks into Pick 'n Pay, takes his Alsation by the lead, and starts swinging it above his head.

'Can I help you, sir?' asks the somewhat-worried assistant.

'Ag, no thanks,' says the blind oke. 'I'm just looking around.'

ROUGH LANDING

The same oke completed a course in parachute jumping. After many successful jumps, he was asked by a reporter: 'How do you know when you're about to hit the ground?'

'Oh, that's easy,' says the oke. 'I just wait till my dog's leash goes slack.'

GYNAES

ENGINE SPECIALIST

Tired of his job, bored with the view, a gynaecologist decides to change his career. He's always enjoyed tinkering with motorcar engines, so he applies for a course at the Witwatersrand School of Mechanics.

For the final exam, he has to strip an engine completely and reassemble it in perfect working order. He gets down to work and anxiously awaits the results. When they arrive, he can't believe his eyes: 150%! He calls his instructor. Surely some mistake?

'No,' says the instructor. 'Let me explain. I gave you 50% for stripping down the engine – a very thorough job. Then I gave you 50% for reassembling it – nothing I could fault there. And then I gave you a 50% bonus – for doing it all through the exhaust pipe!'

HANSIE & THE BOYS

MAIDEN OVER

'Cricket, cricket, cricket!' complained Hansie's wife. 'That's all you ever think of. I bet you don't even remember the day we were married.'

Hansie: 'Of course I do. That was the day when Pat Symcox scored a hundred against the Aussies.'

MEMBERS ONLY

Ali Bacher accidentally lands up in the Ladies during the English tour of '98. He's taking a shower when he hears these female voices. Streaking past the packed female cloakroom with a towel over his head, he makes a beeline for the exit.

Says the first lady, 'It's definitely not my husband.'

Says the second lady, 'It's definitely not my lover.'

Says the third, 'It's definitely not a member of Lords.

EYE ON THE BALL

Hansie gets given out by the umpire for the umpteenth time, caught behind. Hansie isn't happy. Like everyone else who was watching the game, he knows that his bat was nowhere near the ball. He walks over to the umpire, smiling, because Hansie never loses his cool.

'Mr Umpire,' he says, 'let's be honest. I didn't touch that ball.'

The umpire says, 'Well, I believe you did.'

Hansie takes a closer look at the umpire and says, 'First time I noticed you got one glass eye, Mr Umpire.'

The umpire gets a moerse skrik. 'What? Nobody ever noticed that before! Please, do me a favour and don't tell anyone.'

Hansie says, 'Okay, I won't. But only if you'll reconsider my case.'

The umpire says, 'Okay, but only if you can tell me which eye is the glass one.'

Hansie takes a good look and says, 'The sympathetic one.'

IN AND OUT

A mother of three filed paternity charges against a well-known test cricketer.

'On what grounds?' asked the judge.

'Lords, Old Trafford, and the Wanderers,' she replied.

SUCKER

'You need glasses, mate,' moaned the dismissed Shane Warne as he passed the man in the white coat.

'So do you, mate,' answered the man. 'I'm selling ice-cream.'

NOT ON YOUR LIFE

The umpire of the cricket match also happened to be the village undertaker. Out of appreciation for what his club had done for him, he solemnly swore, 'I will bury, free of charge, any member of the club who passes away while I am still undertaker of this village.'

Suddenly, a shot rang out. The umpire and his club-mates spun around and saw that a Scotsman had just shot himself.

BALLS UP

'Oh Allan,' sighs the soon-to-be Mrs Donald, 'I'm so looking forward to that moment when Jonty and the boys make an arch for us, holding up their bats, just like they did for Hansie.'

'I'm afraid that won't be possible, skattie,' says Allan, carefully removing his lip-gloss in the mirror.

'What do you mean?' huffs his fiancée. 'Why on earth not?'

'Hansie is a batsman,' says Allan. 'That's why they held up their bats.'

'So?'

'I'm a bowler.'

MOTHER'S MILK

Makhaya Ntini was practising his bowling skills in a village somewhere in the Transkei. Every afternoon during practise a local outjie would bring him a cup of fresh milk, saying: 'This is from my mom'. This went on for two years, and Ntini loved it.

One day Gogga Adams visited Makhaya and witnessed this milk routine. He walked over to the young Transkeian and requested a cup of fresh milk for himself. The youngster said he'd ask his mom, and returned after half an hour.

'Sorry Gogga,' said the piccanin. 'My ma says the other tiet is for the baby.'

PULL THE OTHER ONE

Just before the big match, the secretary receives a message from the guy at the turnstiles. 'There's an umpire down here with two friends. Wants to know if they can come in.'

'No way,' replies the secretary. 'The man's obviously lying.'

'How can you be so sure?' asks the guy at the turnstile.

'Did you ever hear of an umpire with two friends?'

GOING BATTY

The cricketer is stretched out on the couch, straight as a wicket, pouring out his woes to his psychiatrist.

'It's terrible,' says the cricketer. 'I can't score runs, I'm a terrible bowler, and I can't hold a catch. What can I do?'

'I suggest you get another job,' says the shrink.

'I can't,' says the cricketer. 'I'm playing for England tomorrow!'

GUNNING FOR RUNS

South African cricket's top guns
Bat slowly and seldom get runs
To emulate Lara
Let's feed 'em cascara
And be sure of them getting the runs

NET 'N OOMBLIK

Gerhardus Liebenberg se vrou bel hom in Londen tydens die Proteas se onlangse Europese toer.

'Kan ek met Gerrie praat, asseblief?'

'Jammer mevrou,' sê die beampte, 'hy's nou net in om te kolf.'

'In daardie geval,' sê Mev. Liebenberg, 'sal ek aanhou.'

COUNT YOURSELF LUCKY

Allan Donald delivers the mother of all fast balls. KER-BLAMMM! It hits the Aussie full on his helmet, goes right through the bars and smacks him full in the mouth.

The poor oke is standing there with his head hanging down, blood pouring from his mouth, spitting out one tooth after the other. Pat Symcox walks up to the oke and says, 'Hell, you can be lucky it was a NO BALL!'

HELLO? HELLO?

His wife's in the maternity ward about to have a baby, so Willem decides to phone from work and find out how things are. Like all prospective fathers, Willem is terribly nervous and dials the wrong number. Which happens to be the main switchboard at the Wanderers.

'Hello, I'm Brandt. How are things going there?' inquires Willem.

'Well, four are out,' says the guy manning the telephone. 'We hope to have another four out before the lunch break, but the last one was out for a duck.'

SOOS DIE WIND

Shaun Pollock boul op 'n kol baie sleg, en 'n klein dogtertjie hardloop op die veld en gee hom 'n pilletjie. 'Waarvoor is dit?' vra die verbaasde Shaun.

'Drink hom gou, dit sal help.'

'Waarvoor?' wou Shaun weet.

'Pappa sê jy boul nie so goed nie,' sê die dogtertjie, 'want dis die wind wat jou pla.'

FEATHERS

In Bloemfontein stap 'n ou tannie na Gerhardus Liebenberg toe nadat hy pas sy paaltjie verloor het.

'Ek wil graag 'n lekker dik verekombers maak, en ek wonder of jy kan help om die vere te voorsien.'

'Hoekom vra antie vir my?' vra Gerhardus.

'Almal sê vir my jy't hierdie seisoen die meeste ducks gehad.'

LAST MAN OUT

Doodsberig in koerant: 'n Bekende krieketspeler het vanmiddag beswyk nadat hy met 'n krieketbal teen die kop getref is. Hy laat 'n paaltjiewagter, drie glippe en 'n man in die gang agter.

HALF-PRICE

Die krieketondersteuner kom by Springbokpark se hek in Bloemfontein aan. Die ou in die kaartjieskantoor sê, 'R120 asseblief.'

'Hier's R60,' sê die ou, 'ek kom net vir die Vrystaat kyk.'

HEAVEN &
THE OTHER PLACE

TRANSPORTS OF DELIGHT

Three men are standing at the gates of heaven. St Peter asks them if they ever cheated on their wives. The first man says, 'All the time.' St Peter gives him a Fiat Uno and admits him to heaven.

The second man says, 'I cheated a couple of times.' St Peter gives him a Toyota Corolla and admits him to heaven. The third man says, 'I never cheated on my wife in forty years of marriage.' St Peter gives him a Rolls-Royce and admits him to heaven.

A week later, the three men meet at an intersection in heaven. The third man is sitting in his car, crying. The other men ask why he's crying, when he's got such a lekker car.

The guy shakes his head and says, 'I just saw my wife, and she was driving a skateboard.'

COLD-HEARTED

These two okes arrive simultaneously at the Pearly Gates.

'How'd you get here?' asks the first oke.

'I froze to death', says the second.

'Shees, that's bad. Must've been a terrible death.'

'Ja,' says the second, 'First you get the shakes, then your lips turn blue, then your hands and your toes turn numb. Then you fall asleep, and after that it's not so bad. What about you?'

'Heart attack,' says the first oke. 'As you can see I was a little on the hefty side. I knew my wife was cheating on me, so one day I arrived home unexpectedly and ran up the stairs. There she was lying on the bed, all alone but looking flustered and guilty as hell. So I rushed down the stairs and into the basement, then upstairs into the attic, then down again into the kitchen. No sign of the other oke. Then I felt this sharp pain in my chest. That's about the last thing I can remember.'

The second oke shakes his head. 'Man,' he says, 'isn't that ironic.'

'What do you mean?' asks the first oke.

'If you had only looked inside the freezer, we'd both still be alive.'

YUPPIE HELL

A young, ruthless, obscenely rich executive pranged his Z3 and went straight to hell. When he got there, he saw one sign that said Capitalist Hell, and another that said Socialist Hell. There was a queue stretching right round the block for Socialist Hell, and no one at all waiting in line outside Capitalist Hell.

The executive asked a guard, 'So what do they do to you in Socialist Hell?'

And the guard said, 'They boil you in oil, whip you, and tie you on the rack.'

The executive gulped. 'And what do they do to you in Capitalist Hell?'

'The exact same thing,' answered the guard.

'Then why is everybody standing in line for Socialist Hell?' asked the yuppie.

'Because in Socialist Hell,' answered the guard, 'they're always out of oil, whips, and racks!'

WAGES OF SIN

These three men have reached their final destination, and are standing in line at the Pearly Gates. St Peter says to the first oke, 'Let's see. You're Mr Jones, the engineer. We've been expecting you. Please follow me.' Jones follows.

At the end of a long corridor, St Peter opens a door and says, 'This is where you'll be staying, Mr Jones.'

Jones walks into a cold, dark, musty room. Water is dripping from the ceiling, and there are instruments of torture on the walls. Chained to the centre of the floor is a huge, slobbering, growling Rottweiler.

'Mr Jones,' booms a voice in the darkness, 'you have sinned!'

St Peter shuts the door, and goes back to the Pearly Gates. 'Ah,' he says to the second man, 'you must be Mr Smith, the doctor. Please follow me.' Smith follows. At the end of a long corridor, St Peter opens a door and says, 'Step inside, please, Mr Smith.'

Mr Smith steps inside. Cold, dark, musty. Rack. Whips. Big dog. 'Mr Smith,' booms the voice, 'you have sinned!'

St Peter shuts the door and goes back to the Pearly Gates. There's one guy left in the line.

'And you must be Mr Brown,' says St Peter. 'The lawyer. This way, please.' Brown walks that way.

At the end of a long corridor, St Peter opens a door. The lawyer peers inside. It's the same kind of room, only colder, darker, and mustier, with even more fearsome torture instruments lining the walls. There is, however, one big difference.

In the centre of the room stands Cindy Crawford, the supermodel. As Mr Brown, the lawyer, steps into the room, a voice booms, 'Cindy Crawford! You have sinned!'

LAWYER LAWYER

A lawyer arrives at the Pearly Gates. St Peter checks out his credentials.

'I note that you reached the very ripe age of 96,' says St Peter. 'That's quite an accomplishment.'

The lawyer looks confused. 'Ninety-six? There must be some mistake. I'm only 34.'

'Not according to your billing hours,' says St Peter.

SPESIALE GAS

Van het die Laingsburg-vloed oorleef, en jarelank vir almal wat wou luister sy oorlewingstog in die fynste besonderhede beskryf. Toe hy uiteindelik te sterwe kom, stap 'n engel in die hemel hom tegemoet. 'Ons het vanaand so 'n klein verwelkoming vir die nuwelinge, Mnr van der Merwe, en dit is die gebruik dat nuwelinge ietsie tydens die geleentheid sal sê.'

'No problem,' sê Van. 'Ek sal hulle vertel op watter dramatiese wyse ek die Laingsburg-vloed oorleef het.'

'Ek wil nie graag u geesdrif demp nie meneer,' sê die engel, 'maar Noag is ook vanaand in die gehoor.'

HIJACK!

HI JACK

What do you call a Spaniard who's just been hijacked?
Carlos.

BYE JACK

The good news is that the hijackers and the car thieves aren't stealing Hi-Ace buses anymore.
Why?
Because they've all been stolen already.

SECURITY GATES

A hijacker and his accomplice have just hijacked a brand-new Be My Wife, swanky new cellphone included. Charging down the highway at 240 kays an hour, the guy behind the wheel phones his cousin Dlamini in Guguletu, instantly forgetting that he's driving a car.

Next moment, the hijackers find themselves standing outside the Pearly Gates.

The Duty Angel checks the Big List, scratches his head, and checks again. No mention of any Gauteng hijackers arriving today. The Duty Angel calls St Peter on the buzzer.

'Sorry to bother you, Chief, but are we expecting a couple of hijackers from Gauteng in a white Bee Em today?'

St Peter checks the database on his computer.

'Can't see anything here,' he says, 'but I'm a bit

snowed under at the moment. Maybe you should come up and have a look for yourself.'

So the Duty Angel tells the hijackers to wait, and he runs upstairs to check the computer. Nope, nothing here. He dashes back down again. Seconds later, St Peter gets a frantic call on the buzzer.

'Chief,' says the Duty Angel, 'you're not going to believe this. They're gone!'

'What, the hijackers?'

'Yes,' says the Duty Angel, 'but that's not all – they've taken the Pearly Gates with them!'

UNHOLY ROW

This nun stops at an intersection in Commissioner Street in Jo'burg. She's driving a little white Uno. Suddenly, from out of nowhere, this oke in a balaclava jumps out, points an AK-47 at the window, and yells: 'Hijack!'

Father O'Flaherty, who happens to be crossing the street at that very moment, calls out to the nun: 'Show him your cross, Sister! Show him your cross!'

The little old nun doesn't hesitate. She rams the door open, sending the hijacker flying. She grabs his rifle, whacks him on the head with it, kicks him in the nuts, and shouts as he hobbles away: 'Voetsek, jou blerrie hijacker!'

BLADE RUNNER

They hijacked my son in the supermarket the other day.

He went in with his rollerblades and came out on bricks.

HOLIDAYS

HAPPY HOLIDAYS

Mr and Mrs Goldenfinger are standing in the check-in queue at Johannesburg International, weighed down with baggage for their long-awaited trip to Miami Beach.

'So? Are you excited?' asks Harry, pointing his brand-new camcorder in Dora's direction.

'Excited? Of course I'm excited,' says Dora, pushing her overladen trolley a fraction of a millimetre closer to the front of the queue. 'But you know something, Harry, I wish we'd brought the piano with us.'

'The piano? Why would we want to bring the piano?'

'Because I left the tickets on top of it.'

FAST FOOD

Famished after a long drive through the middle of nowhere, Van is overjoyed to find a fast-food joint offering everything from hamburgers to doughnuts. He steps inside and orders a hamburger to go.

The chef nods, grabs a raw patty from the shelf, and slaps the patty under his arm to flatten it for cooking. Van is disgusted. He calls the manager over to take a look.

'Oh, that's nothing,' says the manager. 'You should see how he prepares the doughnuts!'

HAPPY DAY

During the last days of the Reich, as the Red Army moved closer and closer in on Berlin, the ailing Führer called an old gypsy fortune-teller to his bunker.

'When will I die?' Hitler wanted to know.

The gypsy peered into her crystal ball and said, 'You will die on a Jewish holiday.'

'What do you mean?' thundered Hitler. 'How can you possibly know that?'

The old fortune-teller shrugged.

'Because any day you die will be a Jewish holiday.'

HONEYMOONS

I WANT SOME MORE

The newlywed bride and groom had been busy honeymooning for three days straight. On the fourth day, the groom rose early and started paging through the paper, thinking it was time to try a slightly different activity.

'Honey,' he said to his wife, 'How would you like to see Oliver Twist?'

And his bride said: 'You show me one more trick with that thing and I'm going home to Mother.'

FOOD OF LOVE

'So how was it?' asks the mother of the newly-wed bride.

'He took my hand and kissed me on the cheek,' she answers. 'And then he went to sleep.'

'I'll tell you what to do,' says Mom. 'Buy a dozen oysters and feed them to Frikkie. It works better than Viagra.'

The next day Mom calls her daughter on the phone. 'So? Did the oysters work?'

'Only seven of them,' replies the bride.

WASHDAY BLUES

The young newlyweds moved into their apartment after a swinging honeymoon in Mauritius.

'Want to go upstairs and do it?' the husband asked.

'Shhh!' said the bride. 'These walls are paper thin. All the neighbours will know what we're about to do. In future, we'll have to ask each other in code. For example, how about asking, "Have you left the washing machine door open" instead?'

So, the following night, the husband asked, 'I don't suppose you left the washing machine door open, did you?'

'No, I definitely shut it,' replied the wife, and she rolled over and went to sleep.

When she woke up a little while later, she was feeling in the mood. She nudged her husband and said, 'You know, honey, I think I did leave the washing machine door open after all. Would you like to do some washing?'

'No, thanks,' said the husband. 'It was only a small load, so I did it by hand.'

WEDDING NIGHT

Mike got married, but he was too dumb to know what to do on his wedding night.

'For goodness sake, Mike', said his wife, 'you take that thing of yours that you play with and you put it where I wee.

So Mike got up and threw his rugby ball into the sink.

CULTURE VULTURE

'Jy't g'n kultuur nie,' sê die jong bruid vir haar man.

'Kultuur?!' gil hy. 'Jy sê ek het nie kultuur nie?! Ek vat jou *Hamlet* toe, ek vat jou *Swanemeer* toe, en gisteraand toe vat ek jou na Pavarotti se konsert toe. Ek vat jou na al daai kak toe en jy sê ek het nie kultuur nie!'

HOSPITALS

WRONG NUMBER

Mike lands up in casualty with a badly burnt ear. 'What happened?' asks the nurse.

'Ag, the usual story,' says Mike. 'I was busy ironing my underpants when the phone rang.'

JUST A SNIP

Van is in hospital. He's very nervous. He's been booked in for a minor operation, but the thought of it is causing him major stress. Trying to take his mind off the prospect, Van turns to the bloke in the next bed. The bloke introduces himself as Abie Cohen.

Van perks up, 'You're not Jewish, by any chance, Mr Cohen?'

Mr Cohen says, 'By any chance? Of course I am.'

So Van confides in his wardmate. 'I'm really worried,' he says. 'I'm here to have a circumcision. Tell me, Mr Cohen, is it painful?'

Mr Cohen winces. 'Painful? PAINFUL? Don't talk to me about painful. After I had mine, I couldn't walk or talk for a year.'

THE TASTE OF MONEY

Van swallowed a R5 piece and was rushed to the emergency ward. His wife called the nurse on duty.

'How's my husband?' she asked.

'Still no change, I'm afraid,' said the nurse.

ONLY THE BEST

Abie is booked into hospital for a minor operation.

'Would you like a local anaesthetic?' asks the doctor.

'Are you crazy?' yells Abie, 'The medical aid is paying for this! Give me the best imported anaesthetic you've got.'

CHECKING UP

The blonde is lying on the gurney in the hospital corridor, just before going into surgery. A man in a white coat walks by, lifts up the sheet, nods, and leaves. This happens a second time. Then a third. Finally, the blonde asks, 'Doctor, when am I going into surgery?'

'Don't ask me,' says the guy in the white coat. 'I'm just a painter.'

HOTELS

SPECIAL BREAKFAST

This oke is sitting in the dining room of his beachfront hotel in Durban. He calls the head waiter and says he'd like to order breakfast.

'I want two boiled eggs, one of them so undercooked

it's runny, and the other so overcooked it's tough and hard to eat. Also, grilled bacon that has been left on the plate to get cold; burnt toast that crumbles away as soon as you touch it with a knife; butter straight from the deep freeze that's impossible to spread; and a pot of very weak, lukewarm coffee.'

'That's a complicated order, sir,' frowns the waiter. 'It might be quite difficult to organise.'

And the guest replies, 'It shouldn't be. That's exactly what you gave me yesterday.'

DO-IT-YOURSELF

McTavish strolled into the foyer of the one-star hotel and said, 'How much for the night?'

The innkeeper said, 'It's R150 for the night, or R50 if you make your own bed.'

'I'll make my own bed,' said McTavish, without a moment's thought.

'Good,' said the innkeeper. 'I'll get you some nails and wood.'

ROOF WITH A VIEW

The busty blonde, who made *Baywatch's* Pamela Anderson look like Twiggy, decided it was too dangerous to do her tanning on the Durban beachfront. So she took the lift to the top of the luxury hotel, and soaked up the sun on the roof.

On the first day of her holiday, she wore her skimpy bikini for the sake of decorum. On the second day, she thought to herself, 'Who's this decorum bloke, anyway?' And she shrugged off the tiny slivers of fabric and stretched out on her stomach for Part One of her overall tan.

Hardly had the blazing sun begun to penetrate her sunscreen, however, than she heard the sound of running footsteps and panting behind her. Quick as a flasher, she pulled a towel over her rear.

'Excuse me, miss,' said the flustered assistant manager of the hotel, out of breath from running up the stairs. 'We really don't mind your sunbathing on the roof, but we would very much appreciate you wearing a bathing suit, as you did yesterday.'

'What difference does it make,' asked the blonde. 'No-one can see me up here, and besides, I'm covered with a towel.'

'Not exactly,' said the embarrassed little man. 'You're lying on the dining room skylight.'

OPENING TIME

It's three in the morning when the desk clerk at the hotel gets a call from an obviously intoxicated guest.

'What time does the bar open?' asks the guest.

'It opens at noon, sir,' says the clerk, and he goes back to reading his novel.

An hour later, the phone rings again. It's the same guy.

'What time did you say the bar opens?'

'Same time as before,' says the clerk, trying hard to be helpful and polite. 'Noon, sir.'

Another hour passes. The first rays of dawn are just beginning to appear on the horison. The phone rings.

'Yes?'

'It's me again. I just wanted to know what time the bar opens.'

'Look, sir,' says the clerk, 'I've already told you twice that it opens at noon. If you really can't wait to get in, I can have room service send something up to you.'

'No,' says the drunk, 'I don't want to get in. I want to get OUT!'

SEVEN-UP

What a lekker hotel! I left a call for seven in the morning and woke up with seven blondes in my room.

HUNTING

SOS

Mike and Vusi went hunting in the woods. In the process of stalking an impressive-looking kudu, they got lost. Very lost. Stuck without a compass, a map, or a kudu, the two men were left to rely entirely on their own wits.

'Moenie panic nie,' said Mike, putting his hand on Vusi's shoulder. 'I'm an expert in survival, and I know exactly what to do. All we have to do is shoot three shots in the air.'

'How will that help us?' asked Vusi, trying not to panic.

'Don't you know anything?' said Mike. 'Three shots in the air is the internationally recognised signal for SOS.'

Vusi nodded. It was worth a try. First shot, second shot, third shot.

Several hours later, growing increasingly hungry and desperate, Vusi turned to Mike and said, 'Well, Mike. We tried three shots in the air and nothing happened. What do we do now?'

And Mike said, 'Ag, don't worry, Vusi, my pal, we can sommer give it another try. We've still got three arrows left.'

STICK TO DUCKS

Mike and Van, last of the Big White Hunters, are sitting in a pub in the Bushveld, bushed after a hard day's big-game hunting.

'You know, Van,' says Mike, 'I've finally decided I'm going to give up hunting elephants.'

'Why's that?' asks Van, pouring himself another tot of Amarula.

'Because I think I'm getting a hernia from carrying these blerrie elephant decoys.'

BEAR NECESSITIES

Two blondes went hunting bears in the woods.

They came upon a sign that said 'Bear Left'.

So they went home.

WOOF

Koos and Piet were invited to go duck-hunting. They were each given a retriever dog and dropped off next to a huge dam at five o' clock in the morning.

By 5 o' clock that afternoon, the two exhausted hunters fell down in the shade of a mopanie tree, totally disillusioned. 'Twelve hours,' said Piet, 'and not one single blerrie duck. I can't understand it.'

'If you ask me,' replied Piet, 'I think we didn't throw the dogs up high enough.'

DUCK, YOU SUCKER

Fed up with having to listen to the boasts of his macho duck-hunting colleagues, the stockbroker from Sandton decides to go out and bag a few ducks of his own one long weekend. He splashes out on the best double-barrelled shotgun credit can buy, and accessorises it with hunting clothes, boots, and designer gear from all the right Sandton City boutiques.

Then he hops into his 4×4 and heads for the country. He treks through bush, vlei, veld, and mountains for hours, occasionally even getting out of his car to admire the scenery. But he doesn't shoot a duck. He doesn't even see one.

As the sun begins to sink in the sky, he heads reluctantly back to the highway and the city beyond. Then, on the verge of civilisation, he hears a faint 'quacking' noise. He leans out of the window and looks up. A duck!

He stops the car, hops out, finds his shotgun, assumes the position, holds his breath, aims, and fires. BLAM! The duck spirals from the sky. The yuppie can't believe his luck. The duck falls into a nearby farmyard.

The yuppie drives closer and climbs over the fence to retrieve his trophy. Suddenly, he finds himself face-to-face with the meanest-looking farmer he's ever seen. 'Where the hell do you think you're going, city boy?' asks the boer.

'I'm going to get my duck,' says the yuppie.

The farmer folds his arms and says: 'My property, my duck.' The yuppie can't believe what he's hearing.

'Come on!' he says. 'I've been out hunting all bladdy day. I saw the duck, I shot it, it's mine.'

The farmer looks him squarely in the eyes and says, 'My property, my duck.'

The yuppie's had as much as he can take. He reaches into his pocket and pulls out the most powerful weapon in his possession. His cellphone. He's going to call his lawyer, the cops, the media … anybody. But he can't get a signal. So he starts whining and arguing again.

The farmer listens in silence, and then he says, 'All right. I'll tell you what, city boy. Out here in the Bosveld, we've got our own way of settling arguments. We call it Last Man Standing. Here's how it works. I kick you in the balls as hard as I can, and then you kick me in the balls as hard as you can, and so on and so forth. Last man standing gets the duck.'

The yuppie thinks it over. He's desperate to have a duck to brag about back at the office on Monday.

'Okay,' he says. 'You first.'

The farmer rubs his hands, stamps his heavy workboots on the ground, and then lets kick with all his might. EINA! The yuppie's eyes roll back in his head. He coughs, wheezes, grits his teeth, clutches his groin. He remains standing. But only just.

After a minute or two, he manages to compose himself. 'Okay,' he says to the farmer. 'Now it's my turn.'

And the farmer says, 'Never mind. You can have the duck.'

BIG WHITE HUNTER

'Yes, I came face to face with a lion once,' said Mike, staring into the flames of the fire outside the Bushveld pub. 'And as luck would have it, I was alone and without a gun.'

'What did you do?' asked the blonde on his arm.

'What could I do?' said Mike. 'First, I tried looking straight into his eyes, but he kept on coming slowly toward me. I moved back, but he kept coming nearer. I had to think fast.'

'So how did you get away?' gasped the blonde.

'Ag,' said Mike, 'I just left him and passed on to another cage.'

BRAVEHEART

Deep in the African bush, Mike and Van are looking for signs of lion. They find some. A set of perfectly-shaped spoor, along with a heap of fresh dung.

'Okay,' whispers Mike, 'you follow the tracks and see where the lion is heading. I'll walk backwards and see which direction he came from.'

LEEUTEMMER

'n Klompie Vlakplaas-manne hou een aand in '83 beraad in die wildtuin saam met 'n aantal Westerse eweknieë. Hulle gesels oor hoe hulle 'n leeu sal jag.

Die Brit sê, 'I'll walk straight up to the lion and show no fear. Lions will never charge if you don't show fear. Then I'll just aim my .375 at his head and shoot him on the spot.'

Die Amerikaner sê, 'I'll tie a chunk of donkey's meat to a tree and get onto the highest branch. Once the lion gets stuck into the meat, I'll shoot him up in the tree.'

Eugene de Kock sê, 'Ek kan sien julle manne ken nie Suid-Afrika nie. Ek sal 'n haas in 'n strik vang en hom opdonner tot hy erken hy's 'n leeu.'

LEKKER TEKKIES

Koos en Piet gaan jag, en Koos dra 'n lekker fensie paar splinternuwe Nike tekkies.

'Waarvoor sal 'n man nou sulke mooi nuwe tekkies dra as jy gaan jag?' wil Piet weet.

'Dis in case 'n leeu op my afstorm,' sê Koos.

'Jy's mal, man,' lag Piet. 'Jy sal mos nooit vinniger as 'n leeu kan hol nie.'

'Ek hoef nie,' sê Koos. 'Ek moet net vinniger as jy kan hol.'

SUKKEL-SUKKEL

Mike en Kallie het gaan jag, en hulle is besig om hierdie reuse koedoe deur die veld te sleep. Hulle het die dier aan die horings beet, maar dit gaan maar sukkel-sukkel. Die eienaar-wildboer sien die petalje, en stel toe die volgende voor: 'Julle moenie die koedoe aan sy horings sleep nie,' sê hy, 'want kort-kort haak die horings aan die bosse vas, en dan vat dit julle weer 'n uur om die horings los te haak. Kry bietjie kop, manne, en vat die dier aan sy agterbene. So sleep julle hom mos nou baie makliker, want daar's mos nou nie horings wat kan vashaak nie. Dis baie eenvoudig, eintlik logies.'

Mike en Kallie maak toe so, en sleep die koedoe nou aan sy agterbene.

So 'n halfuur later sê Mike, 'Hell ou Kallie, ons is darem nou al 'n moerse ent weg van ons bakkie.'

INNOCENTS ABROAD

GOING UP

Oom Giel and his son, Pieter, were on their first visit to the big city. Fresh from their merino farm in the Karoo, they were amazed by everything they saw. But one thing in particular caught their eye. A lift in the lobby of a skyscraper.

They stood there for a while, watching the shiny silver doors slide apart and move back together again. 'What's that, Pa?' asked Pieter.

'I've got no idea, my son. I've never seen anything like it in my life.'

As they gaped, with eyes as wide as saucers, a hefty old tannie shuffled up to the lift and pressed a button. The shiny doors opened, the tannie shuffled in, the shiny doors whispered shut. Lights flashed above the doors, and there was a pinging sound. More lights, more pinging.

Then the doors opened again, and a beautiful, busty blonde in her early twenties sashayed out. Oom Giel turned to his son and said, 'Wat staan jy so en kyk, seun … gaan haal jou ma!'

DISTINGUISHING FEATURES

Having lost the race to find suitable employment back home, Mike and Kallie are taken on as casual labourers on a construction site in London. They enjoy the work, they enjoy getting paid in pounds, they enjoy the company of their fellow brickies and sparkies and trench-diggers.

As proud citizens of the Rainbow Nation, they're particularly happy to enjoy an after-hours dop every now and then with the only black member of the workforce. One day, sadly, the black guy slips on a scaffold and plummets KER-SPLAT to the ground below.

The cops are on the scene almost immediately. 'Did any of you know this fellow?' asks a Bobby, whipping out his spiral notebook.

'Ja,' says Mike.

'What can you tell me about him?' asks the constable.

'Nothing much,' shrugs Mike. 'All I know for sure is that he had two arseholes.'

The policeman pauses with his pen in the air. 'What on earth do you mean?'

'Well,' continues Mike, 'every now and again, me and Kallie would join him for a dop, and the barman would look up from the counter and say, "Here comes that black guy with the two arseholes."'

FAIR SWAP

Mike falls in love with this beautiful Moroccan lady. They're standing in the departure lounge at Casablanca Airport, waiting for the plane. A handsome young Moroccan can't keep his eyes off the girl. He goes up to Mike.

'I'll give you ten camels if I can have her.'

'Ten camels!' booms Mike. 'You must think I'm mal. Gimme a carton and she's yours.'

ZEBRA CROSSING

Koos, from Loeriesvlei, daar onder in die Bosveld, sets foot in Gauteng for the first time in his life. He tries to cross a street in Sandton, but every time he steps off the pavement, a Porsche or a BMW or a 4×4 nearly knocks him over.

A spietkop sees the struggling Koos and shouts, 'Hei, there's a zebra crossing just a little way down the street.'

Koos says, 'Well, I hope he's having better luck than I am.'

IRISH

BANG BANG

Did you hear about the Irish cowboy?
Rick O'Shay.

AYE AYE

How can you identify an Irish pirate?
He's the one with patches over both eyes.

SECRET WEAPON

Seamus O'Flannagan hobbled into the pub on a crutch, with one arm in a cast and a bandage wrapped around his head.

'Good heavens,' said the bartender. 'And what happened to you, O'Flannagan?'

'I got into a tiff with Riley,' said O'Flannagan, manoeuvring himself onto a barstool.

'Riley? He's just a wee fellow,' the bartender said in surprise. 'He must have had something in his hand.'

'Aye, that he did,' said O'Flannagan. 'A shovel it was.'

'Dear Lord. And didn't you have anything in YOUR hand?'

'Aye, that I did,' said O'Flannagan. 'Mrs Riley's left tit. A beautiful thing it was, but not much use in a fight!'

HANDS OFF

'Paddy,' asked the barmaid, 'what are those two big bulges in the front of your trousers?'

'Ah,' said Paddy. 'They're hand grenades. Next time that queer O'Flaherty comes feeling my balls, I'll blow his bloody fingers off.'

TAKE YOUR PICK

How do you confuse an Irishman?

Show him three shovels and tell him to take his pick.

TRAFFIC SIGNAL

Seamus O'Flannagan was summoned to court for killing a dog by running it over with his car. The magistrate asked Seamus how he could possibly have missed seeing the dog in his headlights, when the animal was clearly visible with its leg cocked against a tree.

Seamus shrugged and said: 'I did indeed see that, Your Honour, sir, but at the time I thought he was turning right.'

WINNING TICKET

'And the winning ticket is number 11,' Father O'Reilly called out at the charity raffle. Everybody looked around to see who had won the prize, but no one had their hand in the air.

'Are you sure you don't have ticket number 11, Father Murphy?' asked Father O'Reilly after a while.

'Ah, so I do,' said Father Murphy. 'I'm sorry, I was looking at it upside-down.'

ALAS, POOR PATRICK

Bud Nelson, New Yorker, flew to Knock Airport in the west of Ireland on business. As he walked down the stairs from the plane onto the runway, he noticed a small Irishman standing beside a long trestle table. On the table was an assortment of human skulls.

'What are you doing, bud?' asked the American.

'I'm selling skulls,' replied the Irishman.

'Oh yeah? And what skulls do you have?' asked Bud.

'Well, I have the skulls of the most famous Irishmen that ever lived,' said the Irishman.

'You do?' said Bud. 'That's great! Gimme some names.'

'Well,' said the Irishman, pointing to various skulls, 'that one there is James Joyce, the famous author and playwright. That one there is St Brendan, the navigator. That's Michael Collins, the leader of the 1916 rising, and that one there is St Patrick, the patron saint of Ireland. God bless his soul.'

'Sorry,' said Bud, 'But did you say St Patrick?'

'Indeed I did, sir,' said the Irishman.

'I gotta have that!' said Bud, and he handed over £150 in cash.

Bud flew back to New York and mounted the relic on the wall in his pub. People came from all over America to view this famous skull. Many years later, now retired, Bud flew back to Ireland for a quiet visit. At Knock Airport, he was walking down the stairs from the plane, when he saw the same Irishman with the same trestle table.

'Hiya there,' said Bud. 'What are you doing?'

'I'm selling skulls,' replied the Irishman.

'And what skulls do you have today?' asked Bud.

'Well, I have the skulls of the most famous Irishmen that ever lived!' said the Irishman.

'You do?' said Bud. 'That's great! Gimme some names!'

'Well!' said the Irishman, pointing to various skulls, 'that one there is James Joyce, the famous author and playwright. That one there is St Brendan, the navigator. That's Michael Collins, the leader of the 1916 rising, and that one there is St Patrick, the patron saint of Ireland. God bless his soul.'

'Wait a second,' said Bud, 'Did you say St Patrick?'

'Indeed I did,' said the Irishman. 'That's very strange,' said Bud. 'You see, I was here about ten years ago and you sold me a skull just a little bit bigger than that one there, and you told me then that it was the skull of St Patrick.'

'I did?' said the Irishman, thinking hard. 'Oh yes! I remember now. Well, you see, sir, this is St Patrick when he was a boy!'

MISTAKEN IDENTITY

McGinty and McMurphy met in the street. McGInty said to McMurphy, 'Have you seen Mulligan lately?'

McMurphy said, 'Well, I have and I haven't.'

McGinty asked, 'And what do you mean by that?'

'It's like this,' said McMurphy. 'I saw a chap who I thought was Mulligan, and he saw a chap who he thought was me. And when we got up to one another … well, it was neither of us!'

AIR DISASTER

This two-seater Cessna crashed in a graveyard outside Dublin. The Irish press reported that 200 bodies had been discovered and they're expecting to find many more.

NICE CIGARS

An Englishman, a Frenchman and an Irishman are captured by the Germans and thrown into prison. The commandant, in a rare moment of compassion, tells the men, 'I'm going to lock you away for five years. But I'll let you have anything you want now, before I throw you inside.'

The Englishman says, 'I'll have five years' supply of the finest English beer!' His wish is granted, and he's locked away with his beer.

The Frenchman says, 'I'll have five years' supply of the finest French brandy!' His wish is granted, and he's locked away with his brandy.

The Irishman says, 'I'll have five years' supply of the finest Cuban cigars!' His wish is granted, and he's locked away with his cigars. Five years go by.

The Englishman is released. He staggers into the sunlight, drunk as a lord.

The Frenchman is released. He staggers into the sunlight, drunk as a Frenchman.

The Irishman is released. He staggers into the sunlight, shouting, 'Anyone got a light?'

WHOOSH

Did you hear about the Irishman who couldn't tell the difference between arson and incest?

He set fire to his sister.

BEAN SOUP

Paddy, the Irish cook, was renowned the world over for his Irish Bean Soup.

'I use exactly 239 beans,' he revealed. 'One more and it would be too farty.'

MASS APPEAL

Old man Murphy lived all alone in his cottage in County Galway. Well, almost all alone – he had a pet poodle who was his most faithful and devoted companion. Sadly, one day Murphy awoke to discover that the poodle had perished in the night.

Since he had been so close to the animal, Murphy carried him across to Father O'Reilly and said, 'Father, do you think you could be so kind as to say a mass for this poor creature?'

Father O'Reilly looked at the ex-poodle, shook his head, and said, 'I'm sorry, Murphy. We cannot hold services for animals in this church. Why don't you take him down the road to that new church, you know, the one where they're always happy and clapping? Maybe they can do something for your dog.'

'Thank you Father,' said Murphy. 'I'll be getting along now. Do you think a donation of £50,000 will be sufficient for the service?'

Father O'Reilly motioned Murphy to sit down again.

'Well now,' he said, 'and why didn't you tell me the dog was Catholic?'

JEWISH

BZZZZZ

Two bees bump into each one day. 'What's the buzz?' asks the first bee. 'Not too good,' says the second. 'I haven't been able to find a decent flower or fruit to gather pollen from all day.'

'Have you tried the bar mitzvah down the road?' says the first bee.

'The bar mitzvah?'

'Yes. They're having a big banquet with plenty of fresh fruit and flowers. Just fly five blocks down, turn left, and keep going until you see the cars.'

So the bee flies fives blocks down, turns left, sees the cars, and zooms inside the hall. A few hours later, the bee bumps into his buddy again.

'How'd it go?' says the bee. 'No, sweet,' says the other

bee. 'Never seen so much fresh fruit and flowers in my life. Got all the pollen I need. What a wonderful bar mitzvah.'

'That's nice to hear. But – and you'll pardon me for asking – what's that little black thing on your head?'

'That's my yarmulke,' says the second bee. 'I didn't want anyone to think I was a Wasp.'

JUST IN CASE

There's this mohel, the oke who does the snipping in the circumcision business. By the time he retires, he's got a whole barrel full of foreskins. He's got no idea what to do with them, so he takes them to the leatherworker across the road. 'Can you make me something out of these?' he asks. The leatherworker says, 'Sure. Come back in two days.' Two days later the leatherworker hands him a wallet. 'A wallet!' shouts the mohel. 'From all those foreskins, you make me one lousy wallet?' The leatherworker shrugs. 'Relax' he says, 'Just rub the wallet a little, and you've got yourself a very nice briefcase.'

GOING FOR A SONG

The little old Jewish lady calls the Classified section of the newspaper and says she'd like to place an ad under 'Obituaries'. The telesales lady says, 'Certainly. What would you like the ad to say, Madam?'

'Hymie Schmendrik died,' she dictates.

'That's it? Hymie Schmendrik died?'

'That's it.'

'But you get four lines in the obituary,' says the telesales lady. 'It's included in the price.'

'All right then,' says the little old lady. 'Hymie Schmendrik died … Cadillac for sale.'

ETHNIC JOKE

These two Jewish guys are walking down the street. The one turns to the other and says, 'Hey, did you hear the one about these two Jewish guys who were walking down the street? The one turns to the other and says ...'

That's as far as he gets. The other guy holds up his hand and says, 'Hold it just a second! Why are you always telling stories about the Jews? We've got enough trouble as it is. Pick on another nationality for a change. Like the Chinese, for instance.'

So the first guy shrugs his shoulders and says, 'Okay. These two Chinese guys are walking down the street. The one turns to the other and says, 'So tell me, Hymie, when is your son getting bar mitzvahed?"

MAMA'S BOYS

The Yiddishe mama has three sons who go abroad and prosper in their respective fields. One day, the sons gather to discuss the gifts they've been able to send to Mama back home.

Says Abie, the lawyer, 'I built a big house for Mama in Houghton.'

Says Moshe, the gynaecologist:, 'I sent Mama a Mercedes Benz with a driver.'

Says David, the chartered accountant, 'You know how much Mama likes to read the Bible. You know how her eyesight is getting worse and worse. I sent Mama this remarkable parrot that recites the whole Bible – all she has to do is name the chapter and verse.'

Soon after, Mama sends the boys a letter of thanks.

'Abie,' she says, 'the house you built is so huge. I only live in one room, but I have to clean the whole house.'

'Moshe,' she says, ''I'm getting too old to travel. So the Mercedes stays in the garage. And the driver is a pain in the tochus.'

'But David,' she says, 'the chicken you sent was delicious!'

HIS 'N HERS

Suzie's in the bathroom, getting ready for the dinner party. Suddenly, she's not in the bathroom anymore.

She's in the bedroom, shrieking at her husband: 'That new maid we hired ... she stole two of our best towels!'

'Which towels do you mean, sweetie pie?'

'What do you mean which towels do I mean! The ones we got from the hotel at Sun City.'

FAMILY TIES

The Jewish mama gives her son two neckties for his birthday. One's red, the other's green. That night, to show his appreciation for the gift, the son puts on the red tie before driving to his mother's to pick her up for dinner.

'What's the matter?' asks Mama, pointing at the necktie. 'You don't like the green one?'

NOT KOSHER

Father O'Reilly and rabbi Goldberg were sitting opposite each other at a multi-denominational banquet. Father O'Reilly speared a slice of roast ham with his fork, took a generous bite, and declared, 'Mmm-hmmm. This ham is absolutely delicious. Tell me, rabbi, when are you going to loosen up a little and try some for yourself?'

'At your wedding, Father O'Reilly,' retorted the rabbi.

LAST RITES

Hymie, 92, after a long and fruitful life, was on the verge of taking his last few breaths. He lay in his bed with his loving wife watching over him.

Outside, a gale-force wind howled, and a driving thunderstorm rattled the windows.

'Sadie, I'm about to die,' croaked Hymie. 'Get me a priest.' Sadie threw her husband a worried look.

'Not only you are about to die, you're also losing your mind. A priest? Don't you mean a rabbi?'

Hymie beckoned his wife to come a little closer.

'You want a rabbi should go out on a night like this?'

ROW ROW ROW THE BOAT

Yeshiva University, the official rabbinical training ground, decides to field a crew in the intervarsity rowing league. No matter how hard they try, no matter how faithfully they train, the Yeshiva crew always finish in the same position. Stone last.

Finally, the coach sends Schmendrik on a top-secret mission to spy on the opposition. Schmendrik hides in the bushes and watches Harvard hard at practise. He rushes back to the Yeshiva.

'Coach, coach!' he yells, 'I've got it! I've figured out their secret! They have eight guys rowing, and only ONE guy shouting.'

NOTHING DOING

During the Sabbath service in the synagogue, the rabbi kneels down, puts his forehead on the floor, and says, 'Before you, oh Lord, I am nothing.'

The cantor – he's the guy who leads the congregation in song – thinks it can't hurt, so he also kneels down, touches his forehead to the floor, and says, 'Before you, oh Lord, I am nothing.'

Watching from the fifth row of the synagogue, Bennie Finkelowitz, the bookmaker, shrugs to himself, gets up, kneels down in the middle of the aisle, puts his forehead on the floor, and says, 'Before you, oh Lord, I am nothing.'

The rabbi nudges the cantor, 'Look who thinks he's nothing.'

MAMMA MIA

This young Jewish oke is seeing a psychiatrist for an eating and sleeping disorder.

'I am just so obsessed with my mother,' he says. 'As soon as I go to sleep, I start dreaming, and everyone in my dream turns into my mother. I wake up in such a state, all I can do is go downstairs and eat a piece of toast.'

The psychiatrist replies, 'What, just one piece of toast, for a big boy like you?'

SHOP TILL YOU DROP

This old bobbela – a Jewish ouma, for those of you not familiar with the term – goes to see her lawyer about a change to her will.

'I want you should put in my will that I must be cremated,' she tells the lawyer, 'and I want my ashes should be scattered on the first, second, and third floors of Woolworths in Sandton City.'

'That's a very unusual request,' says the lawyer. 'Can I ask you why you want to have this done?'

'Because that way,' says the bobbela, 'at least I'll know my daughter will come to visit me once a week.'

LITTLE BUBILA

Mrs Finkelowitz is sending her only son to school for the first time.

'My little bubila,' she says, pinching him on the cheek, 'this is your first time at school, so I want you to be a good boy, okay bubila? And when you come back from school, my little bubila, I want you to tell me everything you learned, okay bubila?'

She pinches him on the other cheek.

'Yes, mama,' he says, and off he goes to school. A little later, he comes home.

'Well, my little bubila,' says his mother, 'what did you learn in school today?'

'Mama,' he says, 'I learned that my name is Irving.'

THE GURU

Mrs Pupkewitz, 67, from Highlands North, goes to see her travel agent. 'I want to go to India,' she says.

'India?' says the travel agent, 'Are you sure? It's filthy,

it's hot, it's filled to the brim with all sorts of strange people ...'

'I want to go to India,' says Mrs Pupkewitz.

'But it's a long journey,' says the travel agent, 'and those trains, how will you manage? What will you eat? The food is too hot and spicy for you. On the roads, they drive like crazy. Elephants, cows, camels, all over the place. You can't drink the water. You can't eat fresh fruit and vegetables. You'll get sick: the plague, hepatitis, cholera, typhoid, malaria ... what will you do? Can you imagine the hospital, no Jewish doctors? Why torture yourself?'

'I want to go to India,' says Mrs Pupkewitz.

The travel agent shrugs. The necessary arrangements are made, and Mrs Pupkewitz goes to India. Undeterred by the noise, heat, dust, and smell, she immediately makes her way to an ashram – a secluded religious community run by a guru.

At the ashram, she joins the seemingly never-ending queue of people waiting for an audience with the guru. An aide tells her it will take at least three days of standing in line to see the guru.

'That's okay,' says Mrs Pupkewitz.

Finally, she reaches the hallowed portals. There she is told firmly that she can only say three words.

'Fine.'

She is ushered into the inner sanctum where the wise guru is seated, ready to bestow spiritual blessings upon eager initiates. Just before she reaches the holy of holies she is once again reminded: 'Remember, just three words.'

Unlike the other devotees, Mrs Pupkewitz does not prostate herself at the guru's feet. Instead, she stands directly in front of him, folds her arms, fixes her gaze on his, and says, 'Sheldon, come home.'

SILENT PARTNER

A Jewish boy comes home from school and tells his mother he has been given a part in the school play.

'Wonderful,' says the mother, 'what part is it?'

The boy says, 'I play the part of the Jewish husband.'

The mother scowls, 'Go back and tell your teacher you want a speaking part!'

FIRST LADY

The first Jewish president of the USA is elected. First thing he does, he calls his mother.

'Mama,' he says, 'I've won the elections. You've got to come to the swearing-in ceremony.'

'I don't know,' she says. 'What would I wear?'

'Don't worry,' says the President-elect. 'I'll send you a dressmaker.'

'But what about food? I only eat kosher.'

'Mama,' he says. 'You're talking to the future President of America. I can get you kosher food.'

'But how will I get there?'

'I'll send a limousine to pick you up. Just come, mama. It's my big day.'

'All right, already. If it makes you happy, I'll come.'

The great day arrives. Mama is seated between the Supreme Court justices and the future members of the cabinet. As the ceremony begins, she nudges the gentleman on her right.

'You see that boy up there, the one with his hand on the Bible?'

The man nods.

'His brother's a doctor!'

BLIND FAITH

What did the blind man say when he was given a piece of matzo?

'Who wrote this rubbish? I can't understand a word of it.'

ALL THAT GLITTERS

Mrs Finkelowitz decides to have her portrait painted for posterity. And, now that you mention it, for prosperity.

Which is why she instructs the artist, 'I want you should paint me with diamond earrings, a diamond necklace, emerald bracelets and a ruby pendant.'

'But you are not wearing any of those things,' says the artist.

'I know,' she said. 'It's in case I should die before my husband. I'm sure he will remarry right away, and I want his new wife to go meshuga looking for the jewellery.'

EASY MONEY

The nursery school teacher has a question for her class of five-year-olds. 'Children,' she says, 'I'll give five Rand to the first child who can tell me the name of the most famous man who ever lived.'

Little Eamon Murphy puts up his hand and says, 'Please Miss, it was St Patrick.'

'Sorry, Eamon,' says the teacher, 'that's not the answer I was looking for.'

Little Hamish McTavish puts up his hand and says, 'Please, Miss, it was St Andrew.'

'Sorry, Hamish,' says the teacher. 'That's not correct, either.'

Finally, little Sammy Cohen, sitting at the back of the class, puts up his hand.

'Please, Miss,' he says. 'It was Jesus Christ.'

'Well done, Sammy!' says the teacher. 'Come up here and get your five Rand.'

As the teacher hands Sammy his money, she says, 'You know, Sammy, you being Jewish, I was very surprised when you said Jesus Christ.'

Sammy shrugs.

'I know, Miss. In my heart, I know the answer is Moses. But what can I say? Business is business.'

KIDS

MUST TRY HARDER

Klein Jannie and his mom are sitting in the doctor's waiting room. Mom is filling out the medical form.

Name ....
Address ....
Occupation...................
Date of birth ....
Marital status ....
Sex ....

And so on. Jannie watches as his mom dutifully answers all the questions, and then he says, 'Ma, now I know why you and Pa got divorced.'

His mother frowns. 'All right, Jannie. You tell me why you think we got divorced.'

Jannie points to the medical form, 'You got an "F" for "Sex".'

ALL ABOARD

Little Johnny is playing with the train set he got for Christmas. His mother is cooking Sunday lunch in the kitchen. As Johnny brings the train to a halt, his mother hears him say, 'This the last stop, you &^%$#!!! So all you *^&% and %$#@ had better get off the *&^*(#% train right now, and hurry the *&^* up!'

Johnny's mother is so shocked, she almost drops the roast chicken on her foot. She storms into the lounge and yells, 'Johnny! You know better than to use such filthy language! You get up from there right now and stay in your room for the next two hours, until you learn how a child is supposed to speak!'

Two hours later, Johnny returns to play with his trains.

'Welcome aboard, all Spoornet passengers,' says Johnny. 'The 2.15pm express to Cape Town will depart in exactly seven minutes. Would all passengers with destinations of Germiston, Pretoria, Potgietersrus, Belville, and Cape Town please board the train now, and remember to watch your step. We wish you a pleasant journey.'

In the kitchen, Johnny's mother smiles sweetly to herself.

Little Johnny continues, 'And if any passenger would like to know why the *&^% we are two hours late, go and ask the *&*^% in the kitchen!'

SNNNNNNIFFF

Little Johnny's father catches him snorting a powdery substance behind the shed.

'Johnny!' he yells, 'what's that stuff you're sticking in your nose? It had better not be cocaine!'

'Don't worry, Pops,' says Johnny. 'It's only Kool-Aid.'

'Kool-Aid? Why would you want to stick Kool-Aid up your nose?'

'Because I've got a cold,' sniffs Johnny.

'Well, Kool-Aid isn't going to get rid of your cold, my boy.'

'I know, Pops,' says Johnny. 'But at least it makes my snot taste lekker.'

MIND YOUR HEAD

The Sunday School teacher has a question for little Johnny. 'Now, little Johnny,' she says, 'What does the story of David and Goliath teach us?'

'It teaches us to duck, Miss,' comes the answer.

O NO

Miss Ramsbottom wrote the chemical terms for water, oxygen and salt on the blackboard:

$H_2O = ?$

$O_2 = ?$

$SO_2 = ?$

'Now class,' she asked, 'who can tell me what H_2O is?'

Little Sally's hand was up in a flash: 'Water, Miss.'

'Excellent,' said Miss Ramsbottom. 'And who can tell me what O_2 is?'

Johnny put up his hand and keenly snapped his fingers. 'Oxygen, Miss.'

'Very good,' said Miss Ramsbottom. She noticed that little Mike had his finger up his nose and wasn't concentrating at all.

'Mike,' she said, 'Now you tell the class what SO_2 is.'

'I dunno, miss.'

'It's because you never pay attention,' sighed Mrs Ramsbottom. 'All right, I'll give you a clue. What does seawater taste like?'

Mike scratched his temple, looked at her dumbly and said, 'I dunno, Miss.'

'Here's another tip,' said Miss Ramsbottom. 'If you've just played a rugby match and you've been sweating a lot, what will you taste if you put your tongue against your arm?'

Little Mike stared at her blankly and said, 'I dunno, Miss.'

Miss Ramsbottom was running out of patience. She raised her voice a degree or two.

'Just think, Mike, think! What do you call the stuff your mom used to throw on your eggs when you were a little boy?'

A huge smile formed on Mike's mouth as he blurted out: 'Johnson's Baby Powder!'

YUM

What's the difference between snot and spinach?

You have to force a kid to eat spinach.

SUM-OF-A-BITCH!

Little Stuart arrived home after his first day at school.

'So, how was it?' his father inquired.

'It was nice,' said Stuart. 'Miss Thompson taught us that two and two the son of a bitch is four.'

There was a moment of shocked silence from the father. Thinking he must have heard incorrectly, he said, 'And what else did this Miss Thompson teach you?'

'She also taught me that three plus three the son of a bitch is six.'

At seven o'clock the following morning, Stuart's dad is sitting in the principal's office. Miss Thompson is called in to explain.

'How can you teach my son that three plus three the son of a bitch is six! He's only seven years old!'

Miss Thompson heaved a sigh of relief, smiled and said, 'Well, what I actually teach them is, "three plus three, THE SUM OF WHICH is six".'

TAP-TAP

The English laaitie and the Boere laaitie are talking about their forefathers.

'My grandfather was tapped on the shoulder with a sword by the King of England, and he became a Knight of the British Empire,' says the English laaitie.

'That's nothing,' says the little Boereseun. 'My oupa was tapped on the head with a knopkierie by Shaka Zulu, and he became an angel!'

HELPING HAND

A little girl is out walking with her grandma. In the middle of the park, they come across a couple of dogs mating.

'What are they doing, Grandma?' asks the little girl.

Turning crimson with embarrassment, the grandmother says, 'The dog on top has hurt his paw, and the one underneath is carrying him to the doctor.'

'They're just like people, aren't they, Grandma?'

'How do you mean?' asks Grandma.

'Offer someone a helping hand,' says the little girl, 'and they'll screw you every time!'

MOENIE NOU KYK NIE, MAAR ...

Die outjie kom by sy ma, kyk vas teen haar wenkbroue: 'Ma, watter woord is beter om te gebruik ... die Vader se naam of die f-woord?'

'Geeneen,' sê Ma. 'Altwee is sonde.'

'Ma, maar as ek nou rêrig moet, watter een moet ek eerder gebruik?' vra die seuntjie.

'Liewer die f-woord,' antwoord Ma.

'Ma,' sê die seun uiteindelik, 'daar sit 'n hottentotsfok teen jou kop.'

TINKLE TINKLE

Little Schucks was approached by the lifeguard at Bloemfontein's municipal swimming pool.

'You're not allowed to pee in the pool,' said the lifeguard. 'I'm going to report you.'

'But everybody pees in the pool,' said little Schucks.

'Ja,' said the lifeguard, 'but not from the diving board!'

I YAM WHAT I YAM

The vicar asked the young lad, 'Now tell me laddie, who went to Mount Olive?'

'Popeye,' said the lad, quick as a flash.

KNOCK-KNOCK

Knock-knock.
Who's there?
Isabel.
Isabel who?
Isabel not working again?

Knock-knock.
Who's there?
Adolf Ball.
Adolf Ball who?
Adolf Ball hit me in the mouth. That's why I'm talking this way.

Kconk-kconk.
Who's there?
Dissel.
Dissel who?
Dissel Lexic.

Knock-knock.
Who's there?
Etiquette.
Etiquette who?
Etiquette you for double-parking if you don't move your car right away.

Knock-knock.
Who's there?
Naas.
Naas who?
Naas place you got here, China.

Knock-knock.
Who's there?
Luyt.
Luyt who?
Luyt my fire, baby.

Knock-knock.
Who's there?
Fivaz.
Fivaz who?
Fivazholes working on the case, and they still can't solve the crime.

Knock-knock.
Who's there?
Joost.
Joost who?
Joost a minute while I look for a gap.

Knock-knock.
Who's there?
Atja.
Atja who?
Gezundheit.

Knock-knock.
Who's there?
Donna.
Donna who?
Donna tell me you already heard-a dis one.

Knock.
Who's there?
Oupa.
Oupa who?
Oupatunity only knocks once.

Knock-knock.
Who's there?
Chantelle.
Well, if you won't tell, I'm not going to open the door.

Knock-knock.
Who's there?
Chekov.
Chekov who?
Chekov ek my sleutels op die tafel gelos het, asseblief.

Knock-knock.
Who's there?
Juluka.
Juluka who?
Juluka like the back end of a bus.

Knock-knock.
Who's there?
Os.

Os who?
Os-tralia.

Knock-knock.
Who's there?
Du Randt.
Du Randt who?
Du Randt is nou 15 tot die Pond.

Knock-knock.
Who's there?
Vakansie
Vakansie who?
Vakansie and his whole blerrie team if they don't win the cricket!

Knock-knock.
Who's there?
Ferdi.
Ferdi who?
Ferdi laaste keer, hou Suid-Afrika blank!

Knock-knock
Who's there?
Huwelik
Huwelik who?
Huwelik nie bly nie.

Knock-knock.
Who's there?
Papparazzi
Papparazzi who?
Papparazzi met Dodi as hy te vinnig ry nie.

Knock-knock.
Who's there?
Hanekom.
Hanekom who?
Hanekom en die henne kraai.

KUGELS

IT'S YOUR CALL

Two kugels are chatting over their Schpritzers at Stephanie's Café. Asks the one, 'Soozee, do you talk to your husband while you're making passionate love?'

Says Soozee, 'Heavens, no! Why would I want to make a phone call at a time like that?'

TABLE MANNERS

Suzy Schmendelberger, socialite, is briefing her maid-of-honour in advance of the dinner party of the year.

'Selina,' she says, 'make sure you don't forget the sugar-tongs.' Selina looks confused. Sugar-tongs?

Suzy grabs hold of the sugar-tongs, show them to Selina, and whispers conspiratorially, 'You see, Selina, when the male guests go to the toilet, they hold their, you know, male members between their fingers, so we really can't have them handling lumps of sugar too, now can we?'

Selina shakes her head in agreement, then nods her head in understanding. Halfway through the evening, Suzy summons Selina with a click of her fingers.

'Selina,' she says, 'where did you put the sugar-tongs?'

'They're hanging in the toilet,' she says, 'just like Madam told me.'

WEIGHTWATCHERS

Two kugels are kugelling over their Schpritzers at Stephanie's. Says the first, 'So, how are things with you and Harry, doll?'

Says the second, 'Don't ask! Things are terrible, doll. He yells at me, criticises me, picks his nose in front of me, never lifts a finger around the house, and on top of all that, I know for a fact that he's having an affair with his secretary. I'm telling you, I'm so stressed out, I've already lost eight kilograms this month alone.'

'Have you thought about leaving the swine?' asks the first kugel.

'Of course I have,' replies the second. 'But first, I want to get my weight down to seventy-five kilograms.'

LAWYERS

ENOUGH IS ENOUGH

What's the difference between a prostitute and a lawyer?

The prostitute will stop screwing you when you're dead.

THANK YOU, FATHER

A truck driver used to amuse himself by running over lawyers he would see walking down the side of the road. Every time he would see a lawyer strolling along, he would swerve to hit him, there would be a loud THUMP, and he would swerve back on the road.

One day, as the truck driver was driving along, he saw a priest hitch-hiking. He thought he would do a good turn, so he pulled the truck over. 'Where are you going, Father?' he asked the priest.

'I'm going to the church just down the road,' replied the priest. 'No problem, Father! I'll give you a lift. Climb in the truck.'

The grateful priest climbed into the passenger seat and the truck driver continued on his journey.

Suddenly the truck driver saw a lawyer walking down the road. Instinctively, he swerved to hit him. Then he remembered there was a priest in the truck, so at the last minute he swerved back on to the road, narrowly missing the lawyer. Even though he was certain he'd missed the lawyer, however, he still heard a loud THUD.

Not understanding where the noise was coming from, he glanced in his mirrors. When he didn't see anything, he turned to the priest and said, 'I'm sorry, Father. I almost hit that lawyer.'

'That's okay,' replied the priest. 'I got him with the door.'

WHERE THERE'S A WILL

A lawyer draws up a will for a little old lady. He charges her R100. She reaches into her handbag and pays him in cash. Only when she has left the office, does the lawyer notice that the little old lady has given him two R100 notes, instead of one. Suddenly, the lawyer is struck with an ethical dilemma. Should he tell his partner?

GULP

How do you stop a lawyer from drowning?

Take your foot off his head.

PLANE TERROR

Did you hear about the terrorist who hijacked a 747 full of lawyers?

He threatened to release one every hour if his demands weren't met.

LEGALLY SPEAKING

This oke stomps into the pub after a rough day at the divorce court. 'Gimme a double brandy and Coke,' he yells at the bartender. He knocks it back and then he shouts out, 'All lawyers are assholes!'

A guy at the other end of the pub goois him a mean look and says, 'You'd better take that back, buddy.'

'Why?' says the oke. 'Are you a lawyer?'

'No,' he replies, 'I'm an asshole.'

WHAT LAWYERS ARE GOOD FOR

A man walks into a bar with a crocodile on a leash. The man asks the bartender, 'Do you serve lawyers here?' Not wanting to lose any business, the bartender grits his teeth and says, 'Sure we do.'

'Great,' says the man. 'Give me a beer, and my crocodile will have a lawyer.'

LEGAL BRIEF

The trouble with the legal profession is that 98 % of its members give the rest a bad name.

CLUCK-CLUCK

What is the difference between a rooster and a lawyer?

A rooster clucks defiance, and you know what a lawyer does to clients.

BORSEL

Wat is die ooreenkoms tussen 'n prokureur en 'n toiletborsel?

Jy haal hulle net uit as jy in die stront is.

JUST HOOT

If you see a lawyer on a bicycle, why should you never swerve to hit him?

It might be your bicycle.

DÉCOR TIP

How many lawyers does it take to wallpaper a room?

It depends on how thinly you slice them.

YOUR HONOUR

You get two kinds of lawyers. Those who know the law, and those who know the judge.

THIS IS A STICK-UP

Two lawyers are waiting in line in a bank. Suddenly, a man in a balaclava bursts in and begins waving his AK-47 meaningfully in the air. After grabbing all he can from the tellers, the robber orders everyone else in the bank to stand against the wall and hand over their cash and valuables.

Hearing this, one of the lawyers stealthily jams something in the other lawyer's hand. 'What is this?' whispers the lawyer, without looking down. 'It's the fifty bucks I owe you,' replies his colleague.

MADIBA

FAST LANE

Joel's just scored the winning goal in the '95 World Cup, the ref's just blown the whistle, and 64 000 South Africans are jumping up and down with joy in the stands. It's the single greatest moment in the nation's sporting history, even if it will later pale in comparison with Louis Luyt's resignation. But for now, the mood is one of sheer, unadulterated jubilation.

Even Madiba, still wearing his No. 6 jersey, is toyi-toyiing happily in the VIP box. His chauffeur, apologising profusely for the disturbance, manages to pluck up the courage to remind the President that he's due for an urgent appointment in Pretoria in half-an-hour's time.

Twenty minutes later, Madiba finally makes it to the Merc. As the chauffeur opens the rear passenger door, Madiba says, 'Move over, China. I'm driving.'

'But … but … but …' buts the chauffeur.

'But nothing,' says Madiba. 'We've got five minutes to get to the Union Buildings. I want to see what this baby can do.'

Turns out this baby can do 242 km/h in a 120 km/h zone. The traffic cop manning the speed trap can't believe his speedometer. He leaps out, stops the car, motions the driver to wind down the window.

'Evening, sir. Naand, meneer. Can I see your …' He

looks at the driver. He looks at the oke sitting in the back seat. 'J-j-just a second,' stammers the cop. He radios his boss back at headquarters.

'Meneer,' he whispers, 'we've got a problem here.'

'What's the problem?'

'Some oke has just zoomed through the speed trap at 242 kays an hour.'

'So? Ticket the oke, man!'

'That's what I'd like to do, meneer. But the problem is, he's a VIP.'

'So? All the more reason to ticket the oke, man!'

'You don't understand, meneer. This oke is not just your everyday, ordinary VIP. This oke is REALLY a VIP, and I mean REALLY.'

'Really?' says the boss, 'Well, who the bliksem is he?'

'Um, that's just the problem, meneer. I don't know.'

'Well, if you don't blerrie well know who he is,' yells the boss, 'then how do you blerrie well know he's a VIP?'

And the cop says, 'He must be blerrie important, Meneer, because Nelson Mandela is his chauffeur.'

FREE AT LAST

Walking through the gates of Victor Verster on the day of his release from prison, Madiba shouted, 'I'm free, I'm free!'

Little Gammat looks at Madiba and said, 'So what? I'm four.'

MARRIAGE

MONEY FOR NOTHING

This oke comes home from work one day to find his wife sitting on the stoep with her bags packed. He asks her where she thinks she's going, and she says, 'I'm going to Las Vegas.'

He asks her why, and she says, 'I just found out that I can make R400 a night doing what I give you for free.'

The oke thinks about this for a while, and then he goes into the house and packs his bags and joins his wife on the stoep.

'And just where do you think you're going?' she asks.

He replies, 'I'm going to Las Vegas too'.

His wife checks him out. 'Why?'

And the oke says, 'I just want to see how you're going to live on R800 a year.'

LAWNMOWER MAN

'Man, it's just too blerrie hot to wear clothes today,' said Van as he stepped out of the shower. 'Skattie, what do you think the neighbours would think if they saw me mowing the lawn like this?'

Mrs Van looked up at him.

'Probably that I married you for your money.'

SHOTGUN WEDDING

A woman goes into a sporting goods store to buy a shotgun. 'It's for my husband,' she tells the assistant.

'Did he tell you what gauge to get?' asks the guy.

'Are you crazy?' she says. 'He doesn't even know I'm going to shoot him!'

THE TRADE-OFF

Koos and Willie, best of buddies, best of neighbours, have been working at the same factory, on the same shift, for years. As they put down their tools one lunchtime, Willie turns to Koos and says, 'You know, China, I've been thinking. I love my wife. But sometimes, man, I get a little bored. I was just wondering … have you ever thought of switching?'

Koos pauses in mid-bite of his fried-egg sarmie. For a

moment, Willie is worried that his pal is going to send him flying to the floor.

Instead, Koos says, 'Hang, that sounds like a great idea. Let's maar talk to our wives, and see what they think.'

So Koos and Willie talk to their respective wives at home that night. Much to their amazement and delight, their spouses – who have also been feeling a bit bored lately – agree that it sounds like a great idea.

Come Friday night, the couples get together to put it into practice. Next morning, Koos says to Willie, 'How was it for you, hey?'

Willie says, 'No, lekker, man. I had a lot of fun. We must try it again sometime.'

'Ja, definitely,' says Koos. 'Let's go next door now and see how the girls made out.'

SEX BEFORE MARRIAGE

Piet and Willie are having a dop together, when the conversation turns to married life. 'You know,' says Piet, 'I had sex with my wife before we were married. Did you?'

'I'm not sure,' says Willie, thinking hard. 'What was your wife's maiden name?'

HAVE YOUR CAKE AND EAT IT

This oke is a real lazy bugger, just like someone else I know. One day his wife says to him: 'The washer of the kitchen tap is worn out. Will you fix it?'

'Do I look like a plumber?' he says, and he walks away.

A few days later, the lady of the house has another small request for the man of the house. 'The bulb in our bathroom has gone. Do you think you could replace it?'

'Do I look like an electrician?' he says, as he plonks himself in front of the TV.

Two weeks later, he comes home from his job at the Post Office. The tap in the kitchen is fixed, and there's a new bulb in their bathroom.

'I see you got some okes to fix the tap and the light,' he says.

'Actually it was this handyman,' she says. 'I phoned him and said if he would come over and fix the stuff I'd either bake him a nice chocolate cake or allow him to have his way with me.'

'So did the cake come out okay?' asks Mr Lazybones.

And his wife says, 'Do I look like a baker?'

AFTER YOU

What's the definition of a gentlemen?

A guy who holds the door open for his wife so that she can carry in the booze.

CHANGING PLACES

The husband says to his wife, 'Why don't we try a different position tonight, honeybunch?'

And the wife says, 'That sounds like a good idea. You stand by the ironing board, and I'll sit on the sofa and fart.'

COLD COMFORT

Why do married women weigh more than single women?

Single women come home, see what's in the refrigerator, and go to bed. Married women come home, see what's in bed, and go to the refrigerator.

SHEER MADNESS

It's the day before his wife's birthday, so Van pops into this exclusive boutique in Sandton City. He knows exactly what he wants. Or at least, he knows exactly what he thinks his wife will want. 'Show me the sheerest piece of lingerie you have in the shop,' he tells the assistant.

She shows him an outfit so sheer, it almost isn't there.

'How much?' asks Van.

'This one is R1 200,' says the assistant.

Van thinks about it.

'Actually, I'm looking for something a little more sheer,' he decides.

The assistant shows him something a little more sheer. 'This one is R1 750,' she says.

'You haven't got anything just a little more sheer than that?' asks Van.

The assistant wanders off to take a look in the XXX-Sheer section of the shop. She returns with precisely the outfit Van has in mind.

'How much?'

'This one is R3 500.'

'I'll take it.'

Back at home, Van can't wait to show the outfit to his wife. 'Try this on, skattie. Then come downstairs and model it for me.'

Mrs Van goes upstairs and opens the box. Bliksem. This thing is sheer. So sheer, that Van probably won't even notice if she's wearing it or not. Probably cost a fortune, too. Mrs Van decides she'll take it back to the shop for a refund in the morning. For now, she'll sommer go out wearing … nothing at all.

So Mrs Van, wearing nothing at all, strikes a pose at the top of the stairs. 'Well,' she says, 'what do you think?'

Van takes a good look. 'Bliksem,' he says. 'You'd think for R3 500, they'd at least iron the blerrie thing.'

SNYKUNS

Koos en Frik sien mekaar by Wepener se koöperasie en Koos vra, 'Hoe gaan dit met die vrou, Frik?'

'Nee, oukei,' sê Frik. 'En daar by jou kant?'

'Gaan maar sleg. My vrou het mos plastiese snykunde ondergaan.'

'Wragtag?' sê Frik. 'Sjym. Was dit 'n groot storie?'

'Moerse,' sê Koos. 'Ek het haar kredietkaart opgesny.'

MAKING IT LEGAL

If marriage were outlawed, only outlaws would have inlaws.

SOFT PAWN

'I bought us this flat above a pawnshop,' said Koos to his brand-new bride.

'Why a pawnshop?' asked Nellie.

'Ag, I thought you'd like to be near your wedding ring,' explained Koos.

STRANGE BEDFELLOWS

A loyal member of the Freedom Front married a young lady who was a staunch supporter of the Democratic Party.

On the first night of their honeymoon, they began arguing about politics. The dispute continued until late in the night. After a few hours the young bride said: 'Darling, there's a split in the DP, and I think if the Freedom Front member stood now, he would get in easily.'

'Too late,' said the Freedom Front man. 'He's already stood as an independent, and lost his deposit!'

PSSSST

Van het laat gekuier die aand, staan die nag op, loop 'n draai en kom terug. Hy skud sy vrou wakker.

'Wat's dit?' vra sy deurmekaar. Van sê, 'Jy gaannit nie glo nie. Ek loop 'n draai, en die lig gaan sommer vanself aan. Toe ek klaar is, daar gaanie lig wragtag sommer weer vanself af.'

'Ai,' sê sy vrou, 'moenie vir my sê jy't alweer in die fridge gepie nie.'

PSSSST AGAIN

Anniversaries are like toilet seats.

Men usually miss both.

VAT SO

Sy't 'n man gesoek en het 'n advertensie in die koerant geplaas.

Sy't duisende briewe teruggekry wat gesê het, 'Jy kan myne kry.'

LOVERBOY

The widow placed a death notice in the newspaper, adding that her husband had died from gonorrhoea.

Her two daughters were horrified. 'You made a terrible mistake!' they said. 'Daddy died of diarrhoea.'

'There was no mistake,' said the widow. 'I'd rather have him remembered as a great lover than the great shit he really was.'

OINK

What's the big difference between men and pigs?

When pigs drink, they don't make men of themselves.

BUURMAN

Van kom by die huis aan, klim uit sy kar en sê nonchalant 'hallo' vir sy vrou. Sy sien hoe die buurman uit sy kar klim met 'n pragtige bos blomme, sy vrou styf teen hom vasdruk en haar 'n soen gee.

'Hoekom doen jy dit nooit nie?' wil Van se vrou weet.

'Nooit,' sê Van, 'ek ken die vrou skaars.'

NOTHING PERSONAL

The blonde was seeking maintenance for her baby.

'Do you know who the father is?' asked the lawyer.

'Yes,' she cried, 'it was Tommy.'

'We need to know his surname if we're seeking maintenance.'

'I don't know,' said the blonde. 'You see, I didn't know him personally.'

MAYORS & MAYORESSES

ONE FOR ALL

Elected mayoress of Blikkiesdorp by a huge majority, Mrs Tshabalala decided she was going to make her mark in local politics.

During the first town council meeting, the engineer suggested the construction of a public urinal.

'What's a urinal?' asked Mrs Tshabalala. It was explained to her in great detail. The Mayoress thought it over and said, 'If we're going to erect a urinal, then we must get an arsenal too.'

BUL EN KOOI

'Wat 'n mooi dier,' sê mev. Burgemeester aan die skoubeampte tydens 'n amptelike besoek aan Koppies se landbouskou terwyl sy en die burgemeester na 'n stoetbul kyk.

'Ja,' sê die beampte, ''n ou grote soos dié dek gemiddeld vyfhonderd keer per jaar.'

'Vyfhonderd keer sê jy?' vra mev. Burgemeester hoogs beïndruk, en fluister in die beampte se oor, 'Sê dit bietjie vir die burgemeester.'

Die beampte maak toe so. 'Baie interessant,' sê die burgemeester. Dis natuurlik met net een koei?'

'Nooit,' sê die beampte, 'dis vyfhonderd verskillende koeie.'

Die burgemeester sê hardop, 'Sê dit vir mev. Burgemeester.'

FRUIT CAKE

It was the last day of the Kransvlei Agricultural Show, and the crowd gathered for the draw of the great raffle.

The mayor put his hand into the hat and drew ticket number 2667. There was a delighted shriek from a young lady in the crowd.

'You receive the third prize,' said the compère, 'which is one week at the Lost City.'

'Yeeeeyyy!' went the crowd.

He went on to draw another ticket, which was 9431. He read out the number, and oom Pottie jumped with delight, waving his ticket in the air.

'Oom Pottie, you receive the second prize, which is a beautiful fruit cake, made from the wonderful fruits of our fertile Kransvlei valley.'

Ou Oom Pottie went ballistic, 'What?' he shouted, 'how can the third prize be a week at Lost City and I get a blerrie fruit cake?'

'We have to remember, Oom,' said the compère, 'that this fruit cake was specially baked for our wonderful show by our wonderful Mayoress.'

'Ag, screw the Mayoress!' shouted oom Pottie.

'No, no Oom,' said the compère, 'that's the first prize!'

MIDLIFE CRISIS

FACELIFT

Caught in the throes of his midlife crisis, this forty-something executive decides to treat himself to a facelift. It costs him R20 000, but he feels really good about the result. On his way home from the clinic, he stops to buy a newspaper.

'How old do you think I am?' he asks the vendor.

The vendor looks him over. 'I'd say you are about 35.' The man beams from ear to ear. 'I'm 47,' he says.

After that, he pops into McDonald's for lunch. He rattles off his order, and says to the counterhand, 'How old would you say I am?'

The counterhand studies his face. 'I'd say you're 29.'

The man smiles so much that his face begins hurting. 'I'm 47,' he says.

He eats his meal and makes his way to the bus-stop. While waiting for the bus, he catches the eye of a little old lady.

'How old would you say I am?' he asks her. She looks up at him and says, 'You know, my eyesight hasn't been too good since I turned 85. But when I was young, I had a sure-fire way of telling a man's true age. Let me put my hand down your pants for a while.'

The man is taken aback for a moment, but since there is nobody else at the bus-stop, he decides to play along.

'All right,' he says, and the little old lady sticks her hand down his pants. After a couple of minutes, she withdraws her hand and says: 'You're 47.' The man is stunned.

'That's brilliant! How on earth could you tell?' The little old lady shrugs.

'I was standing behind you at McDonald's.'

FULL PHYSICAL

On the day of her 50th birthday, Mrs Van goes to see her doctor for a full physical. Back home, she gloats: 'The doctor says I have the body of a 30-year-old.'

'That's nice,' says Van, slouching on the couch with a beer in his hand. 'And what did he say about your big fat arse?'

'Nothing,' replies Mrs Van. 'Your name never even came up.'

MIKE

DRINK 'N DRIVE

Mike, the mechanic, is working under a car when some brake fluid drips into his mouth. He spits it out immediately, but something about the aftertaste makes him say to himself, 'Hang, this stuff isn't that bad, you know.'

So next day, while he's under another car, he opens his mouth wide and swallows a little of the oily black liquid. He licks his lips. Man, that's lekker. Eventually, Mike is drinking a full can of the stuff every day.

One lunchbreak, he decides to tell his buddy. His buddy explodes, 'Are you crazy, Mike? You can't drink that stuff! Brake fluid is poison, man! It'll destroy you! You'd better give it up!'

And Mike says, 'Ag, don't worry about me, pal. I can stop any time.'

VIP

Mike went to see Dr Vusi, the urologist, about the results of his fertility tests. He sat in the waiting room for two hours, flipping through old Farmers' Weeklies and twiddling his thumbs, before the doc was ready to see him.

Mike took his seat and glared at the doc. The doc looked at Mike and said, in his heavy Zulu accent, 'The tests show that you are impotent.'

Mike stripped his moer, shot up from the chair, and said, 'Well, if I'm so blerrie important, why did you make me wait for two hours?'

DUM-DUM

Mike and Nellie were sitting in the local restaurant in Keetmanshoop.

'Hold on, don't move,' Mike warned Nellie in mid-mouthful.

'Why, what's the matter?'

'There's a very dangerous fly buzzing around your mouth. Keep still.'

'Oo-ee,' shrieked Nellie. 'What is it?'

'It looks like a dum-dum fly,' said Mike.

'A dum-dum fly? What's a dum-dum fly?'

It's something that hangs around the back end of cows.'

'Hang on,' said Nellie. 'Are you saying that my face is like the back end of a cow?'

'It's got nothing to do with me, poepsie,' shrugged Mike, 'but you'll have to convince the fly.'

IN THE NUDE

Not many people know that Mike Schutte is also an accomplished artist. Anyway, a beautiful-looking woman once asked Mike to paint her in the nude.

'Sorry,' he said, 'I don't do that sort of thing.'

'I'll pay you twice your usual fee,' said the woman.

'Forget it,' said Mike.

'How about if I increase your fee FIVE times?'

'Okay,' shrugged Mike, 'but you'll have to let me at least wear my socks. I need somewhere to hold my brushes.'

FIRST, CATCH YOUR RAT ...

Said Nellie to Mike, 'I'm sick and tired of these blerrie rats in our house.'

Said Mike to Nellie, 'Ja, me too. We must get some rat poison to put in their holes.'

Said Nellie, 'Okay, but who's going to hold the rats?'

NEVER ON A SUNDAY

Little Mike ran up to his toppie one Sunday morning and said, 'Pa, there's an oke at the door with a moustache.'

'Tell him I've got one already,' said Mike.

'No,' said little Mike, 'You don't understand. He wants to know if you'll be a Jehovah's Witness.'

'Ag no, man,' said Mike, trying to find the comic supplement. 'Tell him I can't, 'cause I never saw the accident.'

Little Mike ran to the door, and returned with another question.

'Hy wil weet wat is Pa se kerkverband.'

'Sê vir hom ek skuld die kerk niks,' said Mike.

A few seconds later, little Mike was back.

'Now he wants to know what religion grandpa belonged to.'

'Tell him grandpa was a Methodist,' said Mike.

'He also wants to know what religion grandma belonged to.'

'Tell him she was a spiritualist.'

'So what does that make us, Pappie?' asked little Mike.

Mike thought about it for a second.

'That's easy,' he said. 'We're Methylated Spirits!'

RUN FOR YOUR MONEY

Little Mike burst into the house and said, 'Daddy, daddy, I ran behind a bus and saved two rand!'

'You could have run behind a taxi and saved ten,' replied Mike.

PIGEON POST

Mike is taking a casual stroll in the park, when a passing pigeon craps right on his head. A woman in the vicinity sees this, and says, 'Hold on, Mike, I've got a tissue in my handbag.'

And Mike snaps back: 'Ag, don't be silly, lady. That pigeon will be miles away by now.'

SPECIAL DELIVERY

Mike goes to see a carpenter. He's got a little job he'd like the guy to do. He pulls out his cigarette box, and reads the dimensions scrawled on the back.

'I need you to build me a box that is 5 centimetres high, 5 centimetres wide, and 15 metres long. Can you do that?'

'I suppose so,' shrugs the carpenter. 'But what are you going to do with a box like that?'

'Well,' says Mike, 'my neighbour moved house and forgot some things, so he asked me to send him his garden hose.'

UITKENNING

Mike is op vir verkragting. Daar is sewe verdagtes, en Mike en die ses ander ouens staan so teen die muur in die polisiekantoor tydens die uitkenningsparade. Die slagoffer kom die vertrek binnegestap om die skuldige uit te ken.

Mike gee haar een kyk en sê, 'Sersant, dis sy!'

SAVED BY THE BELL

Mike het slaapprobleme gehad en gaan dokter toe.

'Dok,' sê hy, 'Ek slaap baie sleg. Wat moet ek doen?'

Die dokter sê, 'Tel elke aand tot tien nadat jy in die bed geklim het, en ek waarborg jou jy slaap soos 'n klip.'

'n Week later is Mike terug. 'Dok,' sê hy, 'dit werk nie. Ek kom net tot by agt, dan spring ek uit die bed uit en dan's ek wawyd wakker.'

'Hoekom dan so?' vra die dokter.

'Ek's 'n bokser.'

ORIGINAL SIN

Standing in line to win a fabulous prize, Mike has to answer an easy question on the TV gameshow.

'And now, Mr Schutte,' says the gameshow host, 'for R10 000 in cash … can you tell me what the word "naive" means?'

Mike jabs his finger on the buzzer. 'Ag, that's easy,' he says. 'It's what Adam did in the Garden of Eden.'

HAVING A BALL

Mike rocks up at a fancy dress party with a movie theme. The invite says you've got to come dressed as your favourite Hollywood movie. Mike is stopped at the door. And no wonder: he's wearing nothing but five tennis balls, dangling from a belt tied around his waist.

'What movie are you supposed to be?' asks the doorman.

'Don't be stupid!' says Mike, barging his way into the party. 'Can't you see I'm dressed as "The Magnificent Seven"?'

IQ TEST

Mike is having his aptitude tested for a top position in the civil service.

'Okay, Mike,' says the tester, 'can you tell me how many days in the week begin with a 'T'?'

Quick as a flash, Mike answers: 'Two. Today and tomorrow.' The tester consults his clipboard and nods. 'Very good. Now for the next question. How many seconds are there in a year? Take your time on this one, Mike.'

But Mike doesn't take his time. In less than a second, he answers: 'Twelve. The second of January, the second of February, the second of March …'

The tester holds up a hand. It's time for the third and final question. 'How many 'die's' in My Sarie Marais?'

Mike frowns. Bites his lip. Thinks. Counts on his fingers. Then sticks his fist in the air and declares: 'Twenty-four! Dee dee-dee dee-dee dee-dee-dee dee-dee …'

Just over a week later, Mike gets the call to inform him that he didn't get the job. Reason? He's too highly qualified.

BO-BLY

'Mike, hou jy van afval en pap?' vra Kallie eendag vir Mike.

'Nee,' antwoord Mike, 'ek hou van bo-bly en styf.'

HOENDER OF EIER

'Mike,' vra die gameshow host, 'wie was eerste, die hoender of die eier?'

Mike dink lank en hard. Toe antwoord hy: 'Ek het nie eers geweet hulle't resies gehol nie.'

SONBRAND

'n Mooi meisie op die strand vra vir Mike, 'Is jy rooi van die son?'

'Nee,' antwoord hy, 'ek is Mike van die aarde.'

KOEBAAI CRUEL WORLD

After losing everything on the stock market, Mike walks into his bedroom and finds his wife in the arms of another man. Mike grabs his .38 Special, points it at his head and says, 'Koebaai. Ek het genoeg gehad.'

'Mike, asseblief, moenie!' shouts his wife.

'Sharrap!' says Mike, 'jy's volgende!'

POOR OKE

Jimmy sees a hearse passing by and asks Mike, 'I wonder who died?'

Says Mike, 'The oke inside the coffin.'

WEES BEREID

Mike en Kallie is op vir moord in die ou Suid-Afrika, en hulle word die keuse gestel: of die galg, of 'n inspuiting met die Vigs-virus. Kallie besluit die galg is meer pynloos en hy kies die galg. Mike hou sy arm uit, smile, en sê, 'Spuit maar in.'

Kallie vra, 'Is jy mal? Weet jy hoe gaan jy ly?'

Mike sê, 'Moenie worry nie, ek dra 'n F.L.'

DRINK EN DRYF

Mike en Kallie sit en kuier in die kroeg.

'Ek sit nie in hierdie bar omdat ek hier wil sit nie,' sê

Kallie. 'Ek sit hier omdat my vrou my na drank dryf.'

'Jy's gelukkig,' sê Mike. 'Ek moes self hiernatoe loop.'

THE FIXER

'Wat het van klein Mike geword?' vra Kallie vir Mike oor 'n dop.

'Hy's mos Amerika toe,' sê Mike.

'O ja? Om te watte nogal?'

'Nee, hy's wat hulle noem 'n sports mekênniek.'

'Nê? Sê Kallie. En wat doen 'n sports mekênniek nogal?'

'Nee, hy fix goete.'

'Hy fix goete? Soos watse goete fix hy?' vra Kallie.

'Nee,' sê Mike, 'hy fix goete soos boxing matches, baseball games ..."

LIBIDO

Mike's libido was at an all-time low. He couldn't afford Viagra, so he bought himself a big book at the CNA. It was called *HOW to HUG*.

When he got home his wife looked at him as if he was crazy, and asked the poor oke why he'd wasted his money on a volume of the Encyclopaedia Britannica.

MISUNDERSTANDINGS

MIND'S EYE

Mr de Kock teaches Biology to the senior class at the posh suburban girls' college. One day, he points his ruler at prim and proper Penny Fauntleroy.

'Miss Fauntleroy,' he says, 'would you please name the organ of the human body which, under the appropriate conditions, expands to six times its normal size, and would you kindly define those conditions?'

Miss Fauntleroy is speechless. She stammers, turns bright red, gathers up her books and storms straight out of class. Undeterred, Mr de Kock turns to her classmate, Felicity Witchwood-Jones.

'Can you tell us the answer, Miss Witchwood-Jones?'

'Yes,' she says. 'It's the pupil of the eye, in dim light.'

'Thank you,' says Mr de Kock. 'And would you be so kind as to convey the following information to Miss Fauntleroy. One, she did not study her lesson. Two, she has a dirty mind. And finally, one day, she is going to be faced with a dreadful disappointment.'

PRETTY IN PINK

This oke arrives at work one Monday sporting two perfect shiners – an ugly, swollen pulp of red, blue and purple on each eye.

'Jeez, Frikkie, what happened to you, my ou?' asks a colleague.

'No, I went to church yesterday,' says Frikkie, 'and I was sitting behind this auntie in a pink dress. Except on her, it looked like a wedding marquee. Anyway, she got up to sing a hymn, and I saw that this pink dress was pinched right up into her massive arse. You know how uncomfortable that can be.

'So I sommer leaned over and gently pulled the dress out of the place where it was being pinched. I mean, I was only trying to do good. But the next thing this auntie turns around, checks me skeef, and stoots me with a right so hard that I land up three pews further.

'So I get up, I shake my head, I gather myself with the little bit of dignity I've got left and I walk back to my original seat. Just as I sit down again the dominee says we must rise for the prayer. So standing there I take a peek through my healthy eye and I see this pink dress is wragtag being pinched once again into that same place.

'So of course I'm telling myself, "Myself, you're not going to pull that dress out again", and while I'm still thinking about this the oke standing next to me leans over and he pulls the blerrie thing out without any warning.'

'But why have you got two black eyes then?' asks the colleague.

'Hell man, I got such a moeruvva skrik, I put my hands together like you do when you pray and I quickly rammed the dress back in again.'

FOUR CANARIES

Hoping to book a table at the most exclusive restaurant in town, this oke dials the number and says, 'Excuse me, is that the Four Canaries?'

A rough-sounding voice says, 'Nee, dis die fôkken Spories.'

The caller is taken aback. 'I beg your pardon! Well, how do I get the number of the Four Canaries, then?'

'Bel die fôkken lughawe, man.'

MOFFIES

DO UNTO OTHERS

They've reached the part of the church service where the collection plate is passed around. Casting his eyes over the usual assembly of copper coins and brass buttons, the preacher spies a crisp new R200 note. He immediately stops the service.

'Brothers and sisters!' he booms, 'someone has truly opened up their heart for us today. Would the person who put the R200 note in the collection plate please stand up.'

Cecil, who owns a hairdressing salon in the neighbourhood, stands up and flashes a huge smile at the congregation.

The preacher says, 'As a small token of appreciation for your generosity, brother Cecil, I'd like to ask you to choose the next three hymns.'

So Cecil looks around the church and says, 'Okay, I'll take him and him and him.'

IF WISHES WERE HORSES

Fitzpatrick and Fitzgerald, the two Irish homosexuals, were strolling gaily down the street when they came upon a leprechaun. 'Well, I'll be buggered,' said Fitzpatrick.

'Let's first see what the leprechaun wants,' said Fitzgerald.

They bent down to see the leprechaun stomping up and down in fury, as leprechauns tend to do when they are discovered. 'Now I'm going to have to grant you three wishes!' seethed the leprechaun.

'Really?' said Fitzpatrick.

'Of course! Don't you know anything about old Irish tradition? Hurry up! I haven't got all day!'

Fitzpatrick and Fitzgerald look at each other in amazement. 'You first,' says Fitzpatrick.

'All right. I wish we had a million dollars.'

Poof!

A brand-new leather suitcase appeared at their feet. Inside: one million dollars in crisp new bills.

'And I wish we had a mansion on a beach in California,' said Fitzpatrick.

Poof!

And there they were, masters of the manor on a beautiful beach in California.

Overwhelmed by their new-found riches, Fitzpatrick suggests to Fitzgerald that they save their third wish for later. The leprechaun agrees. A week or so later, Fitzpatrick and Fitzgerald are lounging around on the patio of their mansion, when they hear a crashing sound coming from the front door. Fitzpatrick gets up to investigate.

They've got visitors. Not just any visitors: it's a party of men wearing white sheets, with pointed hoods on their heads. One of the men has a rope in his hands.

Fitzpatrick screams. He turns to Fitzgerald and says, 'I think this might be a good time to use our third wish.'

Fitzgerald, getting ready to run like the wind, manages to answer, 'I'm afraid I already used our third wish about a week ago.'

'And what did you wish for?'

The men in white sheets draw nearer.

'I wished that we were hung like black men.'

BE UPSTANDING IN COURT

Did you hear about the two gay judges?
They tried each other.

WOODY

What do gay termites eat?
Woodpeckers.

ADAPT OR DYE

Did you hear about the three gay guys who attacked a woman walking down the street?
Two of them held her down, and the other started doing her hair.

CLICK

The young man was introduced to the Queen.

'And what do you do for a living?' asked Her Majesty.

'I'm a photographer, Ma'am,' he replied.

'How remarkable,' said the Queen. 'My brother-in-law is a photographer.'

'How odd,' said the photographer. 'My brother-in-law is a queen.'

HELLO TEACHER

This sales rep was on assignment in the platteland. He knocked on the door of a guest house in the Karoo.

'I'm afraid we don't have any spare rooms,' said the proprietor, 'but you're welcome to share a room with the little redheaded school teacher.'

The salesman could hardly contain his excitement. 'Thank you very much,' he said. 'I promise I will be a real gentleman.'

'That's good,' said the proprietor. 'So is the little redhead school teacher.'

STRAIGHT TALK

A husband and wife were having a heated argument in a pub. The moffie leaned over to his partner and said, 'See, I told you, these mixed marriages never work.'

QUEEN OF THE BALL

The top industrialist was getting increasingly worried about his son's poor performance at university. Finally, he phoned the dean and asked for an explanation.

'I have good news and bad news,' said the dean. 'Your son has failed all his exams miserably, and he is a homosexual.'

The distraught industrialist cried out, 'Then what can the good news be?'

'He's been voted Rag Queen.'

IN THE CLOSET

Mike says he loves women so much, he must be a lesbian.

MOTHERS-IN-LAW

KA-BOOM

Mike phones his doctor in a state of total panic.

'Doctor doctor,' he says, 'I swallowed a live bullet! What should I do?'

'Eat a couple of cans of baked beans,' advises the doc, 'and stand in front of your mother-in-law.'

BRUSH-OFF

It's the day after Mike's big birthday. His mother-in-law asks Nellie, 'So how does Mike like that toilet brush I gave him for a present?'

'Ag, he doesn't mind it,' says Nellie, 'but he still prefers to use toilet paper.'

HAVE A NICE DAY

A guy goes to the doctor for a check-up. The next day, the doctor calls him back.

'I have some really bad news for you,' he says. 'I've checked the results of your tests with some of my colleagues. I'd really like to be able to tell you otherwise, but I'm sorry to say you have one more day to live.'

'One day!' yells the guy. 'What, you mean, like, today is the last day of my life?'

The doctor nods. 'I'm afraid there's nothing more we can do for you. And don't worry about the bill – I've spoken to your medical aid, and they're going to take care of it.'

Gee thanks, thinks the guy, as he heads for the bar to drown his sorrows and figure out what to do next. One drink follows another, and by the time he gets home, it's 9.30 p.m.

He staggers his way up to the bedroom. Pausing on the threshold, he thinks: may as well go out with a bang.

So he throws his clothes off, gets into bed, and makes wild, passionate sex until the sun comes up. Exhausted, utterly spent, he finally flops into the bathroom. There stands his wife with a mudpack on her face.

'What are you doing in here?' he asks her.

'Shhhhhh!' she says. 'You'll wake my mother.'

KOM MAAR SAAM

Ek neem altyd my skoonma saam met vakansie, want ek's bang ek moet haar soen as ek haar groet.

VERLOOFRING

Sy kom wit geskrik by die huis aan en vertel haar man dat sy buite die winkelsentrum beroof is. Haar handsak met al die kontant en kredietkaarte is weg. 'Gelukkig het ek darem my verloofring gered,' sê sy.

'En hoe't jy dit reggekry?' wil hy weet.

'Ek het dit ongemerk in my mond gedruk.'

'Plaas jy jou ma ook saamgeneem het,' sê hy, 'dan kon jy jou handsak ook gered het.'

MOVIES

THE MOVIE GAME

Some alternative stars and titles for popular Hollywood movies:

Mission Impossible – Roelf and Bantu

Mrs Doubtfire – Dr Zuma

Dances with Wolves – Balke Toe met Barend

True Lies – TRC

Gone with the Wind – A Fart in the Lift

A Few Good Men – The ANC

Look Who's Talking – Confessions of die Groot Krokodil

Sister Act – Pieter-Dirk Uys

Jungle Book – Die SA Grondwet

The Birdcage – Monica Lewinsky's Mouth

The Addams Family – Goggo se Mense

One Flew over the Cuckoo's Nest – One Flew over the Union Buildings

Blazing Saddles – Parliament Seats

Kindergarten Cop – George Fivaz

Schindler's List – The Lift Repairman's Working Schedule

Out of Africa – Coming to America

Back to School – The Department of Education

Trading Places – The New South Africa

Mr Mom – Evita Bezuidenhout

Days of Thunder – Tri-Nations Rugby

Romancing the Stone – Screwing Mick Jagger

Cape Fear – A Windy Day in the Cable Car

Sudden Impact – The Unexpected Taxi

Boomerang – Boesak

Get Shorty – Tackle Kevin Putt

Bad Boys – Toks en Balie

MUSICIANS & THEIR INSTRUMENTS

NAME THAT TUNE

Schucks shuffles into the pub. He looks like he's got the worst hangover in the world. In fact, he's stone cold sober – but he's got plans. He sits down with a sigh, orders four double whiskeys, knocks them back, and pops a fistful of Prozac into his mouth. The barman has been in the game long enough to see that this oke has a problem.

'Look,' he says, 'I know this is none of my business, but are you okay, pal?'

Schucks looks at the barman. Of course he's not okay. But he's glad to have someone to talk to.

'I write these beautiful songs,' says Schucks, 'I mean really, really beautiful. But the record companies keep on rejecting them. I know they're good, but no one else seems to think so.'

Trying his best to be nice, the barman asks Schucks to play him a song on the piano. Trying his best to be humble, Schucks flatly refuses. The barman insists.

'Ag, okay,' shrugs Schucks, and he sits down at the piano.

The barman secretly grits his teeth. He's expecting to hear a mangled mess of sour notes and off-key chords. Instead, he hears a melody so sweet and beautiful, it brings tears to his eyes. As the final notes drift into the ether, the entire pub bursts into spontaneous applause.

'Hell man, that was magnificent!' says the barman, as he pours Schucks a double whiskey on the house. 'I can't understand how anyone could possibly reject such a beautiful song. What's it called?'

'That one?' says Schucks. 'It's called "I Love the Bokke So Much I Could Shit".'

BLES MY SOUL

Why are the girls mad about Bles Bridges?
   Because of the vibrato in his voice.

GUMS

What has one thousand legs and no teeth?
   The front row at a Bles Bridges concert.

SAX AND VIOLINS

The muso comes home every night carrying five violins
under his right arm and three saxophones under his left.
He walks into the living room and plonks the violins and
the saxophones on top of the TV.
   His wife freaks out, 'Take that bloody stuff off!'
   'Why?' asks the muso.
   'There's enough sex and violence on TV as it is!'

PUMP ORGAN

Luigi arrived at the doctor and said, 'My wife she's-a
pregnant again!'
   The doctor throws his hands up in the air. 'Didn't you
wear the condom as I instructed?'
   'Si Doc,' said Luigi. 'But we don't a got an organ so I
stuck it over the trombone. It's a the only music
instrument in-a da house.'

THEY'RE PLAYING OUR SONG

They were making love with romantic music playing in the
background. Suddenly there was an irritating noise over
the hi-fi. 'Let me put the Dolby on quickly,' he said.
   'Don't worry,' said the blonde. 'I'm on the pill.'

DUMB AND DRUMMER

Did you hear about the bass player who locked his keys
in the car?
   He had to break a window to get the drummer out.

Did you hear about the drummer who was so dumb, he lost one of his sticks and became a conductor?

How do trumpet players park in the handicap spots?
   They put drumsticks on the dash.

Why do drummers have lots of kids?
   They're terrible at the rhythm method.

This oke goes into a store, walks up to the counter and says, 'I'd like a Marshall HiWatt 360 watt amplifier and a Fender geetar with the fried rose tremolo ...'
   The guy stops him right there and says, 'You're a drummer, aren't you?'
   'Uh, yeah. How did you know?'
   'This is a travel agency.'

What's the difference between a saxophone and a vacuum cleaner?
   You have to plug in the vacuum cleaner before it sucks.

What's the difference between a saxophone and a fish?
   You can tuna fish.

DRUM SOLO

When his boat is wrecked in a tropical storm, this oke just manages to make it to the shore of a jungle island. He is greeted by the local chief, but he can hardly hear a word because of the persistent pounding of drums in the background.
   'What are those drums for?' asks the shipwreck survivor.
   Cryptically, the chief replies, 'The drums must not stop.'
   The man stays the night in the village. All through the night, the drums keep going. He gets up in the morning, not having had a wink of sleep, and he says to the chief, 'Please, can't you do something about those drums?'

The chief replies, 'The drums must not stop.'

Finally, in exasperation, the guy asks why.

And the chief says, 'Because when drum solo stop, sax solo start.'

TRADESMAN'S ENTRANCE

Three men die in a plane crash and are waiting to enter heaven. St Peter asks the first man, 'What did you do on Earth?'

'I was a doctor,' says the man.

'Go right through those Pearly Gates,' says St Peter. He asks the second guy.

'I was a school teacher.'

'Go right through those Pearly Gates,' says St Peter. 'And how about you?' he asks the third guy.

'I was a musician.'

'Al right,' says St Peter. 'Go around the side, up the freight elevator, through the kitchen …'

EARPLUGS

Why do bagpipe players walk while they play?

To get away from the noise.

NAAS

HOMECOMING

'What's the first thing you do with your wife when you get home after an overseas rugby tour?' Carel once asked Naas.

'That's obvious,' smirked Naas.

'Okay,' said Carel, 'what's the second thing?'

And Naas said, 'I take off my boots.'

FACE IT

Schucks is walking around Loftus with a black eye when he bumps into Naas.

'What happened to you?' inquires the Blond Bombshell.

And Schucks says, 'I walked up to the ticket booth at the gate, and the oke asked me for my ticket. So I said, "my face is my ticket." Then he said '"Well, sorry, but I've got strict instructions to punch all tickets", so he moered me.'

SNOTKLAP

During his playing years, Naas wasn't very popular outside Blou Bul country. But one day, kicking against Province at Loftus, he missed a crucial penalty and Province won. A young schoolboy was so disappointed, he walked straight up to Naas after the match and gave him a snotklap.

To which an ardent Province supporter remarked, 'That's the first case in history where the fan hit the shit.'

ON THE BALL

Always aware of the need to maintain a high standard of personal grooming, Naas once walked into a pharmacy in Europe and said: 'I'd like some deodorant, please.'

'The ball type?' asked the assistant.

'No,' said Naas, 'it's for under my arms.'

TOILET HUMOUR

In sy speeldae het 'n Province supporter eendag gevra wat is die verskil tussen Naas en 'n plaastoilet?

Albei hou van 'n long drop.

NOTHING DOING

Much sought-after in the rugby world of a few years back, Naas was once contracted to play with the Italian club,

Rovigo. During his first practice session, the Italian coach took Naas aside and laid down some of the ground rules.

'Naas, we train very hard every day of the week. On Monday we play touch rugby for four hours until your tongue is hanging out. Then on Monday night we relax and we all play pool. You like?'

'Sorry,' said Naas. 'I don't play pool.'

'No problem,' said the coach. 'On Tuesday we run up a the hill for three hours until we all pass a out. Then on Tuesday night we drink until we all pass out. You like?'

'No fanks,' said Naas. 'I don't drink.'

'It's a fine,' said the coach, 'because on Wednesday we train in the gym until all the muscles are stiff. Then we all go for a the long, nice massage. You like?'

'I hate massages,' said Naas.

''Ats-a okay', said the coach. 'Thursday is the big day when we make two hours contact until we all bleed. Then on Thursday night we get the girls, we just lie still and the girls they make all the moves.'

'I'm not interested in girls,' said Naas.

'Whats-a matter?' asked the coach, 'you a bloody moffie?'

'Certainly not,' said Naas.

'Oh shit,' said the coach, 'there go Friday nights too!'

BOTTLE BLOND

Naas was always very popular at Newlands, if only as a target for the beer-bottle throwers. Asked how he felt about such treatment from the partisan home crowd, Naas shrugged: 'Ag, I wouldn't mind so much if they'd only empty the bottles first.'

PASS THE PASTA

Naas's nickname in Italy was 'Pasta'. Whenever he touched the ball, the Italian crowd would be on their feet shouting: 'Past-a ball and stop-a kicking you fool!'

TO DIE?

Naas's first match in Italy was also the one in which he performed his one and only tackle. He tackled Enrico Vallas, the big Italian prop from the club L'Aquila, right out of the game. Problem was, the tackle was so late, that had it been any later it would've been under the showers.

Vallas, dik de donner in, grabbed Nasie by his collar and shouted: 'Hey, you come-a here to die?'

To which the trembling Naas replied: 'No, I come-a here yesterdie.'

THAT'LL BE THE DAY

They say Naas had a unique way of motivating his players before a big match. He would say: 'Boys, vandag gaan ek tackle.'

RUGBY GENIUS

In Naas's heyday, the early eighties, they used to have this ultimate test of intelligence at Loftus. Eighty thousand staunch Blou Bulle packed in on the stands like sardines.

(Actually they call those East stands at Loftus the 'blackhead' stands, 'cause everyone just wants to squeeze you out.)

The MC called Naas to the middle of the field and asked him: 'What's two and two?'

Naas said, 'Four.'

To which the Loftus crowd rose as one fan and shouted, 'Gee hom nog 'n kans!'

SKOP EN SKOP

Waarvoor staan NAAS?

NASIONALE ASSOSIASIE vir AANHOUDENDE SKOPPERS.

HELP FROM ABOVE

Naas was having an off-day. When he missed the third penalty in a row, he kicked the little heap of sand in disgust and said, 'Bliksem.' The referee was his ouboet, Darius, a dominee.

'Cool it, Naas,' said Darius. 'Swearing won't get the ball over the post. Just relax, keep your head down and say a silent prayer before you kick at the posts again.'

Next penalty. Naas misses again. 'Bliksem,' he said, stamping his foot even further into the hallowed turf of Loftus.

'Please, kleinboet,' said Darius. 'You're setting a very bad example as captain of your team. Besides, we're both Christians, and you won't get any help from above by swearing like this. Next time you attempt a kick at post, rather say Amen, and the ball might well go over.'

So Naas goes for it again, right in front of the posts. This time the ball keeps low, heading straight for the corner flag. Naas says, 'Bliks ...', rethinks, and says 'Amen.'

What followed was a fierce bolt of lighting, a tremendous flash of thunder and a strong gust of wind which picked the ball up from the corner flag and steered it straight through the posts.

'Amen!' shouted Naas.

'Bliksem,' said Darius.

MOO

On which hand does Naas have a tattoo of a cow?
On de udder hand.

BEATING THE BENZ

Often a victim of my pranks, Naas finally got me back when I used him in a video shoot one day. I arrived late for the shoot, and Naas and crew were waiting impatiently for me outside a studio in Parktown.

As I took the turn into the driveway in my Merc 230E,

Naas shouted: 'Schuster, wat's die verskil tussen 'n ou wat 'n Merc ry en 'n koei?'

'You got me,' I said.

To which Naas replied: 'By die koei sit die poephol aan die buitekant.'

NEW SOUTH AFRICA

LONG DROP

Van the farmer has this state-of-the-fart two-seater out-house. One morning he happens to be sharing it with Vusi.

'Damn,' says Van, pulling up his pants. 'I dropped a 50 cent piece. Vusi, get down there and take it out.'

'Aikona,' says Vusi. 'You do it yourself. This is the New South Africa.'

On his way out, Vusi takes a R10 note from his pocket, and throws it down the hole.

'What did you do that for?' asks the bewildered Van.

'Just trying to help you out,' shrugs Vusi. 'I didn't think you'd go down there for a 50 cent piece.'

IT'S THE PITS

One day on the plaas, Vusi is leaning over the water pit to retrieve the bucket. Whoops. He leans a little too far.

Farmer Van, busy watching the rugby in his voorkamer, hears Vusi's terrifying screams and rushes to the scene as soon as the ref blows the halftime whistle. Van looks into the 20-metre pit, cups his mouth with his hands, and calls out, 'Vusi! Het jy seergekry?!'

'Ek weet nie, Baas,' replies Vusi. 'Ek val nog.'

A split second later, Van hears a loud thump as Vusi's body hits the ground.

'Vusi,' yells Van, 'het jy iets gebreek?'

'Aikona,' says Vusi, 'ek het nog niks gesien om te breek hierso nie.'

VOETSEK!

Juffrou Rosie sê vir haar graad 6-klassie in Vryburg dat hulle vandag tydens Geskiedenis-periode 'wie het dit gesê' gaan speel. As hulle antwoord korrek is, kry die leerling die res van die Vrydag af.

Sy kyk eerste na Sakkie en vra, 'Sakkie, wie het dit gesê: "Never in the field of human conflict, was so much owed by so many to so few"?' Sakkie steek sy hand op en sê, 'Winston Churchill, 1940, juffrou.'

'Pragtig Sakkie,' sê juffrou. 'Sien jou Maandag. Goed, wie het dit gesê: "There will be no majority rule in Rhodesia during my lifetime"?' Klein Vusi steek sy hand op en sê, 'Ian Smith, 1967, juffrou.'

'Baie mooi Vusi, sien jou Maandag.'

Vet Frik agter in die klas lol die heeltyd met Thandi se hare, sy vererg haar en skielik steek sy haar passer diep in vet Frik voor haar se boud. Frik spring blitsig op uit sy stoel, gryp sy agterwêreld vas, gluur woes vir Thandi en gil, 'Voetsek jou m**d!'

Die juffrou swaai geskok van die swartbord af om en vra: 'Wie het dit gesê?' Daar's 'n geskokte stilte voor Frik sê: 'Eugene Terreblanche, 1981. Sien juffrou volgende Vrydag!'

STILL WAITING

Vusi is on his way to deliver a parcel in the company bakkie. A taxi swerves in front of him, causing him to lose control and roll the bakkie. As the bruised and battered Vusi crawls through the window of the overturned vehicle, a passer-by rushes over to Vusi: 'Het jy seergekry?'

'Uh-uh,' says Vusi. 'Die baas hy was nog nie hier nie.'

SOEK WERK

Die foon lui op die boer se plaas en dis 'n swart man aan die anderkant wat sê hy soek werk as 'n kombuiskok.

'Nee dankie,' sê die boer, 'ek het 'n kok.'

'Maar ek is 'n special cookboy.'

'Dankie, maar my kok is 'n baie special cookboy.'

'Ja, maar ek is a very very very special cookboy,' sê die ou.

Die boer is nou al lekker de dinges in en sê, 'Johannes is my cookboy nou al vir twintig jaar en hy is 'n very very very special cookboy.'

Toe antwoord die swart man, 'Dis oraait, Oubaas, dis Johannes wat praat. Ek check net 'n bietjie op oppie Oubaas.'

GETTING THERE

This white oke is standing next to this black oke at the urinal. The white oke looks down and says, 'Man, I only wish I had one like yours, hey.'

The black oke says, 'You can! Just tie a string around it, put the string down your pants leg, and hang a weight on the end of the string. You'll have one like mine in no time.'

A few weeks later, they meet again. The black oke says, 'So how's it working?'

The white oke says, 'Great … I'm halfway there.'

The black says, 'What do you mean?'

The white says, 'It's black.'

TWO BAGS FULL

This big plaasboer pulls up at a filling-station in Worcester. Gatiep is doing the filling-up, when he notices a bag of coals and a heap of cow dung on the back of the bakkie.

'Ek sê, Meneer,' tunes Gatiep, 'what are you going to do with the coals and the cowshit?'

The boer isn't in a mood for small talk. 'I'm going to make myself a hotnot,' he growls.

'O ek sien,' nods Gatiep. 'And if you wanna make a whitey, you'll only use the shit, hey.'

WHISKEY FOR TWO

Van tells Vusi to go and buy him a bottle of J&B at the off-sales of the local hotel. Vusi jumps on his bicycle and is back in no time, carrying a whiskey-shaped bottle wrapped in brown paper.

'Sorry baas Van, they don't have J&B, so I got you a bottle of Ek en Djy.'

'Ek en djy?' echoes Van. 'There's no blerrie whiskey called Ek en Djy.'

So Vusi unwraps the bottle and points to the label: 'Look, Black and White.'

NO JOB, NO FOOD, NO MONEY

TAKEN FOR A RIDE

The bergie is making his way back to Cape Town. It's a sweltering day, and he's been standing next to the main road for hours. Plenty of hiking, but not a hitch in sight. So he decides to walk over to a farm road in the hope that some good-natured farmer will pick him up.

Sure enough an oke comes past in a fancy Merc. 'Want a lift, my friend?'

The tramp checks out the swanky jammie, the aircon, the six-pack on the passenger seat. He looks at the long road, the scorching sun. He looks at the driver.

'No thanks. You can open your own fôkken gates.'

STAR OF THE SHOW

This larney woman in Upper Houghton was throwing a party for her granddaughter. No expense had been spared: she'd hired a caterer, a jumping castle, a make-up artist, and a clown. Just before the first guests were due to arrive, two vagrants rang the doorbell.

Feeling a little more touched than usual by the plight of the poor, she told the guys they could have a meal and R20 each if they would help chop some wood at the back of the house. They readily agreed, and got down to work chop-chop.

The guests arrived, and the party was going with a bang. Then came a call from the clown. He was stuck in a traffic jam on the N1, and he didn't see how he was going to make it in time for the party.

Hugely disappointed, the woman told the kids. She went into the house and flipped through the Yellow Pages. No luck. Then she happened to gaze out of the window. She saw one of the vagrants doing cartwheels across the lawn, leaping in the air, howling like a monkey, and swinging himself around on the branches of a tree.

The woman went outside. 'That was brilliant!' she said. She turned to the other vagrant, who was also watching with fascination.

'Do you think your friend would consider repeating his performance for the children at the party? I would pay him R50!'

'I dunno,' said the vagrant. 'Let me ask him. HEY WILLIE! FOR R50, WOULD YOU CHOP OFF ANOTHER TOE?'

ODD JOB

Mike kry die affirmative-klap en loop van huis tot huis op soek na odd jobbies. In Sandton sê 'n ryk ou vir hom, 'You can paint the porch at the back of the house.'

Na twee ure klop Mike aan die ou se deur en sê, 'Ek het hom sommer twee coats gegee, Meneer. En by the way, dis nie 'n Porsche nie, dis 'n Z3.'

SOEK 'N LIGHT

Die ou staan buite die hekke van Loftus en bedel, erg gekletter. So tussen die bedel deur vang hy kort-kort 'n teug aan sy half-jack in 'n bruin kavdoes. Op 'n kol sien hy een van sy vodde tekkies se veters is los, stap na 'n ou en vra, 'Hei, drink jy?'

'Nee,' sê die ou.'

'Nou hou vas my borrel la'k my skoen kan vasmaak.'

Hy tel naderand 'n stompie op, en vra vir die eerste die beste ou, 'Het jy vir my 'n light ou pêl?'

'Voetstek man, jy's gesuip,' sê die ou en stap aan. Dis min of meer die standaardreaksie wat hy by almal kry, totdat daar so 'n klein outjie met 'n vriendelike gesig verbykom. Ons tramp waai sy stompie tussen twee borriegeel vingers voor die ou se neus en sê, 'Ek soek 'n light, ou pêl.'

'Seker,' sê die ou, en steek die tramp se stompie aan. Die tramp is baie beïndruk met die vriendelike ou. 'Luister, ou pêl', sê hy, 'jy's 'n moerse nice ou. Almal vloek my, en jy gee sommer vir my 'n light. Sê my, wat's jou naam, toe?'

'Ek's Paulus,' sê die ou. Die tramp se oë rek. 'Paulus? Wragtag, hê? Sê my, ou Paulus, het daai Korinthiërs ooit vir jou teruggeskryf?'

LET THEM EAT GRASS

This Sandton yuppie is driving down the road in his brand-new silver Merc, when he sees two okes eating grass on the pavement. He can't believe his eyes. He stops, rolls down the automatic window, and says, 'Hey, why are you guys eating grass?'

The one oke answers, in between mouthfuls of kikuyu, 'We haven't got any money for food.'

'Come along with me,' says the yuppie.

'But Sir, what about my friend?' asks the man.

'Bring him along too,' says the yuppie.

'But I have a wife and five children,' says the second man.

'Bring them along too,' says the yuppie.

The poor okes can't believe their luck. They gather their

belongings, load up the wife and kids, and hit the road in air-conditioned luxury.

As the needle begins to hover around 240, one of the okes taps the yuppie on his shoulder and says, 'Sir, you are too kind. Not many people would stop to pick up people eating grass on the side of the road.'

'I know,' says the yuppie. 'But my lawnmower is in for repairs, and you should just see the size of my lawn at home!'

NUNS

BOOTS & ALL

Mother Superior rises early one morning and walks through the convent to the breakfast hall. A passing nun greets her and says, 'I see you got up on the wrong side of the bed this morning, Reverend Mother.'

She's puzzled, but she lets it pass. A few moments later another nun approaches and whispers, 'Good morning Reverend Mother. I see you got up on the wrong side of the bed this morning.'

Just outside the breakfast hall, a third nun looks at her and says, 'I see you got up on the wrong side of the bed this morning, Reverend Mother.'

By this time Mother Superior is totally baffled. 'Listen Sister,' she says, 'you're the third one this morning to say that to me. What exactly do you mean?'

'Well, Reverend Mother,' the nun replies, 'you're wearing Father Murphy's boots.'

KNOW THY ENEMY

Sister Bernadette was strolling home through the village, as was her habit, when a drunk staggered out of the King & Castle and bumped right into her.

'Young man!' warned the nun, 'alcohol is the elixir of the devil!'

The young man looked at her and said, 'Begging your pardon, Sister, but how would you know? Why don't you try a drink before you jump to such hasty conclusions?'

Sister Bernadette thought about this for a moment, and then agreed that she would be better qualified to wage war against alcohol if she had a better understanding of the enemy.

'All right, young man,' she said. 'Go back in there and bring me a drink. Just make sure it is in a paper cup.'

So the guy went back to the counter and ordered two drinks, one in a paper cup. The bartender leaned over and said, 'Don't tell me that crazy Sister Bernadette is freeloading again!'

OLD TOPPIES

THANKS FOR THE MEMORY

This ou toppie of 92 is sitting on the park bench, crying his eyes out. A policeman comes over and asks the old man what's wrong.

'Well,' says the oupa, 'I just got married recently to a twenty-five-year-old woman. Each morning she makes me a wonderful breakfast and then we make love. At noontime she makes me a wonderful lunch and then we make love. At dinner time she makes me a wonderful supper and then we make love.'

The policeman looks at the old man and says, 'You shouldn't be crying! You should be the happiest man in the world!'

So the old man says, 'I know! I'm crying because I don't remember where I live.'

GET STUFFED

This old tannie who lived in the Bushveld had two pet monkeys. One died. Followed, not too long after, by the other. Since she had been very fond of the animals, the tannie took both monkeys to the local taxidermist.

'Do you want them mounted?' he asked.

'Ag no,' she said. 'Just sommer shaking hands will do.'

FORGET ABOUT IT

Abie and Harry, both in their eighties, are sitting on the park bench, schmoozing about this, that, and the other. Mostly, the other.

'As I was saying,' says Harry, and he pauses with his hand in the air. 'What was I saying?'

Abie looks at him. 'You were talking about your memory.' Harry thanks him.

'That's right. I was saying how terrible it is how you lose your memory when you get old.'

'It's not so terrible,' says Abie. 'You should just do what I do.'

'What do you do?' asks Harry.

'I take a tablet.'

'You take a tablet? What's it called?'

'It's called a … it's called a …'

'It's on the tip of your tongue?'

'No, I swallowed it already when I woke up this morning. It's called a … it's called a … tell me, Harry, you know that flower, that beautiful flower with the thorns and the wonderful scent …'

'A rose?'

'That's it!'

'The tablet is called a rose?'

'No, schlemiel, not the tablet, my wife!'

And Abie yells across at the little old lady dozing on the other end of the bench: 'Rose! Rose! What's the name of that tablet I take for my memory again?'

HAIRSPRAY

A little boy and his grandfather are raking leaves in the yard. The little boy finds an earthworm trying to get back into its hole. He says, 'Grandpa, I bet I can put that worm back in that hole.'

The grandfather replies, 'I'll bet you five bucks you can't. It's too wiggly and limp to put back in that little hole.'

The little boy runs into the house and comes back out with a can of hairspray. He sprays the worm until it is straight and stiff as a board. Then he puts the worm back into the hole.

The grandfather hands the little boy five bucks, grabs the hairspray, and runs into the house. Half-an-hour later, the grandfather comes back out and hands the little boy another five bucks. The little boy says, 'Grandpa, you already gave me five bucks.'

The grandfather replies, 'I know. That's from your grandma.'

HELLO?

A little old lady's phone rings late one night. She picks it up and says, 'Hello?'

'Hello,' says the deep voice on the other side of the line. 'I know what you want. I know that you'd like me to push you down on the bed and rip all your clothes off, lick your body all over and make wild and delirious love to you.'

The little old lady looks at the phone in amazement and replies, 'You can tell all this from a single "Hello"?'

HALE AND HEARTY

Abie is watching television late one night, when he suddenly keels over with the remote control in his hand. It's nothing to do with the programme. It's his heart. The paramedics are on the scene within minutes, and Abie is in ICU before you can say 'cardiac arrest'. But Abie's lucky.

Not only does he pull through; he recovers completely.

The doctor says, 'It's amazing, Abie. I've just had a look at the tests, and you've got the same heart strength and function that you had when you were a twenty-year-old.'

'Are you telling me I don't have to take it easy from now on, doc?'

'Well,' says the doctor, 'I wouldn't advise you to ski down Everest on one leg or bungee-jump backwards off bridges. But other than that, you can go ahead and do whatever you used to do in your younger days. You're fit as a fiddle.'

Abie leaps out of bed, rushes home, and tells his wife the good news. 'Do you know what this means?' he says. 'We can have wild, passionate sex, just like we used to when we were 20!'

Dora smiles weakly. She's not 20 anymore. Not that Abie could care. He makes an amorous advance. Then another. Then …

'Are you 100% sure about this, Abie?' asks Dora. 'Sure I'm sure!' he says. 'You want to argue with the doctor?' No, she doesn't want to argue. But she would, just for safety's sake, like to see a letter from the doctor stating that the sort of thing Abie has in mind is not going to prove injurious to his health.

So Abie agrees. 'Okay,' he says. 'First thing tomorrow.'

First thing the next day, he's back in the doctor's office. 'You want a letter from me?' asks the doctor. 'All right. I'll give you a letter.'

The doc scrawls it out in his own handwriting: 'This is to certify that Abie Gundelfinger, a patient of mine, has the heart strength and function of a healthy twenty-year-old, and is fully capable of engaging in any such sexual activities as he may from time to time desire.' The doc signs it with a flourish.

'Abie,' he says, 'what's your wife's first name again?'

Abie looks at the letter, and says, 'Doctor, do you think it would be too much trouble if I asked you to make it out "To Whom It May Concern"?'

KOEKIE SEEP

Die ou dame doen inkopies in die supermark, toe sy haar seep laat val. Die ou net agter haar tel die op en sê, 'Dame, u het u koekie seep laat val.'

'Dankie,' sê die ou dame, 'maar dis nie my koekieseep nie, dis my gesigseep.'

CHECK-UP

Abie shuffles into the doctor's room for his annual medical check-up. The doc asks all the right questions, taps all the right joints, squints into all the right orifices. Finally, he says, 'You're fit as a fiddle, Abie. You'll live to be eighty.'

'But I am eighty!' yells Abie.

'So what did I tell you?' says the doc.

DOWN, BOY

Harry, 92, goes to see his doctor. 'Doc,' he says, 'I need to have my sex drive lowered.'

'What?' asks the doc, 'you need to have your sex drive LOWERED?'

'Yes,' says Harry. 'It's all in my head. That's why I need to have it lowered.'

SILLY BANKER

Old oom Koos has a mild case of Alzheimer's. He only forgets really important things, such as his bank manager's name.

'What's my bank manager's name again?' oom Koos asks his wife.

'Theunis,' says tant Sannie. 'And don't forget you have an appointment with him first thing tomorrow.'

'I won't forget,' says oom Koos. 'First thing tomorrow, appointment with … what did you say his name was again?'

Tant Sannie sits oom Koos down on the chair. 'Now listen nicely, Koos,' she says. 'The only way you're going to remember is if you use a little word-association trick. Think of a word that rhymes with "Theunis".'

Oom Koos thinks long and hard. 'Penis?'

Tant Sannie looks shocked. But if it does the trick, she's prepared to go along with it.

'All right. Now say the two words over and over to yourself, and I promise you, won't forget.'

Oom Koos wanders off, happily mumbling to himself, 'Theunis, penis. Theunis, penis. Theunis, penis. Theunis …'

First thing next morning, Oom Koos strides into his bank manager's office, stretches out his hand, and says, 'Morning Giel!'

PAP EN …

A few years went by and oom Koos's Alzheimer's spilled over onto to his farmhand Jakob. Yet another bank manager had been appointed in the meantime, and he had arranged to introduce himself to Oom Koos at the farm the following morning.

A fierce veld fire broke out on the farm that night. Oom Koos fought the fire right through to the early hours of the next morning, when he suddenly remembered his appointment with the bank manager.

'Jakob,' he said. 'Go back to the farm and tell the bank manager I'm still fighting the fire and can't be there to meet him. I've forgotten his name, so make sure you get it so that I can phone him back.'

Three hours later Van arrived back at the farm and walked over to Jakob.

'So did the bank manager come?'

'Ja Baas, he was here,' said Jakob. 'Short little fat baas with the thick goggles.'

'And what's his name?'

'Hau Baas,' said Jakob, removing his hat to scratch his head. 'That name is the funny Afrikaans name but I cannot remember him. But one thing I can remember from that name is what that name means for me.'

'What's that?'

'That name it means, "Ek eet hom in die more en ek eet hom in die aand". That's all I can remember from that name.'

'Jakob,' said oom Koos, 'it's very important that I get this man's name. You've got to think, my ou pal. Dink.'

At four o' clock the following morning, oom Koos heard a frantic knocking on the door, followed by Jakob shouting: 'Baas Koos! Baas Koos!'

Oom Koos skrikked his gat off and rushed to the front door. 'Wat's dit, Jakob? Nog 'n veldbrand?'

'Aikona Baas,' said Jakob. 'You know that name which is meaning "Ek eet hom in die more en ek eet hom in die aand" ...'

'Ja?'

'I have got that name!'

'Ja??'

'It's Pap-en-pfuss!'

MONSTER

Oom Tos gaan dokter toe, hy't meer probleme as 'n tweedehandse Alpha. Die dokter ondersoek hom en sê, 'Kom volgende week weer dan bring Oom vir my 'n bloedmonster, 'n urienemonster, 'n stoelgangmonster en 'n spermmonster.'

Oom Tos hoor nie so mooi nie en vra vir tannie Toeks, 'Wat sê die dokter?'

Tannie Toeks kyk vir oom Tos en sê, 'Hy sê jy moet jou onnerbroek vir hom los.'

TEST OF STRENGTH

Abie, 82, marries the love of his life. Suzie, 22. They decide they want to have kids. The old-fashioned way. Abie goes to ask his doctor about the chances.

'Nothing's impossible,' says the doctor. 'Let's run some tests and see what we come up with.'

He hands Abie a specimen jar, points him in the direction of the bathroom, and says: 'Bring me a specimen.' Abie gets the picture. He heads off to the bathroom. Half-an-hour later, he's still not back. An hour and a half later, he's still not back.

The doctor knocks on the bathroom door.

'Are you all right in there, Abie?'

Abie opens the door.

'No, doc,' he sighs. 'This isn't going to work. I've tried everything. I've worn out my left hand, I've worn out my right hand, I've run cold water over it, I've run hot water over it, I've even thumped it a few times on the edge of the sink. But no way can I get the top off this specimen jar!'

WHAT'S THE PROBLEM?

Abie, 67, and Rachel, 62 are sitting in the doctor's office. The doctor says, 'What can I do for you?'

Abie says, 'It's our sex life, doctor.'

'What seems to be the problem?'

'Well, it's a little hard to explain,' says Abie. 'We were wondering if you could maybe watch us doing it, and then tell us what you think.'

It's an unusual request, but the doctor nods his agreement. He turns to a fresh page in his medical notebook, the patients disrobe, and they do it.

'Well?' asks Abie.

'I must admit,' says the doc, slightly befuddled, 'I can't see anything wrong. For people of your age, your sex life appears to be very healthy. All I can say is keep it up!'

The couple thank the doc, and they go on their way. The following week, they're back. Same request, same procedure. This continues for a couple more weeks, until the doctor says, 'Look, you've got to tell me what's going on. I don't really understand the nature of your problem.'

'Well, it's simple,' explains Abie, buttoning up his shirt. 'I'm married, and we can't go to my house. Rachel is married, and we can't go to her house. The Holiday Inn charges R250. The Hilton charges R550. You charge R150, and we get 75% back from the medical aid!'

RISE AND FALL

Two toppies in their late seventies are sitting on a park bench, soaking up the sunshine and watching the people go by. Along comes a poppie in a miniskirt so short, if it were any shorter it would have been a scarf.

Oom Allie turns to oom Sakkie and says, 'Sakkie, you remember that blouvitterjoel stuff they gave us in the army in 1939?'

'Ja,' says oom Sakkie. What about it?'

'I think it's finally starting to work.'

SKIN LIFT

Abie has just turned 75, but he doesn't look his age. He looks 97. Finally, fed up with avoiding his wrinkled reflection in mirrors and shop-windows, he decides to have something done about his appearance.

He goes to see a world-renowned surgeon who has developed a radical procedure called a skin lift.

The doctor explains: 'What we do is stretch your skin and pull all your wrinkles to the top of your scalp. You'll look years, maybe even decades younger.' Abie decides to go for it.

Several days later, on his way out of the hospital, he bumps into an old friend. Of course, the guy doesn't recognise him. Finally, he says, 'Abie? Is that you?'

'Yes,' says Abie. 'It's me.'

'But you look so much younger! I don't remember you having a dimple on your chin, either.'

'That's not a dimple,' says Abie. 'It's my belly-button.'

The other guy bursts out laughing.

'If you think that's funny,' says Abie, 'just take a look at what I'm wearing for a tie.'

SLEEPING PILL

The little old lady goes to see her doctor. 'How's everything?' he asks.

'Fine,' she says. 'I'd like some birth control pills.'

The doctor is taken aback. 'Birth control pills? Mrs Smith, you're 75 years old. What possible use could you have for birth control pills?'

'They help me sleep better.' The doctor is taken even further aback.

'How in the world do birth control pills help you sleep better?'

'I put them in my granddaughter's orange juice and I sleep better at night.'

AIRING HIS VIEW

The old Scandinavian fighter pilot was being interviewed on camera for a World War II commemorative special.

'Vell,' said the old guy, 'vee used to fly up dere and dogfight dem Krauts. Ya, vee used to shoot dem German fokkers outta da sky.'

'For the benefit of our viewers,' interrupted the reporter, 'we should explain that the term Fokker refers to a specific type of German fighter plane.'

'Vell, ja,' said the old Scandinavian pilot, 'but those fokkers were Messerschmitts.'

OLD FARTS

Oom Koos and oom Willie are sitting on the stoep of the old-age home, watching the sun sinking slowly in the western sky. Neither says a word; they've known each long enough not to have to bother with small talk at a time like this.

After a while, oom Koos begins leaning a little to the right. Then a little more. Seeing this, a nurse comes rushing out onto the stoep, and she props oom Koos back into an upright position.

Oom Koos doesn't say a word. He just keeps gazing at the twilight sky. A few more minutes go by, and he begins leaning a little to his left. Then a little more. The nurse rushes out again, and gently eases oom Koos into a fully vertical position.

She goes back inside. Oom Koos turns to his stoepmate and says, 'You know, Willie, that Susanna really is one of the nicest nurses in this place.'

'Ja,' nods oom Willie, 'I must say I've got no complaints about her.'

'Well, I've got one,' says oom Koos.

'Really?'

'Ja. I just wish she would let me finish having a blerrie fart every once in a while.'

CHEAP PRESCRIPTION

The ou omie comes out of the doctor's room, holding some pills in his hand and looking very upset.

'What's the matter?' asks his old friend.

'The doctor says I've got to take these pills for the rest of my life.'

'So?' says the old friend. 'We all have to take pills every day.'

'Ja,' says the omie, 'but the doctor only gave me four.'

ONE-HORSE TOWN

This ou toppie and his ou vrou wife stop at Bronkhorstspruit to fill up. The petrol attendant looks at the Cape registration plate and says, 'I see you're from Beaufort-West.'

The ou antie is a heard of hearing and shouts: 'WHAT DID HE SAY?'

The ou toppie says: 'HE SAYS HE SEES WE'RE FROM BEAUFORT-WEST.'

'Oh,' says the antie.

The petrol attendant says: 'BEAUFORT-WEST IS MAAR A ONE-HORSE TOWN, HEY?'

The antie asks, 'WHAT DID HE SAY?'

The old man yells back, 'HE SAYS BEAUFORT-WEST IS MAAR A ONE-HORSE TOWN.'

'Oh,' says the antie.

The petrol attendant leans over and whispers to the ou toppie, 'I had the worst sex in my life in Beaufort-West.'

The antie asks: 'WHAT DID HE SAY?'

The ou toppie shouts: 'HE SAYS HE KNOWS YOU.'

OOM PW

TUTU MUCH

Oom PW was going vir his three monthly haircut in George. So the barber starts making conversation:

'Oom PW, I see ou Tutu doesn't want to leave you alone, hey?'

No reaction from oom PW, except an angry twitch of the mouth. The barber goes on cutting and after a while he says, 'I saw ou Tutu in the newspaper this morning, big smile on his face at your TRC hearing.'

No reaction again, just a slight colour change in oom PW's face.

'They say chances are good ou Tutu's going to send you to jail.'

Suddenly oom PW explodes: 'You're supposed to cut my blerrie hair man! Why do you keep on buggering around with Tutu?!'

'Sorry oom PW, but I have to. Everytime I mention ou Tutu the few hairs on your head stands regop and then I can cut them.'

AND WHO ARE YOU?

Oom PW wanted another dop on the plane from George to Cape Town, but the Indian air hostess said, 'Sorry, the bar has now been closed.'

Oom PW waved his famous forefinger under her nose in no time and said angrily, 'Do you know who I am?'

The hostess said, 'No, but I can find out for you.'

SAY CHEESE

Oom PW is gevra om te poseer vir 'n koerantfoto in sy mooi tuin by Die Anker buite George. Die kameraman het gekorrel, en toe die kamera laat sak.

'Kan oom asseblief glimlag?'

'Maar ek glimlag mos,' sê PW.

OU DOC

BLAF BLAF

Old Danie 'Doc' Craven, the doyen of South African rugby players and administrators, had a unique way of selecting his first team at the University of Stellenbosch. He would stand next to the field during practices with his dog Bliksem by his side.

If Bliksem thought a hooker was very good, he would bark twice, and Doc would select that hooker. When Bliksem thought a lock was up to scratch, he would bark four times. A good scrumhalf? Nine times. And so on.

'But,' said Doc, 'when Bliksem suddenly took off like a rocket with his tail between his legs, barking his head off, I knew it was a bitch on heat behind the grand stand.'

DRINK UP

Doc would also take Bliksem along to Newlands whenever Northern Transvaal played against Province.

Whenever Naas Botha failed to tackle an opponent, Doc would buy Bliksem a beer. Poor Bliksem. He eventually died of cirrhosis of the liver.

NIGHT OUT

Doc was full of good advice for rugby players. He once said, 'A rugby player should always take one night a week off, and tell his girlfriend that he's going to spend the night with his pals.'

His final bit of advice: 'Never waste that night on your pals.'

BALLS

Old Doc was a rugby man through and through. 'If God wanted us to play soccer,' he once said, 'He would have given us round balls.'

RUN LIKE THE WIND

Doc used to enjoy telling the tale of this Matie 'Cheese and Wine team' – a name often used for low-ranking student rugby teams – that went to play a match in Montagu.

Now these okes left Matieland after lunch on the Friday afternoon, and went on a full-scale tour of the wine route on the way to Montagu. One of the players was a prune farmer's son, and this oke had bags and bags full of dried prunes which the manne devoured together with many crates of the cheaper Cape wines.

The prune and wine party went on until the early hours of the following morning, and by the time the team had to take to the field against Montagu's thirds at ten on Saturday, the combination of dried fruit and cheap plonk was beginning to take its toll.

Initially, with great effort and self-discipline, the players were able to suppress their flatulence. But if you have ever attempted to play rugby after a heavy meal, you will know that there are some things that are just not possible to suppress. In polite company, one might be able to get away with these occasional indiscretions.

But a rugby scrum is not polite company. And nor were these indiscretions occasional. Eventually, the Montagu manne could take no more. Pulling their heads out of the scrum, they complained bitterly to the ref.

Having never had to deal with a situation of this nature before – and let's face it, it's not something you're going to find in the rule book – the ref turned his nose up in the air and decided to ignore the gathering storm. As fate would have it, it wasn't too long before the ref found himself at the bottom of a loose scrum.

Now he got the message. Rulebook or no rulebook, he turned to the Matie forwards and seethed, 'If I hear one more, just one more player dropping his guts, I'm going to penalise you, you get me?'

The Matie manne nodded, but barely had the next scrum gone down when the prunes and wine spoke loudly again. The ref blew his whistle shrilly, put his hand into the air and awarded a penalty to Montagu. The flyhalf took the ball, and as he was placing it to go for posts, the ref said, 'Sorry, you're not allowed to kick for posts.'

'Hoekom nie, meneer?' asked the surprised Montagu flyhalf.

To which the ref said, 'Jy kan nie pale toe skop vir 'n poep nie.'

PARENTHOOD

THAT'S MY BOY

These four okes are telling stories in a bar. One leaves to take a leak. There are three guys left.

The first guy says, 'Man, I was worried that my son was going to be a loser because he started out washing cars for a local dealership. Turns out that he got a break, they made him a salesman, and he sold so many cars that he bought the dealership. In fact, he is so successful that he just gave his best friend a new Mercedes for his birthday.'

The second guy says, 'I was worried about my son, too, because he started out raking leaves for a real estate firm. Turns out HE got a break, they made him a commissioned salesman, and he eventually bought the firm. In fact HE'S so successful that he just gave his best friend a new house for his birthday.'

The third guy says, 'Ja, I hear you, man. MY son started out sweeping floors in a brokerage firm. Well, HE got a break, they made HIM a broker, and now he owns the brokerage firm. In fact, he's so rich that he just gave HIS best friend one million bucks in stocks for his birthday.'

The fourth guy comes back from the can. The first three explain that they are telling stories about their kids so he says, 'Well, I'm embarrassed to admit that my son is a MAJOR disappointment. He started out as a hairdresser and is STILL a hairdresser after 15 years. To make things worse, I just found out that he's gay and has SEVERAL boyfriends.

'But, I try to look at the bright side: his boyfriends just bought him a new Mercedes, a new house, and one million bucks in stocks for his birthday.'

MAN EN VROU

Klein Frikkie, sewe, vra sy ma een middag na skool, 'Kan ek en ma bietjie man en vrou speel?' Sy vind die voorstel half vreemd, maar besluit om saam te speel.

'Ou vrou', sê Frikkie terwyl hy sy skooldas afhaal en op die rusbank neergooi nes sy pa altyd maak, 'ek het 'n harde dag gehad. Skink daar vir my 'n lekker dop, man.'

Frikkie plak homself voor die tievie neer met sy voete op die koffietafel, en ma gooi vir hom 'n lang glas Oros. Na 'n ruk sê Frikkie, 'Ou vrou, skep daar vir my 'n lekker bord kos, man.'

Ma bedien vir Frikie 'n lekker kaas en tamatie snackwich. Hy eet homself trommeldik, vat aan sy maag, los 'n vet burp nes sy pa altyd maak en sê, 'Ou vrou, trek uit jou klere dan gaan lê ons so bietjie skuins, man.'

'Wat?!', vra die ma geskok.

'Jy't gehoor wat ek sê,' kom dit van Frikkie, 'trek uit, dan loop en lê ons so bietjie op die bed.'

Sy ma is hoogs ontsteld, stop die speletjie summier, gryp vir Frikkie aan die oor en lei hom die gang af tot in sy kamer: 'Nou doen jy jou huiswerk en ek wil nooit weer sulke goed uit jou mond hoor nie, het jy my gehoor?'

Baie bekommerd vertel sy daai aand die storie vir Frikkie se pa. 'Aag ou vrou,' sê hy, 'dis maar net 'n speletjie, man. Ek sal niks ernstigs daarin lees nie.'

So twee dae later kom Frikkie van die skool af met dieselfde storie, en sy ma besluit sy speel enduit saam, want die ding puzzle haar vreeslik. Dis weer 'n dop wat geskink word, nog 'n snackwich, en toe kom die skuins-lê storie weer.

Sy gaan toe maar badkamer toe, trek uit, en trek haar japon aan. Sy vind Frikkie op die dubbelbed net in sy onderbroekie met haar man se leesbril op sy neus besig om die koerant te lees, presies soos sy pa altyd maak. Sy's nou diep bekommerd, maar gaan lê toe maar hier eenkant op die bed.

Na 'n rukkie sit Frikkie die koerant neer en haal die bril van sy oë af. Die ma dink, 'Wat nou?' Frikkie skuif nader. Sy dink, 'WAT NOU?' Frikkie sit sy hand om haar lyf en fluister sexy saggies in haar oor: 'Ou vrou, dink jy nie dis tyd dat ons vir Frikkie 'n BMX koop nie?'

HELL OF A PARTY

It's two o' clock in the morning. This oke is lying in bed, burning with rage and worry because his two teenage daughters haven't come home from the party. At 3.30 a.m., they finally turn the key in the lock, and tiptoe past their parents' bedroom.

The father says, 'Goodnight, daughters of Satan.'
And the girls say, 'Goodnight Daddy.'

TWINS

Proudly pushing the pram, Mike is parading his twin baby boys down the street. A friend stops to cluck and coo. 'Man, Mike,' he says, 'they're absolutely identical! How do you tell them apart?'

'By their balls,' answers Mike.

'Really?'

'Ja. The one bawls all day and the other bawls all night.'

TICK TICK BANG

Two friends, an Italian boy and a Jewish boy, come of age at the same time. The Italian boy's father presents him with a brand-new new pistol. On the other side of town, at his bar mitzvah, the Jewish boy receives a beautiful gold watch. The next day at school, the two boys are showing each other what they got.

'Nice watch,' says the Italian boy.

'Nice pistol,' says the Jewish kid.

They decide to trade.

That night, when the Italian boy is at home, his father sees him looking at the watch.

'Where did you getta thatta watch?' asks the man. The boy explains that he and the Jewish kid did a trade. The father blows his top. 'Whatsa matta with you! Somma day, you gonna getta married. Then maybe somma day you gonna comma home and finda you wife inna bed with another man. Whatta you gonna do then? Looka atta you watch and say, "How longa you gonna be"?'

IT'S A MIRACLE

A mother and her daughter are at the gynaecologist's office. The mother asks the doctor to examine her daughter.

'She's been having some strange symptoms and I'm worried about her,' the mother said. The doctor examines the daughter carefully. Then he announces: 'Madam, I believe your daughter is pregnant.'

The mother gasps. 'That's nonsense! Why, my little girl has nothing whatsoever to do with men!' She turns to her little girl. 'You don't, do you, dear?'

'No, Mummy,' she answers. 'Why, you know that I have never so much as kissed a man!'

The doctor looks from mother to daughter. Then he looks from daughter to mother. Then, without saying a word, he gets up and walks over to the window. He stares out in silence, until the mother feels compelled to ask, 'Is there something wrong out there, Doctor?'

'No, Madam,' says the doctor. 'It's just that the last time anything like this happened, a star appeared in the East. I was just looking to see if another one was going to show up.'

WHATSITSNAME

The new mother, a blonde, gets out of bed for the first time since her Caesar. Wearing nothing but her robe and fluffy slippers, she shuffles down the corridor to the nurses' desk, where she asks the duty nurse for a telephone book.

'What are you doing out here!' says the nurse. 'You should be in your room resting.'

'I want to search through the phone book for a name for my baby,' says the blonde.

'You don't have to do that here,' tut-tuts the nurse. 'The hospital gives all new mothers a booklet to assist them in picking a first name for their baby.'

'No, you don't understand,' says the blonde. 'My baby already has a first name.'

BIG DAY

Van asks his boss if he can have the day off. 'Why?' growls his boss.

'Because my wife is going to have a baby,' says Van.

'Well, why didn't you say so, jou doring!' says the boss, pumping Van's hand and sending him on his way.

First thing next morning, Van's boss stops him in the corridor and says: 'So? What was it, Van? A boy or a girl?'

And Van says, 'It's too early to tell, boss. We have to wait nine months to find out.'

BIRDS AND BEES

A little girl runs out to the backyard where her father is working. 'Daddy,' she asks, 'what's sex?'

Daddy sighs. He puts down his hedge-clippers. He's read all the books on progressive parenting, and he knows it's better to tell the truth, right now, plain and simple.

So he sits his little girl down, and he starts explaining about the birds and the bees. Except, of course, he isn't talking about birds or bees.

By the time he's run through the basics of the human reproductive process, the little girl's mind is boggling. As she runs off, Daddy asks, 'So what did you want to know all about sex for?'

And she says, 'Oh, Mommy said I must tell you lunch will be ready in a couple of secs.'

AROUND THE TWIST

Way back in the sixties, when rock 'n roll was king, Koos was chewing the fat with his daughter's date for the evening.

'So, Billy,' said Koos, lighting up his pipe, 'do you also like to screw?'

Billy almost fell of the couch. 'Sorry, Oom?' he asked.

'I was just wondering, because my daughter seems to like screwing a lot. In fact, she actually won a prize for her screwing last year.'

Now Billy really did fall off the couch. Picking himself

up, he nodded weakly and said, 'Well, yes, Oom, I suppose I do like screwing, now that you mention it.'

'Well, you be sure to have a good one tonight, then!' said Koos, as his daughter came down the stairs in her beehive, her high-heels, and her frilly satin dress.

The young couple set off on their date. But a few minutes later, Koos's daughter was back. Her beehive was in a mess, and her dress was in disarray.

'Daddy!' she shouted, 'How many times must I tell you? It's the twist, do you hear me, the TWIST!'

PARROTS

PRETTY POLLY

This ou tannie goes to see her dominee. 'Dominee,' she says, 'I've got a problem.' The dominee tells the tannie to tell all.

'I have these two female talking parrots,' she says. 'But they only know how to say one thing.'

'And what is that?' asks the dominee.

'"Hello, we are prostitutes",' says the blushing tannie. '"Do you want to have some fun?"'

The dominee is shocked. But he has a solution.

'Bring your parrots over to my house. I have two wonderfully-behaved male parrots, who I taught to pray and read the Bible. My parrots will teach your parrots to stop saying that terrible phrase, and they'll learn to worship instead.'

The tannie is delighted. She brings her female parrots over to the dominee's house. Sure enough, the dominee's parrots are praying away in their cage. The tannie puts her parrots in with them.

'Hello,' say the female parrots. 'We are prostitutes. Would you like to have some fun?'

And the one male parrot looks at the other and says, 'Put the Bibles away, Polly. Our prayers have been answered!'

BIRD IN THE HAND

Sharp-eyed Vusi sees this parrot strutting around in the middle of the park. Having heard the little homily about the value of a bird in the hand, he tiptoes towards the fine-feathered creature.

Slowly, Vusi reaches out a hand, but no sooner has he touched the parrot then it squawks: 'Los my uit, jou bliksem!'

Leaping into the air with fright, Vusi retorts: 'Hau, sorry baas! Ek het gadenk die baas is a hoenner!'

ABRACADABRA

There was this magician aboard the Titanic who had this parrot as an assistant, with whom he had developed good repartee. Whenever he performed one of his tricks, the parrot would squawk, 'It's up his sleeve', or 'It's under his hat.'

While the magician was in the middle of his show, the Titanic hit the iceberg and sank. The magician swam all through the night while the parrot fluttered overhead. He swam the whole of the next day, and the parrot was still fluttering overhead. On the evening of the second day the parrot finally settled on the magician's head.

'Okay, I give up. What did you do with the bloody ship?'

PET SHOPS

BUDGIES

Mike and Kallie walk into a pet store. Mike says to the salesman, 'I want four budgies.'

'Certainly, sir,' says the salesman. 'Would you like two male and two female, or do you prefer all male or all female?'

Mike shrugs his shoulders. 'Ag, any kind. Just give me four budgies.'

And the salesman says, 'Any particular colour budgies you're looking for, sir? We have yellow, blue, green, pin ...'

Now Mike starts getting fed-up. 'I couldn't care less about their colour, man! Just gooi four budgies in a box for me. Is that so hard?'

The salesman smiles meekly and rushes to comply. He hands Mike his box of budgies, Mike pays, and then he gets into the car with Kallie.

'Okay, Kallie,' he says, 'let's go to the Magaliesberg.' So they drive to the top of a big mountain in the Magaliesberg. Mike gets out, reaches into the box of budgies, and grabs one in either fist.

Then, as Kallie looks on, Mike flaps his arms wildly and jumps off the edge of the cliff. SPLAT. Kallie looks down, shakes his head, and says, 'Shit, man, this budgie jumping really isn't all it's cracked up to be!'

BIRD OF PREY

Kallie walks into the pet shop in Danville and sees a beautiful little bird in the cage. 'I'd like to buy this bird,' he says to the owner.

'Sorry,' says the owner, 'that bird is not for sale. Anything else?'

'But why can't I buy this one?'

'He's too dangerous,' says the owner.

Kallie can't believe it. 'This harmless little voëltjie is too dangerous?'

'Ja,' insists the owner. 'You might not believe it, but this little bird is called the Danville Destroyer. Watch this.'

He begins talking to the bird. 'Danville Destroyer,' he says, 'telephone directory.'

With that, the bird flies over to the telephone directory and violently rips it to pieces. Within seconds the directory is in shreds. The bird settles on the owner's finger again.

'That's incredible,' whistles Kallie, who's had to deal with a few tough birds in his time.

'You haven't seen anything,' says the owner. He talks to the bird again. 'Danville Destroyer,' he says, 'chair.'

The little bird wastes no time as it charges like a missile towards the chair, viciously tearing the stuffing from the cushion before reducing the legs to sawdust. With barely a feather ruffled, the little bird settles on the owner's finger again.

Kallie is amazed. 'I have to have this bird, man. Price is no object.'

The owner's eyes lights up. 'Okay,' he says, 'you can have it for R5 000.'

As Kallie starts putting the cash on the table, Schucks walks into the shop. He can't believe what he's seeing.

'Jeez, ou Kallie, have you just bought the pet shop?' he asks.

'No', says Kallie, I bought this little bird for only R5 000.'

'This little feathered snotkop for R5 000?' asks Schucks. 'This blerrie oke saw you coming, ou Kallie.'

'No ways,' says Kallie, 'this is a moeruvva vicious bird. It's called the Danville Destroyer.'

Schucks scoffs and says, 'Danville Destroyer, my ass.'

POLICE

POLICE FILE

This cop had just finished his shift one cold July evening and was sitting at home with his wife. 'You won't believe what happened this evening, skattie. In all my years on the force I've never seen anything like it.'

'Really, liefling?' she says. 'Tell me what happened.'

'Man, I came across these two okes down by the river. One of them was drinking battery acid and the other was eating fireworks.' His wife looks up from her knitting. 'Drinking battery acid and eating fireworks! What did you do with them?'

'Ag,' says the cop, 'I charged the one and let the other one off.'

AHEAD OF HIS TIME

Mindlessly, motherlessly drunk, Gatiep staggers up to a cop after a night on the town. 'Hey, Ossifer!' he yells in his ear, 'can you tell me the time?'

'It's one o'clock,' says the cop, hitting Gatiep once over the head with his baton.

'Bliksem,' says Gatiep, rubbing the affected area, 'I'm glad I didn't ask you an hour ago.'

HELLO ME

The policeman saw Van entering a house through a window at three in the morning. He rushed over and pulled him out of the window, with Van protesting furiously.

'It's my own house, offisher,' he said, inviting the cop inside to prove it.

'Look offisher, that's my little budgie. That's my TV, that's my chair, and this is my bedroom, and that's my wife.'

He paused for a moment.

'And that oke in bed with her, that's me.'

POLITICIANS

OPPIE KOPPIE

Hoekom dra politici hoedens?
    Sodat hulle weet watter kant om af te vee.

DIT KOS NET EEN RAND

Trevor Manuel klim op die gravy train en besoek Disneyland. Mickey Mouse sien hom, hou sy linkerarm uit en sê, 'Hi, check my Trevor Manuel watch.'

BULLFROG

The politician walked into the doctor's surgery with a frog
on his head.
'Where did you get that from?' asked the doctor.
'It started as a wart on my arse,' said the frog.

BOESAK

Daar is 'n man genaamd Boesak
Die WRK-mense laat sy moed sak
hy is gesekwestreer
en word hy dalk gekastreer
Dan's onse Boesak twee keer platsak.

TUTU

There was an old man called Tutu
Who never let the TRC doedoe
He woke up oom PW
And said 'Jy moet weergee
Why you blew Khotso House moer toe.'

WINNIE

There was a lady called Winnie
Who staunchly denies she's a meanie.
Moenie haar moer pomp nie
Deur te praat van 'n stompie
wat gerook is deur haar sokker team nie.

MANUEL

The reason he's called Manuel
Is om geld met sy hande te tel
Ekonomie stop nie
Toe hy alles laat vrot nie
En die rand val tot innie hel.

MUFAMADI

There is a man called Mufamadi
Met wie ek nie graag wil praat nie
Hy maak tronkdeure oop
Sodat skelms kan loop
En nou's ek nie meer veilig op straat nie.

ZUMA

Daar is 'n tante genaamd Zuma
Ek sien haar onlangs by Bruma
sy't haar veldtog geanker:
'Waar rook trek is kanker'
g'n ghwai meer? … eina ma' toema'

THE GREAT ESCAPE

When Safety and Security Minister Mufamadi visited the Leeukop Prison, he was particularly impressed by the beautifully landscaped gardens.

'It's ou Fred's work,' said the head warden proudly. 'He's an expert gardener, a total perfectionist and a model prisoner.'

'I would like to meet this man,' said Minister Mufamadi.

A meeting was arranged, and the Minister was extremely impressed by ou Fred. He had racks and racks of books in his prison cell: literature, art, horticulture, you name it.

'You shouldn't be in here, Fred,' said the Minister.

'I've been telling them that for years,' said Fred. 'The only reason I am here is because they lost some legal papers about my case.'

'Don't worry, Fred,' said the Minister. 'I will have this thing sorted out by the end of the week.'

Ou Fred was elated. Minister Mufamadi shook his hand and left.

As he walked away, a brick suddenly whacked the Minister on the back of his head.

Ou Fred peeked around a corner and said, 'You won't forget, will you?'

POMMIES

BIG BEN

Mike Schutte jols into London for a sightseeing holiday. After about two minutes, he gets hopelessly lost. So he stops this oke with a pinstripe suit, bowler hat, and umbrella, and he says, 'Excuse me, Meneer, but can you tell me where the Big Ben are?'

The Pom looks down his nose at Mike and says, 'Certainly, my good man. But may I first point out that it is not considered proper English to end a sentence on the word "are".'

So Mike says, 'All right, can you tell me where the Big Ben are, jou poephol?'

OLD BOYS

Three English gentlemen, all properly attired, are sitting in a train compartment while travelling through the English countryside. All three are busily engrossed in reading their *London Times*. Naturally, not having been properly introduced, they are not speaking to each other. It's going to be a long, quiet journey.

Finally, one gentleman puts his paper down and declares, 'Sir James Hyde-White. Brigadier, retired. Oxford, '59. Married. Two sons, both Royal Marine officers.' He nods, and promptly goes back to reading his paper.

A short while later, the second gentleman puts down his paper and declares: 'Sir Jonathan Colin-Simpson. Brigadier, retired. Eton, '61. Married. Two sons, both Royal Air Force pilots.' He nods, and promptly goes back to reading his paper.

A few stations down the track, the elder gentleman puts down his paper and declares: 'McTavish. Ian McTavish. Sergeant-major, retired. Coldstream Guards, 1940 through '45. Not married. Two sons. Both brigadiers.'

PRIESTS

HEAR YE, HEAR YE

Father O'Reilly opens the sliding-door of his confessional box, and a voice booms out in the darkness, 'Father, I had sex with a beautiful pair of eighteen-year-old nympho-maniac twins on five separate occasions this week!'

It takes a lot to shock Father O'Reilly. It takes a lot to outrage him. 'What kind of a Catholic are you?' he demands, shocked and outraged.

'I'm not a Catholic,' says the voice.

'Then why are you telling me this?'

'I'm telling everybody!'

SWEET AND SOUR

The beautiful young Irish lass entered the confessional and said, 'Forgive me, Father, for I have sinned.'

The priest said, 'Confess your sins and be forgiven.'

The young woman said, 'Last night my boyfriend made wild, passionate love to me seven times.'

The priest thought long and hard and then said, 'Take seven lemons and squeeze them into a glass and then drink it.'

'Will this cleanse me of my sins?' asked the girl.

'No,' said the priest, 'but it will wipe the smile off your face.'

WHALE OF A TALE

The dominee winds up sitting next to a snarling young punk rocker on the plane. The dominee greets him politely, and then begins reading his Bible. The punk says: 'Come on, preacher man. You don't really believe the stuff you're reading, do you?'

The dominee says, 'I do. It's the Bible.'

'I know,' says the oke. 'But it's full of fairytales. Like that one about the whale swallowing a man. Surely you can't tell me you believe that?'

'I can,' says the dominee. 'It's in the Bible.'

'Ag no, man. How is it possible for an oke to spend a whole week in a whale's stomach?'

'I can't tell you that,' says the dominee, 'but I'll ask Jonah that one day when I'm in heaven.'

'And what if this Jonah oke isn't in heaven?'

'Then you can ask him.'

PSYCHIATRISTS

SPLIT THE BILL

Did you hear about the oke who had a multiple personality disorder?

He had to stop seeing his shrink because his medical aid wouldn't pay for all the other personalities.

FOR BETTER OR WORS

'Doctor,' says the patient, 'my wife thinks I'm crazy because I like sausages.'

'Nothing wrong with that,' says the doctor. 'I like sausages too.'

'Sexy little buggers, aren't they?'

LIGHT MY FIRE

A man walks into the psychiatrist's office, sits down, takes out a pack of cigarettes, removes a cigarette from the pack, unrolls it, and stuffs the tobacco up his nose.

'I can see you need my help,' says the shrink.
'Yes, doc,' says the guy. 'Got a match?'

I AND I

A man walks into a psychiatrist's office and says: 'Doctor, I have an identity problem. And so do I.'

PEEPING TOM

This oke is having problems with his sex life, so he goes to see a psychiatrist. In a bid to get to the root of the problem, the shrink reels off a list of questions. Among them, 'Do you ever watch your wife's face while you're having sex?'

'Well, yes,' says the oke. 'I did, once.'

'And how did she look to you?'

'She looked extremely angry.'

Aha, thinks the shrink. Now we're getting somewhere.

'Tell me,' he says, 'why do think your wife was angry on this occasion?'

'Well, that's easy,' says the oke. 'She was watching us through the window.'

PUBS & BARS

LOOK WHO'S TALKING

This oke walks into a bar and orders a beer. 'Listen,' he says to the bartender. 'If I show you the most amazing thing you've ever seen, is my beer on the house?'

'We'll see,' says the bartender. So the guy pulls a hamster and a tiny piano out of a bag, puts them on the bar, and the hamster begins to play. 'Not bad,' says the bartender, 'but I'll need to see more.'

'Hold on,' says the man. He then pulls out a bullfrog, and it sings 'Old Man River'. A patron jumps up from his table and shouts, 'That's the most incredible thing I've ever seen! I'll give you R2 000 right now for the frog.'

'Sold,' says the guy. The patron takes the bullfrog and leaves.

'It's none of my business,' says the bartender, 'but you just gave away a fortune.'

'Not really,' says the guy. 'The hamster is also a ventriloquist.'

HEARD IT BEFORE

An Englishman, an Irishman, a Scotsman, a Mexican, an Italian, a priest, a rabbi, and a nun walk into a bar.

The bartender looks up and says, 'What is this? Some kind of joke?'

HOWZIT COUSIN

Mike sidles up to the brunette sitting on her own at the bar. Before he can sidle up too far, the brunette feels compelled to make a small confession. 'Listen, pal,' she says, 'There's something I think you should know. I'm a lesbian.'

'Ag, that's okay,' says Mike. 'I've got a cousin who lives in Beirut.'

CRAZY NIGHT OUT

It's a quiet night down at the local pub. So quiet, that the only topic of conversation is the fact that it's so quiet down at the local pub.

'It's always like this on a Tuesday night,' sighs the publican, sharing his woes with a regular. 'I've tried everything I can think of, but I just can't seem to get people in here at this time of the week.'

A man in a tweed jacket, sitting by himself in the corner, puts down his drink and walks up to the counter.

'Sorry to interrupt,' he says. 'I couldn't help overhearing

your conversation. I'm a doctor at the lunatic asylum up the road, and I'm trying to integrate some of the more sane individuals into the community. Why don't I bring some of my patients along, say next Tuesday. You'll have some customers, and my patients will have a much-needed night out.'

The publican is a little dubious at first. It sounds like a crazy idea. But the more he thinks about it, the more it begins to make sense. What's he got to lose?

'Okay,' he says. 'Bring your patients. Let's see how it works out.'

Next Tuesday night arrives, and with it, a busload of customers from the lunatic asylum up the road. Leading the way is the man in the tweed jacket.

'Give these guys whatever they want,' he tells the publican. 'Put it on my tab, and I'll settle at closing time.'

The publican barely has time to nod his agreement before the rush begins. Eating, drinking, making merry, the patients enjoy a raucous yet well-behaved night on the tiles. It's the busiest Tuesday the publican has seen in years.

At midnight, he rings up the total on his cash register. Ka-Ching! Three thousand five hundred Rand and change! The man in the tweed jacket comes over to the counter.

'This has been a great night,' says the publican. 'Because I'm so grateful, I'm going to give you a little discount. Make it R3 250 straight.'

'Great!' says the man in the tweed jacket. 'Have you got change for a dustbin lid?'

HAPPY HOUR

The Russian, the Irishman, and the Italian are standing on the pavement after work, trying to decide where to go to have a couple of dops.

The Irishman says, 'Let's go to O'Learys. With every third round, the bartender will give each of us a free Guinness.'

The Italian says, 'That sounds good, but if we go to Baldini's, we'll get a free bottle of wine with every third round.'

The Russian says, 'That sounds fine, but if we go to Ivanof's, we can drink for free all night, and then we can go out and get laid in the parking lot.'

'That sounds too good to be true!' says the Irishman. 'Have you actually been there?'

'No,' replies the Russian. 'But my wife goes there all the time.'

POINT OF ORDER

This oke walks into a bar and sits down at the counter. Nothing unusual about that, and nor is the bartender's response: 'Hi. What'll you have?'

'I'll have a Scotch, please,' says the guy.

'Here you go,' says the barman. 'That'll be R7,50.'

The guy gives the barman an odd look. 'What are you talking about? I don't owe you anything for this.'

The barman leans across the counter, and is just about to lay down the law, when a guy sitting a few bar stools down pipes up. 'Wait a second. I'm a lawyer. Legally speaking, this guy is in the right. In your original offer, which constitutes a binding contract upon acceptance, there was no stipulation of remuneration.'

The bartender looks at the lawyer. 'Huh?'

'What that means is that he doesn't owe you any money. You could take him to court if you wanted to, but ...'

The bartender can see he's not going to win this one. 'Okay,' he says to the guy, 'you beat me for a drink. But don't let me ever catch you in here again.'

The next day, the same guy walks into the bar. 'What the hell are you doing here?' yells the bartender. 'I can't believe you have the audacity to come back!'

'What do you mean?' says the guy. 'I've never been in here before in my life!'

The bartender looks at the guy again. 'I'm very sorry,' he says. 'This is uncanny. You must have a double.'

To which the guy replies, 'Thank you. Make it a Scotch.'

HOOG TYD

Tolla stap die pub binne en vra vir die kroegman, 'Ek soek 'n dubbel whiskey. Hoeveel is dit?'

Die kroegman sê, 'R12,65.'

'Nee hel, dis te hoog,' sê Tolla. 'Gee my 'n dubbel gin. Hoeveel is jou gin?'

'Nege Rand sewentig,' sê die kroegman.

'Nee heng, dis te hoog. Wat van 'n klein glasie wyn. Hoeveel is 'n klein glasie witwyn?'

'R4,50,' sê die kroegman.

'Ja, dis oukei. Gee my 'n glasie wyn.'

Die kroegman draai om om die wynbottel van die rak af te haal.

Tolla kyk, en kyk weer, 'Hei, barman,' sê hy, 'watse ding is daai in jou nek?'

Die kroegman vat verleë aan 'n yslike bruin moesie net bo sy kraag. 'Dis 'n moesie,' sê hy. 'Hoekom?'

'Nee,' sê Tolla, 'ek het gedink dis jou poephol want alles is so hoog in die plek.'

RABBIS

TRUE CONFESSIONS

The rabbi is talking to the Catholic priest outside the church. 'Tell me, Father,' he says, 'from where do you get the money to make your church so beautiful?'

'We hear confessions,' says the priest. 'Come inside and I'll show you.'

So the rabbi joins the priest in the confessional. In walks the first penitent.

'Father, it's been one week since my last confession and I have committed adultery three times.' The priest says, 'For your penance say a Hail Mary and put five Rand in the collection box. Your sins will be forgiven.'

The next penitent walks in and says, 'Father, it's been one week since my last confession and I've committed adultery three times.' The priest says, 'For your penance say a Hail Mary and put five Rand in the collection box. Your sins will be forgiven.'

So the rabbi says, 'Do you mind if I have a go?' Sure, says the priest, and they change places. In walks the next penitent.

'Can I help you, my child,' says the rabbi. The penitent says, 'Father, it's been one week since my last confession and I've committed adultery two times.'

The rabbi says, 'Go out and do it a third time! We have a special today … three for five Rand!'

SKIN JOB

What's the difference between a rabbi and a cactus plant?

A cactus plant pricks your skin.

ON THE HOUSE

A priest, a pastor, and a rabbi are walking down the road on a hot day. They pass a busy bar. Because they're a priest, a pastor, and a rabbi, they're able to resist the temptation to nip inside and have a quick dop. Any case, they don't have the money. Then the priest has a brilliant idea.

'Wait here,' he says to his colleagues. He goes inside, orders a Scotch, downs it, and gets up to leave. As he does so, the bartender hands him his tab. 'But son,' says the Father, 'I already paid for the drink!'

The bartender looks annoyed, confused, and then sheepish. "Sorry, Father,' he shrugs. 'It's really busy in here. I must have forgotten.'

The priest walks out and tells the pastor and rabbi about his experience. The pastor strolls in next. He orders a Martini, downs it, and gets up to leave. Same story. Confusion, apologies, blessings bestowed on the bartender.

Now it's the rabbi's turn. He orders a double brandy and soda, gulps it down, and gets up to leave. The bartender hands him the tab. 'But my friend,' says the rabbi, 'I paid you when I ordered the drink.'

By now, the bartender is in no mood to argue. 'I do apologise, rabbi. I don't know what's going on today, but you're the third man of the cloth I've done this to.'

The rabbi shrugs. 'Don't worry, my boy. Just give me change for the R50 I gave you, and I'll be on my way!'

ROAST SURPRISE

The elderly rabbi, recently retired from his duties in the congregation, finally decides to fulfil his lifelong fantasy. To taste pork. He goes to a fancy hotel in the off-season, enters the empty dining-hall, and sit downs at a table in the far corner.

The waiter arrives. The rabbi scans the menu, looking around nervously all the while. Finally, he says: 'Bring me a roast suckling pig.'

As the rabbi waits for his order, wrestling quietly with his conscience, in walks the Schmendelberg family, faithful members of his former congregation.

'Rabbi!' they cry, 'how wonderful to see you! You're eating alone? A rabbi shouldn't eat alone! We'll join you!'

So they join him at the table. The rabbi, shocked into silence, feels the sweat running slowly down his brow.

Just as he is about to excuse himself, in walks the waiter with a huge domed platter in his hand. He lifts the lid with great ceremony, revealing the roast suckling pig in all its finery.

'This place is amazing!' declares the rabbi. 'You order a baked apple, and look what you get!'

FORBIDDEN FRUIT

Father O'Reilly and rabbi Rabbinowitz are sharing a compartment on a train. After exchanging formalities and indulging in the usual polite small talk, the priest leans across and says, 'I know that in your religion, you're not supposed to eat pork, rabbi ... but have you actually ever tasted it?'

The rabbi says, 'I must tell the truth. Yes, I have, on the odd occasion.'

A few minutes later, the rabbi leans across and says: 'In your religion, Father, I know you're supposed to be celibate. But tell me ...'

Father O'Reilly interrupts him. 'Yes, I know what you're going to ask. And yes, I have succumbed, once or twice.'

There is silence for a while. Then the rabbi peeps around the newspaper he is reading and says, 'Better than pork, isn't it?'

RACIAL DISCRIMINATION

RACE BAR

This Chinese oke wanders into a bar and sees this black oke standing behind the counter. 'Hey, nigger,' he says, 'pour me a jigger.' The black oke isn't impressed.

'You can't come in here and talk to me like that!' he yells. 'How would you like it if I started calling YOU names? In fact, let's switch places. You get behind the bar and I'll come in as a customer.'

The Chinese oke agrees, and gets behind the bar. The black oke goes outside. A few seconds later, he strolls back in and says, 'Hey Chink, fix me a drink.'

And the Chinese oke says, 'Sorry, we don't serve niggers here.'

HONKY TONK

Van walks into a pub in Jo'burg after work. The place is abuzz with merrymakers. The hard beat of kwaito music is thundering from the speakers. Van orders a beer, checks out the happy black people, and turns to Vusi, the barman.

'Ja, swaer. Can you believe that only six years ago there used to be a race bar in this pub.'

Vusi takes Van's empty beer bottle from the counter.

'There still is. So piss off.'

TRY NEXT DOOR

A man of Polish ancestry walked up to the counter and asked for a Polish Meatball Sandwich. The man at the counter muttered, 'What a Pollack.'

The Polish man said, 'I resent that. If a Jew came to your counter and asked for a kosher salami on rye, would you call him a stupid Jew?'

'Probably,' replied the clerk.

'And if an Italian came in here and asked for spaghetti and meatballs, would you insult him too?'

'Probably,' the clerk replied.

'Then you're nothing but a bigot,' said the Pole. 'Why do you have to insult everybody who is not like you?'

'Because this is a HARDWARE store,' said the clerk.

MIXED MARRIAGE

Young Hymie, the busiest stockbroker on Wall Street, calls his mother to break the big news.

'Momma, I'm getting married,' says Hymie.

'You're not marrying a goy, are you?' asks his worried mother.

'Oh no, momma,' says Hymie. 'She's a Goldberg.'

'Oy, thank goodness for that. So tell me, what is her first name?'

'Whoopie.'

RAINBOW NATION

HAPPY HAPPY

One day, Winnie Mazikidela-Mandela, Eugene Terre'Blanche, and Dr Zuma are travelling in a light aeroplane.

Winnie says, 'I'm going to throw R50 out of the window and make 50 people happy.'

Eugene says, 'That's nothing. I'm going to throw R100 out of the window and make 100 people happy.'

'So what?' says Dr Zuma. 'I'm going to throw R200 out of the window and make 200 people happy.'

The pilot, overhearing all of this, finally says, 'You know, why don't you all jump out of the window and make everybody happy?'

FLYING HIGH

Madiba, an American, and an Italian are sitting next to each other in a plane. Suddenly the American declares, 'I know where we are!' He sticks a hand out the window, pulls it back in and says, 'We're over New York harbour. I felt the Statue of Liberty.'

A little while later the Italian sticks his hand out and announces, 'I know where we are! We're over the Italian city of Pisa.' The other guys ask how he knew that, and he says, 'I felt the leaning tower of Pisa below me.'

Sometime later, Madiba sticks his hand out of the window, drags it back in, and says, 'I know where we are. We're over Durban Beach.' So how did he know? 'Someone stole my watch.'

BYOB

What do you call Madiba when he arrives for dinner without his wife and a bottle of white wine?

Persona non Graça.

APPELTJES

In die hoogte van apartheid stap 'n Hollandse dame eenkeer 'n groentewinkel in Amsterdam binne.

'Kunt ik uw helpe, mevrou?' vra die Hollandse groentesmous.

'Ja,' se die dame, 'ik will graag een dosyn appeltjes hebbe, dank u wel.'

Die smous vra, 'Uw kom net op de rechte tijd. Ik hebbe vandag Nederlandse appeltjes, Belgiese appeltjes, Duitse appeltjies, en Engelse appeltjes. Welke appeltjes wil u dan hebbe?'

'O,' se sy, 'enige appeltjes. Maar maak tog seker dat het niet Zuid-Afrikaanse appeltjes zein, mijnheer.'

'Zuid-Afrikaanse appeltjes?' vra die smous verbaas. 'Mevrou, ik hebbe doch geen Zuid-Afrikaanse appeltjes niet. Het geeft tog die verbod om enige Zuid-Afrikaanse produkten te verkopen voor de afschuwelijk apartheidsbeleid.'

'Wel jonge,' sê sy, 'solang het niet Zuid-Afrikaanse appeltjes zein, dan kope ik hun tog enige tijd.'

'Goed dan, mevrou, wat wil uw dan hebbe? De Nederlandse appeltjes, de Belgiese appeltjes, de Duitse appeltjies, of de Engelse appeltjes?'

'Geeft dan voor mij een dozyn Belgiese appeltjes alstubelieft,' vra die dame. En hy kry toe 'n dosyn van die beste Belgiese appeltjes gereed, en sit dit op die toonbank neer.

Sy kyk hulle so, kyk hulle weer, en vra, 'Mijnheer, bent jy dan heelemaal erg overtuigd dat bent niet de Zuid-Afrikaanse appeltjes?'

Die smous frons, want hy het dit al mos gesê. 'Mevrou, ik zegd weer, dat bent dog de beleid van de Nederlandse regering om geen Zuid-Afrikaanse appeltjes te verkope. Wij hebben de uitroepen gehoren van de Bishop Tutu, van de Alan Boesak, van de ANC met des groote struggle, so dan geeft wij dog nimmer aan de kliënte de opsie van de Zuid-Afrikaanse appeltjes.'

'Dan bent ik wel heel tevrede,' sê die dame. 'So wil ik dan net een dosyn Belgiese appeltjes, danke.'

Hy draai die appeltjies netjies toe, die dame neem die pakkie, en net voor sy die deur uitstap draai sy om en sê, 'U segd dat uw bent heelemaal seker en totaal geheel en al overtuigd dat ben niet de Zuid-Afrikaanse appeltjes in deze kardoesie?'

Die ou wil hom vererg, maar bly maar beleefd. 'Mevrou,' sê hy, 'zeg mij dan wat hebbe uw so erg tegenover de Zuid-Afrikaanse appeltjes?'

Sy kyk daai sakkie so en sy sê: 'Ik wil dog niet de appeltjes hebbe dat de zwartes met de hande betaste.'

GONE TO POT

Tolla rocks up at the hardware store in Garies. He looks around, stocks up with some provisions, and tells the storekeeper: 'I need a lekker big kaffir-pot.'

The storekeeper cringes as his assistant, Vusi, glares assegais at Tolla. The storekeeper pulls Tolla to one side.

'Tolla,' he whispers, 'this is the New South Africa. You can't say 'kaffir-pot' anymore. You have to call it a cast-iron pot now.'

'Okay,' nods Tolla, 'I understand.'

He pays for the pot, looks at Vusi, and turns to the storekeeper.

'Now can your cast-iron please help me to load my stuff?'

SITTING BULL

Kallie Knoetze and FW were sitting next to each other at a rugby test at Ellis Park, just a short while after FW had announced the release of Nelson Mandela.

The national anthems were played, but Kallie didn't rise for the occasion.

'Staan op, Kallie!' said FW. 'They're playing "Die Stem".'

'Not 'n donner,' said Kallie. 'As soon as I stand up, you'll give my seat away to the blacks!'

BREAK IT UP

Mrs van Poggenpoel, Grade One teacher at Ventersdorp Primary, is talking to her class after break.

'And what did you do during break, little Jannie?' she asks the boy in the front row.

'I played with my ball,' he says.

'If you can spell "ball",' says teacher, 'you can go home early today.

So Jannie spells, 'B-A-L-L'.

'Very good,' says teacher. 'And how about you, little Annie … what did you do during break?'

'I played with my doll,' says Annie.

'If you can spell "doll",' says teacher, 'you can go home early.'

So Annie spells, 'D-O-L-L'.

'Excellent!' says teacher. She wanders around the class, and stops in front of little Vusi's desk.

'And what did you do during break, little Vusi?'

'I had to run away from all the other children,' says Vusi. 'They were being nasty to me because I'm black.'

'All right,' says teacher. 'If you can spell "racial discrimination" …'

RIDDLE-ME-REE

What do you call a dog with steel testicles and no hind legs?
    Sparky.

What did the Indian Ocean say to the Atlantic Ocean?
    Nothing. They just waved.

Why do mice have small balls?
    Because not that many of them know how to dance.

Why did the squirrel sleep on his stomach?
    To keep his nuts warm

How can you tell which end is which on a worm?
Put it in a bowl of flour and wait until it farts.

How do you tell the difference between a cow and a bull?
Milk them both. The one that smiles is the bull.

What did the girl melon say to the boy melon when he proposed to her?
'We're too young … we cantaloupe!'

How do you make a handkerchief dance?
Put a little boogie in it.

What do you call a fly without wings?
A walk.

And a fly without wings or legs?
A roll.

These two peanuts were walking down the road.
One was assaulted.

Why did the chicken cross the road?
Because he saw the zebra crossing.

What does DNA stand for?
National Association of Dyslexics

A big moron and a little moron were sitting on a fence. The big moron fell off. Why?
Because the little moron was a little more on.

The man who invented the 'Hokey Pokey' recently died. You know how they buried him?
They put his right leg in, they put his right leg out, they put his right leg in, and they shook it all about.

Why is 6 scared of 7?
Because 7 8 9 and 10.

What do Eskimos get from sitting on the ice too long?
Polaroids.

What did the German say to the ticking clock?
'Ve haf vays of making you tock.'

Why has Mike Schutte got a hole in his pants pocket?
So he can count to six.

What's brown and sticky?
A stick.

What's brown and sounds like a bell?
Dung!

Why was Adam the first engineer?
He supplied the spare parts for the first loudspeaker.

Did you hear about the two blood corpuscles named Romeo and Juliet?
Shame. All their love was in vein.

Did you know that diarrhoea is hereditary?
It runs in your genes.

What do you call someone who lives at the North Pole, has a heavy South African accent, and supplies electricity to people for a living?
An Eskom ou.

What's the difference between a Rolling Stone and a Scotsman?
One says 'Hey you, get off of my cloud'; the other says 'Hey, McCloud, get off of my ewe.'

What's black and white and eats like a horse?
A zebra.

What's the difference between a vitamin and a hormone?
You can't hear a vitamin.

What's six inches long, has a bald head and drives Jewish women wild?
An American dollar note.

What's got 75 balls and screws old ladies?
Bingo.

Why should you never fall in love with a tennis player?
To them love means nothing.

Naas: How do you keep an asshole in suspense?
Leon: How?
Naas: I'll tell you later.

Leon: What's the first sign of impotence in a man?
Naas: Tell me.
(Leon whispers something inaudible.)
Naas: Sorry?
Leon: (shouts) His inability to hear!

Did you hear about the cannonball artist who was shot into the sky and became a star overnight?

How did Sol Kerzner injure himself?
He sat on his wallet and fell off.

Did you hear about the eighty-year-old man who streaked at the flower show?
He won the prize for best dried arrangement.

'Where does your mom come from?'
'Alaska.'
'Don't worry, Alaska myself.'

What has one wheel and flies?
  A wheelbarrow full of cow manure.

Hoekom is jou hond se naam Vis?
  Want hy byt nie.

My dog doesn't have a nose.
  How does he smell?
  Blerrie bad.

Wat is 'n Vrystaatse moffie?
  'n Ou wat meer van meisies as van rugby hou.

What's the difference between a banana and a vibrator?
  A banana doesn't start shaking when you eat it.

MADE IN JAPAN

Did you know that 85% of all Japanese men have Cataracts?
  The rest drive Rincolns and Chevrorets.

VLOOM-VLOOM

Did you hear about the Japanese car-thief?
  Tommy Tookamota.

AH SO

Did you hear about the Japanese callgirl who went broke?
  Nobody had a yen for her.

ROYAL VISIT

ROYAL FARTY

A series of exclusive dispatches from our intrepid correspondent on the recent British royal visit to South Africa ...

On their latest visit to South Africa, Chief Gatsha introduced Queen Elizabeth and Prince Charles to the nearly extinct Gung-Gung tribe deep in the remotest part of the Transkei.

On arrival the Chief Gung-Gung had just finished brewing his very tasty Gung-Gung beer, especially known for its gas-building qualities.

The Queen, Prince Charles and Chief Gatsha joined in the Gung-Gung beer feast, and it wasn't long before Queen Elizabeth accidentally let out out an enormous fart, shaking Gatsha in his soles.

Blushing like a hotplate Queen Elizabeth immediately turned to Charles, 'Will you stop that, Charles?' to which the bewildered King-to-be asked, 'Which way did it go, Mother?'

Later in the afternoon Chief Gung-Gung was showing the Queen and her son around Gung-Gung land, when Chief Gatsha let out a whopper of a fart. 'How dare you do that before the Queen of England?' inquired the disgusted Prince Charles.

'Sorry,' said the Chief. 'In fact I didn't know it was her turn.'

Still later Chief Gung-Gung took the Queen, Prince Charles and Gatsha on an agricultural tour of Gung-Gung land when one of the horses pulling the cart farted shamelessly. Gatsha blushed profusely and said: 'I'm awfully sorry about that, Mama.'

'No need for concern, Chief Gatsha,' said the Queen. 'In fact, we thought it was the horse.'

Finally, after another few Gung-Gung beers and three hours on the horsecart, the Queen got up from her seat, stretched herself out with dignity and said, 'Aaah. Sitting down in the same position for so long caused my behind to fall asleep.'

To which Chief Gatsha replied: 'Yeees. In fact, we heard it snoring all along, mama.'

Walking towards the Gung-Gung River late that afternoon and donning a loincloth for the evening's tribal celebrations, a bee made its way underneath Prince Charles's loincloth and stung him full on the crown jewels. Hearing her son's terrifying screams, the Queen rushed out from underneath her luxury veld shower, frantically inquiring from Chief Gatsha, 'What happened to my son?'

Chief: He was stung by a Gung-Gung bee, mama.

Queen: Where was he stung?

Chief: Lapaside the river, Mama.

Queen: I mean on which part of his body was he stung.

Chief: That, in fact, I cannot tell you, Mama.

Queen: Come on, you idiot! My son might be dying out there! I need to know where the bee stung him!

There was a beat as Gatsha lowered his eyes and the Queen suddenly realised she was standing in front of this man with nothing on accept her earrings. She instantly grabbed a turksvyblaar and covered the necessary.

Chief: In fact, Mama, let me put it to you this way. If the bee had stung you there, he would have missed.

Before daylight the following morning Prince Charles, Chief Gatsha and his vicious Rottweiler hopped into the 4×4 for a Gung-Gung lion-hunting safari.

The Chief secured a huge chunk of donkey's meat up in the tree ran for cover. Minutes later a massive male lion appeared out of nowhere, jumped into the tree, made itself comfortable on a branch and started tearing away at the meat.

'Now,' whispered the Chief from behind a thicket of bush, 'you take the gun, Charlie, and I'm going to get back into that tree and shake the branches until the lion falls out. Then my well-trained Rottweiler will grab the lion by the balls and drag him over to the bakkie.'

'Jolly excellent, Chief!' said Charles, 'I always knew there was method in this dark continent's madness.' But as the Chief started walking over to the tree, Charles suddenly remembered something, 'By the way Chief, where do the gun and I fit into the picture?'

The Chief turned and paused briefly before he said, 'In fact, my prince, if I happen to be falling out of that tree before the lion, you make bleddie sure you shoot the Rottweiler!'

RUGBY

TRY AGAIN

The ref was blatantly biased towards the Kakamas first XV, and disallowed a very obvious try. The Keetmanshoop manne protested heavily.

'What the hell was wrong with that try, Mr Ref?'

The ref couldn't believe that anyone could ask such a question. He replied, 'Ons druk nie sulke kak drieë op Kakamas nie.'

PALE TOE

'Elke keer as die Gauteng Lions wen,' vertel Van, 'spring my hond op sy agterbene en klap hande.'

'Wragtag?' sê Piet, 'en wat maak jou hond as hulle verloor?'

'Hy maak somersaults,' sê Van.

'Hoeveel somersaults?' vra Piet.

'Hang af hoe hard ek hom skop.'

O GENADE

Die outjie was 'n verwoede Blou Bul-ondersteuner. Hy vra toe vir sy pa of dit sonde is as hy die aand sy gebedjie opsê en vra dat Liewe Jesus die volgende dag die Blou Bulle teen WP moet laat wen.

'Miskien moet jy maar net iets van die WP ook sê,' kom die raad van sy pa.

Die outjie bid toe so: 'Liewe Jesus, sorg asseblief dat die Blou Bulle môre vir die WP 'n hengse pak slae gee, en help die WP net so klein bietjie, nie omdat hulle dit verdien nie maar enkel en alleen uit genade, amen.'

DRUK HOM SO

Die toets is verby en dis 'n gedruis om uit die stadion te kom. Hulle staan gepak soos sardientjies en dit stamp en dit stoot vir 'n vale. Die klein outjie se kop word die heeltyd hier van agter af teen die ou grote voor hom se rug gestamp.

Die kolos vererg hom, swaai om en vra vir die kleintjie, 'Wie de hel dink jy stoot jy so?!'

Die kleintjie sê, 'Ek weet nie. Wat's jou naam?'

GROOT PAMPOEN

Wat is die verskil tussen Francois Pienaar en Aspoestertjie?

Aspoestertjie het by die bal uitgekom.

DAY OF UNREST

Arnold Schoonwinkel, the prominent SA referee, is an old varsity chom of mine. He's a goeie oke, no frills, no fuss, sommer lekker down to earth and a good Christian to boot.

A few seasons ago, Arnold was refereeing a Sunday Currie Cup match in George between South Western Districts and Gauteng Lions, when a fight broke out amongst the forwards. The okes were donnering mekaar uitmekaar, when Arnold shouted: 'Boys, stoppit asseblief, dis Sondag!'

EBONY AND IVORY

In the days before the All Blacks came back to South Africa to get the hiding of their lives, there was a team of all-black rugby players who used to go by the name of the Luiperds.

One day, the Luiperds took on a visiting French side in a game that was so dirty, the score was counted in broken teeth rather than points. At the reception after the match, the master of ceremonies said, 'Ladies and gents, we all saw that today's match was a very physical one. But history was made between black and white today. We cannot steer away from integrated rugby any longer. Rugby is like a piano. Harmony can only be achieved if you play the black and white notes together. And that is exactly what happened today on the rugby field.'

The French captain was asked to reply to the speech. He rose and said, 'What ze master of ceremonies has just said might be true, but I would just like to say that if you keep hitting ze white notes as hard as you hit zem zis afternoon, you will f*** up the piano!'

GROEN EN GOUD

Ek sit eendag op Ellispark en sien hoe die Goue Leeus, met ten minste tien Springbokke, 'n hewige drag slae teen die Vrystaat op die lyf loop. Ek vra vir Jimmy Abbott wat alleen op drie stoele langs my sit, 'Wat's fout met jou manne?'

'Ek weet nie,' sê Jimmy. 'Hulle lyk blerrie goed op papier maar hulle is maar k*k op gras.'

BIG BOOBS

Overheard at a Currie Cup rugby match at Newlands, where Free State were making mincemeat of Province:

'Province is the same as a Cross-your-heart-bra. There's a lot of support, but no cup.'

ACTION REPLAY

According to people who think they know a lot about rugby, the big problem with the Gauteng Lions is that they don't have any fast forwards.

Nonsense. I know for a fact that they've all got fast forwards on their video-machines at home.

BETTER ON THE SMALL SCREEN

The best rugby banner I've ever seen was during a Currie Cup Final between the Gauteng Lions and the Free State Cheetahs in Bloem a few seasons ago.

The Free State Stadium was undergoing some renovations at the time, so the match was played at the Springbok Park cricket field, where some of the spectators were standing a few hundred metres from the action on the field.

A short little Vrystater who was engulfed by the masses was waving a banner reading: 'Ou vrou, tape asseblief die game want ek kan f***l sien!'

FLYHALF

I was invited to a fancy rugby dinner party in Pretoria some years ago. It was real tiresome stuff, with the elderly chairman boring everyone to tears with his long-winded and not-very-witty speech.

Uli leaned over to me and said: 'Isn't there something you can do?'

I thought about it for a while, and then I took a paper napkin and scribbled something on it. It was passed on to the chairman, and he had hardly read it when he turned bright red, coughed and spluttered, brought his speech to a hasty conclusion, and sat down.

'Brilliant!,' said Uli. 'What did you write in that note, Leon?'

'I just wrote, 'Your fly's open.''

ARM IN ARM

What do you call a beautiful woman on the arm of a Gauteng Lions rugby player?

A tattoo.

GLUG-GLUG

They say that a certain very good-looking provincial scrumhalf has been nicknamed 'Sasol' by his teammates.

Why Sasol?
Because he's got a pomp in every dorp.

CUSTODY BATTLE

Little Johnny's parents are getting a divorce. The judge orders them to bring their son to court for the custody decision. The judge looks down at Johnny and says, 'Son, I have decided that I am going to let your mother take care of you.'

Johnny bursts out crying. 'I don't want to live with my mother,' he says. 'She beats me.'

The judge pauses for a moment, and then he says: 'All right. You can live with your father.'

Little Johnny bursts out crying again. 'I don't want to live with my father,' he says. 'He beats me too!'

Now the judge is getting a little exasperated. 'Okay, son,' he says, 'You tell me … who DO you want to live with?

And Johnny answers: 'The Gauteng Lions. They never beat anybody!'

NAILBITING MATCH

Jimmy and Mike were watching the Gauteng Lions take on the Blue Bulls at Ellis Park. Kallie arrived just as the final whistle blew.

'What was the score?' asked Kallie.

'Nil-nil,' answered Jimmy.

Kallie nodded to himself. 'And what was the halftime score?'

'Dunno,' said Mike. 'We only arrived after halftime.'

HOLY WAR

My Bible teacher once asked me in primary school, 'Who beat the Philistines?'

I said, 'Sorry juffrou, I only follow Currie Cup rugby.'

Then my Geography teacher asked me, 'Name two seasons of the year.'

Quick as a flash, I said, 'Rugby and cricket season, juffrou.'

ROLLING BACK

The scrumhalf and the hooker were discussing the ins and outs of their favourite sporting activity. And they weren't talking about rugby. 'You know those serial numbers you get on condoms?' said the scrumhalf.

'I've never seen serial numbers on condoms,' said the hooker.

'Well, then you've never had to roll them back that far.'

COP A FEEL

Sexy Suzie, sizzling under the beefy fullback's manful touch, held up a manicured hand and said, 'Before we go any further, skattie, you must get protection.'

So he called the Flying Squad and asked them to send two policemen up to the hotel room without delay.

RHINO HORN

'I hear you're going out with a rugby player,' said the Sandton socialite to the other Sandton socialite over iced tea one morning. 'Is he any good in bed?'

'Not much,' she confessed. 'But I managed to persuade him to take some rhino horn pills. You know, they're supposed to be an aphrodisiac.'

'Did they help?'

'Oh yes. But now every time he sees a Land Rover, he charges it!'

NICE TRY

A rugby referee died and went to heaven. Stopped by St Peter at the gates, he was told that only brave people who had performed heroic deeds and had the courage of their convictions could enter. If the ref could describe a situation in his life where he had shown these characteristics, he would be allowed in.

'Well,' said the ref, 'I was reffing a game between the Boks and the All Blacks at Ellis Park Stadium. The Bokke were two points ahead with one minute to go. The All Blacks wing made a break, and passed inside to his lock. The lock was driven on by his forwards, passed out to the flanker who ducked blind and went over in the corner. However, the flanker dropped the ball before he could ground it, and as the All Blacks were clearly the better side all game, I ruled that he had dropped the ball down, not forward, and awarded the try.'

'Well, that was fairly brave of you,' said St Peter, 'but I will have to check it in the book.' A few minutes later, he returns and says, 'I'm sorry – I can find no record of this. Can you help me trace it? When did it all happen?'

And the ref looked at his watch and said: 'About 15 minutes ago ago.'

WHAT'S THE SCORE

In the heat of the big match, this oke gets an opponent's boot right on the place where it hurts an oke most. The first-aid guy rushes over to the scene and starts massaging and pouring water over the strategic injury.

'Stoppit!' yells the oke, 'don't wash 'n rub 'em, just count 'em!'

TRY AGAIN

In my rugby-playing days, there was only one thing that stopped me from becoming the world's greatest flyhalf. And that was the fact that I wasn't the world's greatest flyhalf. I just wasn't bang enough, and on top of that, I was a terrible kicker.

One day, we lost a crucial match because I had missed an easy kick over the posts. I walked over to my coach and said: 'Coach, I'm sorry. I'm so cross with myself I could kick my own arse.'

'Ja,' he said. 'And you'd probably miss too.'

SHORTARSE

I started off playing scrumhalf. I was very short. I hated this position, 'cause it gave me a heng of an inferiority complex. Every time the scrum went down I thought they were talking about me. Also I wasn't short enough for a scrumhalf. Doc used to say 'a scrumhalf is the guy in the team with the shortest arse and the longest pass.'

BIG STINK

Upset by a ref's stupid decision, I once blurted out: 'Hey, Mr Ref, you stink, man!'

He picked up the ball, paced out another fifteen yards, turned around and shouted: 'And how do I smell from here?'

SALESMEN

LET'S PARTY

The sales rep arrives at this farm in the Free State late on a Friday afternoon. Having clinched a deal with Van for a new mealie stroper, Van and the rep relax on the stoep with a Klipdrift and Coke when Van says, 'Johnny, I'm gooiing a moeruvva party here on my farm tonight.'

'That sounds lekka,' says Johnny.

'Ja man', Van goes on. 'We're gonna dop, then we gonna dop some more. Then we gonna fight, then we gonna dop again. Then we gonna dance, then we gonna dop some more until we're falling over. Then we gonna dop again, and then we're gonna have some sex. How's about you coming over tonight?'

Johnny: 'Hell, thanks Van. That sounds lekka. What should I wear?'

Van: 'No, come as you are, man. It's only going to be you and me.'

IN THE B-B-BEGINNING

Poor old Job Rossouw can't find a job anywhere. Nothing with to do with affir-affir-affirmative a-a-a-action; it's just that Job suffers from a very noticeable sp-sp-sp-speech impe-pe-pe-pe-diment. Finally, he manages to land a position at a company that sells Bibles.

There are six reps in the company. At the end of the week they compare sales. Ten Bibles here, seven there, three here. Nothing to brag about. The boss is very worried, until a proud Job walks into the office.

'Hu ... hu ... hundred and fo ... fo ... fo ... forty', stutters Job.

The boss and the other reps can't believe what they're hearing: 'Hundred and forty Bibles for the week?' asks the boss.

'N ... n ... not for the wee ... week. Ju ... ju ... ju ... just fo ... fo ... today.'

The boss says, 'That's amazing, Job. Please tell all my reps how you did it.'

'Well I ju ... ju ... just asked them i ... i ... if they wa ... wanted to b ... b ... buy a Bible. If they said n ... n ... no, I said okay, then I'm q ... q ... quickly going to read it to you.'

ONE WAY

Young Frikkie the salesman arrives on oom Koos's farm late in the afternoon. Because it's a long way to the next dorp, Frikkie asks oom Koos if he can stay the night.

Oom Koos has heard all about travelling salesmen, so he says, 'No fine, Frik. Just as long as you don't try anything funny with my little Bettie.'

During dinner that evening, Frikkie can't keep his eyes off Bettie. She's only 18, but there isn't too much about her that's little. From the look in her eyes, and the footsie-footsie under the table, Frikkie begins to get the feeling that the attraction is mutual.

'We've only got two bedrooms on this plaas,' says oom Koos, getting up from the table. 'And I share with no-one.'

Frikkie's eyes light up, but then oom Koos adds, 'You'll notice that I've spread mealie-meal on the floor between the two single beds in Bettie's room. If I see even a single footprint in that mealie-meal, my dogs will have your nuts for breakfast. Verstaan, Frik?'

Frikkie nods. That night, him and Bettie lie in their separate beds, wide awake, without saying a word. Then Bettie whispers, 'Frikkie?'

'Ja, Bettie?'

'Can't you do the pole-vault?'

Another long silence before Frikkie answers. 'Ja, I can, Bettie. But how am I going to get back?'

THE WHOLE TOOTH

Joe was told that if he didn't sell at least 100 toothbrushes by the end of the week, Vusi would get his job. At the end of the week he had sold twice as many. The boss was highly impressed. He called Joe into his office and asked him how he did it.

'Well,' said Joe, 'I erected my own little hawker's stand outside Pick 'n Pay and put some crisps and a new dip on a little table. It was for free, and there was a constant stream of people. I'd invite them to try my new dip, which was made from garlic, vinegar and chicken shit. They'd try it, spit it out and go, 'Aaargh!'. That's when I would say, "Would you like to buy a toothbrush?"'

SCHOOLDAYS

GROWN-UPS

The end-of-year holidays are over, and the nursery school kids have moved up the ladder to Big School. Mrs Ramsbottom welcomes them warmly, and delivers her customary opening address.

'Children, you are no longer babies. You are no longer little toddlers. You are big people now, so you can all start acting like grown-ups. From today, class, I want you to stop using baby language, and to start using grown-up words whenever and wherever you can.'

The class nods in agreement. Mrs Ramsbottom smiles. She's really not that much of a dragon after all.

'Hello, little Timmy,' she says to the boy in the front row. 'And what did you do during the holidays?'

'I went to stay with my Nanna,' he says. An icy glare.

'No, no, Timmy. You went to stay with your grandmother. Use the grown-up word, please.'

Behind little Timmy sits little Suzie.

'Hello Susan,' says teacher. 'Now, what did you do during the holidays?'

'I went for a ride on a big choo-choo,' says little Suzie. Mrs Ramsbottom sighs.

'No, you did not. You went for a ride on a train. That's the grown-up word. Understand?'

Suzie understands. At the back of the class sits little Johnny. Mrs Ramsbottom approaches, with an edge of circumspection in her step.

'And what did you do during the holidays, little Johnny?'

'I read a book, Miss.'

'Oh, excellent,' says Mrs Ramsbottom, much relieved. 'And what was the book called?'

'Winnie the Shit,' says little Johnny, beaming with pride.

FRAGINA

Dis die begin van die nuwe skoolkwartaal en die nuwe Engelse juffrou by Spuitfontein Hoërskool het 'n groot probleem: haar van.

'Meneer,' sê sy so half blosend vir die skoolhoof, 'soos Meneer weet is my van "Fragina". Dis baie belangrik dat Meneer tog nie die "r" sal weglaat wanneer meneeer my vanoggend tydens saal voor die leerlinge verwelkom nie. Mense het al voorheen die glipsie gemaak, en soos Meneer kan dink was dit 'n groot verleentheid. Asseblief, Meneer.'

'Ontspan, Juffrou,' sê die hoof. 'Ek sal doodseker maak.' So sit die hoof hardop en oefen die volgende halfuur lank, 'Fragina ... Fragina ... Fragina ...' tot hy dit so in sy kop ingedril het dat hy oortuig is hy kan nie verkeerd gaan nie.

Tydens saalbyeenkoms open die dominee en stel daarna die skoolhoof aan die beurt. 'Geagte lede van die ouerkomitee, onderwysers, kinders,' begin die hoof, 'julle sien 'n aantal nuwe gesigte op die verhoog vanoggend, en dit is vir my 'n besondere voorreg om ons nuwe leerkragte aan julle voor te stel. In die eerste plek, baie hartlik welkom aan ons nuwe Engelse juffrou ... eee ... juffrou ...' en die skoolhoof slaan 'n total blank.

Hy kyk na die juffrou, sy kyk angsbevange na hom, en skielik glimlag hy verlig want hy onthou van die 'r'.

'Natuurlik ja, Juffrou Droos.'

IE-YOOOOOW!

Miss Ramsbottom asked her Grade One class, 'What is one plus one?'

Young Vusi put up his hand: 'Ie-two, Miss.'

WHAM! She klapped him on his head. 'Not ie-two, Vusi, only two. What is five and four?'

Vusi's hand was up again. 'Yes Vusi?' asked the teacher.

'Ie-nine, Miss.'

WHAM! Another whack on Vusi's head. 'Nine, Vusi, not 'ie-nine'. Okay, here's a difficult one: what is six and five?'

Vusi thought about it carefully before saying, 'Leven, Miss!'

WHAM!

'Eleven!' said Miss Ramsbottom.

HELLO DEAR

The Grade One teacher is calling on her pupils to identify animals from their pictures. She holds up a picture of a horse and asks, 'Johnny, can you tell me what this is?'

And Johnny beams with pride as he says: 'It's a horse, Miss.'

'Very good. And now you, Billy, can you tell me what this is?'

She holds up a picture of a lion.

'It's a lion, Miss.'

'Excellent!' she says.

Now it's little Sammy Cohen's turn. The teacher holds up a picture of a deer. 'Can you tell me what this is, Sammy?'

Sammy looks long and hard at the picture. 'I don't know,' he says. The teacher looks at him in amazement. 'But surely you do, Sammy! Look, I'll give you a little clue. Think about what your mother calls your father.'

Sammy looks even longer and harder at the picture. Then the light of realisation dawns in his eyes.

'Teacher,' he says, 'you mean, that's a schmuck?'

STRESS

The Grade One class is instructed by Miss Ramsbottom to perceive stress in their own homes, and draw a little picture of it.

Next morning she notes that Sannie has drawn a small bottle of nail polish remover next to a piece of cotton wool. 'Tell us how this causes stress in your home, Sannie.'

'One night my mommy was taking nail polish off her nails with this nail polish remover on a little piece of cotton wool. Then she took the little piece of cotton wool and threw it into the toilet, and then my daddy went for a poo smoking a cigarette, and then my daddy threw the stompie into the toilet bowl through his legs and then there was a big explosion. This has caused my daddy lots of pain and my mommy lots of stress.'

'Good,' says Miss Ramsbottom.

After going through the same ritual with various pupils, she walked over to little Schucks and studied his picture, which was a single dot on an otherwise blank sheet of paper. Miss Ramsbottom frowned: 'Can you explain this dot to us, Schucks?'

Schucks shook his head and said, 'That's not a dot, that's a period. My sister hasn't had two in a row and it's been freaking out our whole family.'

ONCE BITTEN

The teacher was telling her Grade Two class the parable of the Good Samaritan. When she had finished she asked, 'Class, why do you think the priest passed the victim without stopping?'

Vusi's hand was up first.

'Yes, Vusi?'

'Because he had already been robbed, Miss.'

CONTAGIOUS

The English teacher challenged the class to make a sentence containing the word 'contagious'. Little Mike's hand shot up in a flash.

'Yes, Mike?' said the teacher.

'The South African Rugby Board have decided to elect a new president in place of Baas Louis,' said Mike. 'It will take that contagious to get back in again.'

NOOIT OP 'N SONDAG NIE

Soos die outjie wat die Sondag nie opdaag vir Sondagskool nie. Die volgende Sondag vra sy juffrou kwaai, 'Waar was jy verlede Sondag, Jimmy?'

'Ek was vol snot van die griep, juffrou,' sê Jimmy, 'maar ons hele gesin het darem 'n godsdiensvideo gekyk.'

'O,' sê die juffrou, 'en watter video was dit nogal?'

'"The Gods Must Be Crazy".'

TAXI!

Die laerskooljuffrou vra die klas moet vir haar 'n voorstelling van Adam en Eva in die paradys teken. Elkeen het sy eie idee: Melanie teken 'n slang met 'n duiwelkop in 'n boom vol appels, Pierre teken Eva plat op haar rug met haar bene wat styfskop in die lug nadat sy die appel geeet het, en Dawie teken 'n wurm wat desperaat spook om by die appel uit te klim.

Klein Leon teken Adam en Eva agter in 'n Mercedes Benz, kompleet met die ster op die bonnet, en agter die stuurwiel sit die chauffeur, die engel Gabriel. Hy't sy een vlerk so op die stuurwiel, en sy ander vlerk hang so oor die oopgedraaide venster.

Die juffrou het die prentjie sooo gekyk, gefrons en gevra, 'Leon, juffrou verstaan nie mooi nie. Wat stel jou prentjie voor?'

Toe sê Leon, 'Juffrou, dit staan in die Bybel dat die engel Gabriel vir Adam en Eva uit die paradys gedryf het.'

BLACKBALLED

Miss Ramsbottom devised a plan during the first period on a Friday morning whereby she could get the attention of the kids. She would ask a question, and anyone who could provide the correct answer would get the rest of Friday off.

'Okay, class,' she said, 'who can tell me who is the Prime Minister of England?'

Nobody knew the answer.

The following week she asked, 'Can anyone tell me what is the square root of seven?'

Again, nobody knew the answer.

Then little Schucks made a plan for the following Friday. He arrived with a couple of black marbles and rolled them along the floor with a clatter.

'Okay,' said Miss Ramsbottom, 'who's the comedian with the black balls?'

'Bill Cosby,' shouted Schucks. 'See you Monday!'

SEX

WAS THAT IT?

Why don't women blink during foreplay?

They don't have time.

WORK OR PLEASURE

A Jew and an Irishman are having a heated debate about the true purpose of sex. The Irishman says it's work. The Jew says it's pleasure.

Unable to reach a conclusion, they agree to continue their research and meet again at a later date. At a later date, the Irishman triumphantly reports that he checked with his priest, and the answer is definitely work.

'Sex is purely for the purpose of procreation, see?'

But the Jew remains unconvinced. He checks with his rabbi and reports his findings to the Irishman. 'My rabbi says it must be pleasure, because if it was work, we'd get the blacks to do it.'

TWICE A DAY

This guy goes to see his doctor and says, 'Doctor, doctor you've just got help me. I just can't stop having sex!'

'Really? How often do you have it?' asks the doctor.

'Well, twice a day I have sex with my wife, TWICE a day!' answers the patient.

'That's not so much,' says the doctor.

'Yes, but that's not all. Twice a day I have sex with my secretary, TWICE a day!' continues the man.

'Well, that is probably a bit excessive,' says the doctor.

'Yes, but that's not all. Twice a day I have sex with a prostitute, TWICE a day!' says the man.

'Well, that is definitely too much,' says the doctor. 'You've got to learn to take yourself in hand.'

'I do,' says the man. 'Twice a day!'

TWO CHANCES

It's bedtime. The married couple are in bed. The wife stops reading, puts down her book, and switches off the light. Snuggling up in the darkness, the husband gently taps his wife on the shoulder and starts rubbing her arm.

The wife turns over and says, 'I'm sorry, honey. I've got an appointment with my gynaecologist tomorrow, and I want to stay fresh.'

The husband sighs, turns over, and tries to fall asleep.

A few minutes later, he rolls back over and taps his wife again. This time he whispers in her ear, 'Do you have a dentist's appointment tomorrow as well?'

HE'LL KNOW

Little Suzie goes to see her mom with her Big Question of the day.

'Mommy,' she asks 'what's an orgasm?'

Mommy gives the usual answer.

'Go and ask your father.'

BIRDS AND BEES

Mike and Nellie are sitting in bed late one night, talking about whatever comes to hand. Then Nellie says, 'Mike, you've really got to talk to little Mike about the birds and the bees one of these days.'

Mike sighs. 'Okay,' he says. 'I'll do it first thing tomorrow.'

So, first thing the next day, Mike corners little Mike in the kitchen.

'Little Mike,' he says, 'you're 14 years old now, and there's something I've got to tell you.'

'Ja, pa?'

'Remember that session I arranged for you with Madame Suzie down at the Ranch?'

Little Mike's eyes light up. 'Oh ja, pa, I remember it well.'

'Well, son,' says Mike, 'it's time that you knew that the birds and the bees do the same thing.'

TALK TO ME

What is it when a man talks dirty to a woman?

Sexual harassment.

What is it when a woman talks dirty to a man?

R2,50 a minute.

POEPSIE

'Am I the first guy to make love to you, poepsie?'

'Of course you are. Why do you men always ask the same stupid question?'

BIG BUSINESS

What did the hooker say to her client?

It's been a business doing pleasure with you.

GOING UP

These two office secretaries are standing shoulder to shoulder in a jam-packed lift. Barely able to move her head, the one secretary whispers to the other, 'Is the guy standing behind us attractive?'

The other secretary just manages to turn around and sneak a peek.

'He's young,' she replies.

'I asked whether he's attractive. I can feel he's young.'

1, 2, 3 ...

Koos has been married for seven years, although it feels a lot longer. The only thing that doesn't feel a lot longer is Koos's ... well, let's just say that Koos and his vrou aren't as close as they used to be. Desperately seeking a solution, Koos goes to see his doctor.

'Doctor,' he says, 'I feel a little embarrassed to say this, but I've been having a hard time having a hard time lately.'

The doctor gets the message. 'Don't worry,' he says. 'It's quite common. I'm sure we'll be able to sort it out.'

Unfortunately, nothing the doctor suggests or prescribes makes the slightest bit of difference. Even Viagra turns out to be a total flop.

'There's only one more thing I can suggest,' says the doctor, scribbling a name and phone number on a piece of paper. 'Go and see this sangoma.'

At this stage, Van will try anything. So he goes to see the sangoma. The sangoma says, 'Yes, I can help you,' and he throws some blue powder on a flame. Whoomph! As Van stares into the billowing smoke, the sangoma grinds some paste into a small container.

'This is very powerful medicine,' he says. 'You must apply it tonight, and while doing so, you must say 1, 2, 3. It will rise for as long as you wish. But remember ... you can only use it once a year.'

'And what do I do when it's, you know, over?' asks Van. 'Then you say 1, 2, 3, 4,' says the sangoma, 'and it will go down again. But be warned. You will not be able to use it for another year!'

Van can't wait. He gets home, gets into bed with his wife, applies the paste as directed, and says out loud: '1, 2, 3.' It works.

Then his wife turns over and says, 'What did you say 1, 2, 3 for?'

FREE SEX

With the needle on the fuel gauge twitching perilously close to 'empty', Mike and Kallie drive their bakkie to the petrol station. 'Hey!' shouts Kallie, looking over his shoulder. 'You've just passed the petrol station!'

'No, man,' says Mike. 'I don't want to go to that one. I want to go to the one with the competition.'

'What competition?'

'You'll see.'

Mike pulls into the petrol station with the competition.

'Fill her up,' he says to the attendant, and then he asks, 'Are you still running that competition?'

The attendant nods.

'What's the prize again?' asks Mike.

'If you win,' says the attendant, 'you're entitled to free sex.'

Mike nudges Kallie in the ribs. 'You see? I told you, man.'

'How do we play?' asks Kallie.

'Well,' says the attendant, 'I'm thinking of a number between one and ten. If you guess right, you win free sex.'

'Okay,' says Kallie. 'I guess seven.'

'Sorry, I was thinking of eight,' replies the attendant.

The following week, Mike and Kallie go back to the same station to fill up.

The attendant says: 'I'm thinking of a number between one and ten. If you guess right, you win free sex.'

'Two,' says Mike.

'Sorry,' says the attendant. 'I was thinking of three. Come back soon and try again.'

As Mike drives off, Kallie turns to him and says, 'You know, I'm beginning to think this blerrie contest is rigged.'

'No way,' says Mike. 'My wife won twice last week.'

WHILE YOU WERE OUT

'You never tell me when you're having an orgasm,' the husband said to his wife.

'That's because you're never home!' she replied.

TOYBOY

Wat is die Afrikaans vir toyboy?

Pompjoggie.

SLIPPERY SOLUTION

A man in a suit, carrying a clipboard in his hand, rings the buzzer on the security gate of a house in the suburbs. The Rottweiler and the Maltese poodle go mal, and then the homeowner answers.

'Sorry to disturb you, sir,' says the guy in the suit. 'I'm conducting market research on behalf of a major pharmaceutical company, and I was wondering if you could answer a couple of questions.'

'Sure,' says the homeowner. 'Fire away.'

'Thanks. Could you please tell me whether you are a frequent or infrequent user of the following product: Vaseline Petroleum Jelly.'

'Frequent, of course,' says the homeowner. 'Been using it for as long as I can remember.'

'And what exactly do you use it for, sir?'

'Three things,' says the homeowner. 'Dry skin, chapped lips …'

'Dry skin, chapped lips,' echoes the guy in the suit, scrawling on his form.

' … and sex.'

'Sex? Uh, I hope you don't mind me asking, sir, but in what way do you use it for sex?'

'We put it on the bedroom doorknob,' says the homeowner.

'The doorknob? And what does that do?'

'It keeps the kids out,' says the homeowner.

TRUE CONFESSIONS

Weighed down with a terrible burden of shame and guilt, Koos goes to see his dominee.

'What's the matter, Koos?' asks the dominee. 'You look like you've got a lot on your mind.'

'Ja, Dominee,' says Koos. 'It's about me and Marie.'

'Is your marriage in trouble?'

'No, Dominee. Quite the opposite, actually. Last night, in fact, we made passionate love for what seemed like hours.'

The Dominee looks intently at Koos. 'And?'

'Well, Dominee, that's what I'm feeling guilty and ashamed about.'

'About making love to your wife? Come on, Koos. That's not a sin.'

'I know, Dominee. But this … well, this was different. I mean, it was really kinky, if you know what I mean. At one stage, I was charging after Marie like a Blue Bull, and then I tackled her from behind and …'

The Dominee holds up his hand. 'You don't have to give me the details, Koos. Believe me, I've seen many marriages crumble because of a lack of physical love in the relationship. Your marriage sounds very healthy to me.'

'Well, yes, it is, Dominee, but …'

'But what?

'Well, the things we did last night, Dominee … I'm just so worried that you're going to ban me and Marie from the church.'

The Dominee bursts out laughing. 'Ban you from the church? For fulfilling your marital obligations to each other? Now why one earth would I want to do a thing like that, Koos?'

'Well, Dominee,' says Koos, clutching his hands to his forehead, 'we've already been banned from flying South African Airways ever again.'

SEX OBJECT

'My wife is a sex object,' says ou Wilbul.

'Why?' asks Leon.
'Everytime I want sex she objects.'

BIG BANG

'As ek en my vrou liefde maak,' sê Smuts van Klapmuts, 'is dit soos Guy Fawkes.'

'Jy bedoel fireworks en donderslae?' vra Leon opgewonde.

'Nee,' sê Smuts, 'ek bedoel een keer 'n jaar.'

SKYDIVING

GO JUMP

Standing in the doorway of the plane, with his extra-large parachute strapped firmly to his back, Mike turns around to ask the skydiving instructor a question.

'If my main chute doesn't open,' yells Mike, 'how long do I have to open the reserve?'

To which the instructor replies, 'The rest of your life.'

FREEFALL

Mike has always wanted to learn to skydive. Finally, he's saved up enough money and courage. After a couple of lessons, he's standing in the doorway of the plane, ready for the jump of his life.

The instructor reminds him: 'You're going to go first, Mike, and I'm going to jump right behind you, so we can go down together.' Mike nods, and sticks his thumb in the air. Then he jumps.

A few seconds later, he looks up to see his instructor in freefall. The instructor pulls his ripcord. The chute doesn't open. Frantically trying to open his reserve, the instructor signals to Mike.

Then the instructor plunges past Mike at a rapid rate. Mike sees him go by, and he quickly undoes the straps of his own parachute.

'Okay, so you wanna race, my China?'

SNUFF

STRONG SNUFF

These two Boere chommies are sitting next to the rugby field on the hoennerstellasie stands in Clanwilliam. The one oke, Oom Sjert, takes out his tin of snuff, opens it and says, 'Demmit, my blerrie snuff is finished.'

He turns to the little eight-year-old Schucks who is kicking a ball behind the stands and says, 'Hei boet, why don't you quickly go and buy the oom a tin of snuff there at ou Doon's keffie.'

He hands little Schucks some money and the empty snuff tin and says, 'Tell him to give you one of these.'

'Fine oom,' says little Schucks, and off he goes. Running over Clanwilliam's B-rugby field he spots a heap of dried dogshit, presumably left over from a recent match. An idea takes root in his ever-scheming mind. Instead of running all the way to the café, why doesn't he just manufacture some snuff of his own?

He picks some of the dogshit up, rubs it between his hands until it's very fine, and carefully puts it into the tin. He replaces the lid and returns to the hoennerstellasies at the rugby field.

'Here is oom's snuff,' he says.

'Thanks,' says Oom Sjert. 'Keep the change.'

Oom Sjert opens the tin of snuff, pinches a small amount between forefinger and thumb, puts it against his huge black and hairy left nostril and inhales deeply, repeating the ritual into his huge black and hairy right nostril.

There's a few seconds of silence with oom Sjert frowning, pleating his nose slightly and sniffing, sniffing. Then he uses both hands to lift up his left leg, turns his veldskoen upwards, looks, but sees no sign of dogshit. He lifts up the other leg, looks under his shoe, still no dog poo. He turns to oom Kallie and says, 'Kallie, het jy gepoep?'

'Uh-uh' says oom Kallie. 'In elk geval nie so lat ek agtergekom het nie.'

Oom Sjert says, 'Then lift up your shoes and check for dogshit. There's a terrible smell that's come through here and hit me smack between the eyes.'

Now it's oom Kallie's turn to look under his shoes, right shoe up, snif-sniff, left shoe up, sniff-sniff. Finally oom Kallie says, 'You know, I got this blerrie cold. My nose is blocked like a drain. I can't smell shit.'

Oom Sjert says, 'Well, take a shot', and hands Oom Kallie the tin of snuff. Oom Kallie takes a lekka liberal pinch of snuff, and a lekka deep drag, left nostril, deep drag, right nostril. He sits back for a second or three, then starts sniffing. Oom Gert is checking him out. Oom Kallie sniffs again, a deeper one this time. Then he turns to oom Sjert and says, 'Ou Sjert, this is blerrie good snuff. It's opened up my nose completely.'

He sniffs again and looks around.

'You're right, man. I can definitely smell dogshit somewhere around here.'

SPIETKOPS

BACKSEAT DRIVER

This traffic cop pulls a farmer over on a small rural road and says, 'Sir, do you realise your wife fell out of the car several kilometres back?'

To which the farmer replies, 'Thank goodness! I thought I had gone deaf.'

HEPPY, HEPPY!

Die ou is diep geswael, en neuk sommer om die eerste hoek teen 'n eenrigting op. Hy sien die blou lig flits, en hy gooi ankers. Die spietkop spring uit sy kar uit, ruk die ou se deur oop en sê: 'Klim uit!' Die ou sit en slinger en val omtrent uit die kar uit.

'Wat dink jy doen jy?', vra die spietkop, 'jy ry soos 'n mal mens hier teen 'n eenrigtingstraat op!'

Hy sê, 'O, is dit wat dit ish? Ek dag die fliek ish klaar en almal ry nou t'rug.'

'Jy's gesuip man!', sê die spietkop.

Hy sê, 'Ja meneer, ek moet nou huishtoe gaan.'

'Waar kom jy vandaan?', vra die spietkop.

Hy sê, 'Ek kom nou net van 'n nuwejaarshpaartie af.

Die spietkop kyk hom aan of hy mal is en sê, 'Meneer, besef jy dis Juliemaand?'

Hy sê, 'Ja, dis hoekom ek nou moet huishtoe gaan.'

LOOK HERE, LADY

Mike Schutte, traffic cop, stops a lady driver and asks to see her licence. She hands it to him and he studies it thoroughly. 'Lady,' he finally proclaims, 'it says here that you should be wearing glasses.'

The lady looks him in the eye and says, 'Well, I have contacts.'

And Mike explodes, 'I don't care who you know! You're getting a ticket!'

VOET INNIE HOEK

Die ou kyk in sy truspieëltjie, sien 'n spietkop agter hom en hy sit voet in die hoek. Die spietkop sit voet in die hoek, en die ou ry nog vinniger … 120 k.p.u … 130 … 160, en dit in 'n beboude gebied.

Hy vat 'n woeste draai, die kar rol, die spietkop gooi ankers, spring uit sy kar en storm nader terwyl die ou bebloed deur die windscreen uitsukkel.

'Is jy van jou blerrie kop af?' vra die spietkop, 'wat jaag jy so?'

'Sorry, ou pêl,' sê die ou, 'maar my vrou het met 'n spietkop weggeloop.'

'Nou wat het dit met jou jaery te doen?'

'Ek het gedog dis jy wat haar wil terugbring.'

NET OM DIE DRAAI

Die ou is stormdronk en ry laat die aand by sy huis in teen 'n hengse spoed. Die spietkop sien hom, jaag hom agterna en sê, 'Hoekom wys jy nie jy gaan draai nie?'

'Hoekom moet ek?' vra die ou. 'Almal weet ek bly hier.'

STUNT DRIVER

Die ou is sterk geswael, vat 'n skerp draai en rol sy kar. Die spietkop kom aangejaag terwyl hy besig is om bebloed deur die stukkende windscreen uit die onderstebo kar te klim. Die spietkop vra onthuts, 'Is jy dronk, meneer?'

Die ou sê, 'Natuurlik, dink jy ek'sh 'n blerrie shtunt driver!'

VOLK HULLE ALMAL

ET was busy doing one of his thundering Volk speeches in Ventersdorp one evening, sweating like a sauna and shouting like a troop commander.

'En daar was, Meneer die Voorsitter, die helde van Bloedrivier!

En daar was, Meneer die Voorsitter, die helde van Majuba!!

En daar was, Meneer die Voorsitter, die helde van Spioenkop!!!'

It was at this point that an old omie who had dozed suddenly woke up. He jumped out of his chair shouting, 'Dis wat ek ook sê, broer Eugene! Te hel met die spietkops!'

MOENIE SKRIK NIE

Die spietkop stop vir Van.

'Moenie skrik nie, meneer, ons wil u net komplimenteer met die pragtige en versigtige wyse waarop u bestuur.'

'Ja-nee,' sê Van, ''n man moet donnersh versigtig ry as jy sho gesuip ish shoos ek.'

TALL TALES

OVER THE TOP

Van, an American and an Englishman are bragging about what's best and what's biggest in their part of the world.

The American says, 'I wanna tell you fellas somethin'. We got a building in New York that goes three storeys higher than the highest cloud in the sky, and I'm not exaggerating' one little bit.'

The Englishman says, 'You do, do you? Well let me tell you something, old chap, we've just manufactured a Rolls-Royce that is wider than the width of the Thames River at it's widest.'

Van says, 'Ag that's nothing. My watsemiekollit is 22 inches long and that's not even including the extra inches when I wake up in the morning.'

A few dops go by. The okes are staring silently into their empty glasses, when the American pipes up, 'Fellas, I gotta confess something. That building in New York I was talking about? Well, that building wouldn't really go up as quite as high as the highest cloud. Maybe an average high cloud would be more accurate.'

The Englishman says, 'Seeing that my American friend is being so honest, I've got to admit that the Rolls I was talking about might not exactly be the width of the Thames. Maybe half the width would be closer to the truth.'

Van says, 'Ja, well, I've also got to admit something. That watsemiekollit I said is 22 inches?'

'Yes?' says the Yank and the Pom.

'It's not really mine. it's my cousin's in Upington.'

MEANWHILE, BACK AT THE RANCH

Van and the American cattle farmer are talking about what's BIGGEST and what's BEST in their neck of the woods.

Van says, 'I've got a cattle farm near Ermelo. It's called STUD OF STUDS, and it covers three hundred and fifty square kilometres.'

He waits for the American's reaction. Nothing. He carries on, 'Nice little piece of land. It's thin country, normally they run about four head of cattle to the square kilometre, but me, I run about thirty-five.'

Now it's the American's turn. 'Yeah well, me and my partner, we run a ranch in Texas,' he drawls. 'Two hundred and ten thousand square miles.'

'Miles?' gulps Van. 'Really?'

'Yeah.'

'What do you call your ranch?' asks Van.

'We call it A B C F X Y Zee Lazy Johnny Sarah B Bar Q with Black Longhorn and Star Spurs Bar Ranch.'

Van is amazed. 'Hell, ou pêl', he asks, 'and how many cattle do you have?'

'We don't have any … never did have one survive the branding.'

TENNIS

TENNIS BALL

A guy's out jogging when he spots a brand-new tennis ball lying in the road. He picks it up and slips it into the pocket of his shorts.

Later, he's standing on a corner waiting for the light to change.

A blonde is standing next to him. She sees the bulge in his shorts. 'What's that?' she says. 'Tennis ball,' he replies. 'Oh, that must be painful,' she says. 'I had tennis elbow once.'

TITANIC

WHAT'S THE DIFFERENCE?

A Korean and a Jew are standing at the bar, silently downing their drinks. Suddenly, the Jew turns around and punches the Korean in the face.

'Hey,' says the Korean, 'what was that for?'

'That was for Pearl Harbour,' says the Jew, and he goes back to his drink. The Korean slams his fist on the counter.

'Pearl Harbour? What are you talking about? That was the Japanese!'

'Japanese, Chinese, Korean, what's the difference,' shrugs the Jew.

They carry on drinking.

Suddenly, the Korean turns around and punches the Jew in the face.

'Hey,' he exclaims, 'what was that for?'

'That was for the *Titanic*.'

'The *Titanic*? Are you crazy? The *Titanic* was sunk by an iceberg!'

The Korean shrugs. 'Iceberg, Goldberg, what's the difference?'

ALMOST THERE

What do you get if you cross the Atlantic with the *Titanic*?
Halfway.

LUCK OF THE IRISH

These three Irish okes were marooned on an iceberg. One had a telescope. In the darkness, he scanned the distant horison.

Suddenly, he slipped the telescope from his eye and shouted, 'We're saved! We're saved!! Here comes the *Titanic*!'

NO BIG DEAL

Hymie and Rebecca were desperately hanging on to the rails at the top of the sinking *Titanic*. Hymie was sobbing his heart out, when Rebecca said, 'Hymie, what are you crying about? It's not ours.'

IT COULD HAVE BEEN WORSE

There were two old Scotsmen were on board the *Titanic*. Halfway across the Atlantic a huge iceberg ripped the side of the ship. I don't have to tell you what happened after that.

An hour later the two old Scotsmen find themselves side by side in the ice-cold water in the dark night, shivering and clinging to a piece of wreckage which is slowly sinking.

One says, 'It could have been worse.'

The other says, 'It could have been worse? How could it ever have been worse?'

'We could have bought RETURN tickets.'

THAT SINKING FEELING

The Englishman was shouting hysterically as he hit the water after having jumped off the *Titanic*.

'I'm sinking, I'm sinking!!'

A German drifted by and said, 'And what are you sinking about?'

VENTRILOQUISTS

YOU TALKING TO ME?

Mike is enjoying a dop after a hard day at the office. (The Post Office.) There's a ventriloquist in the pub, loudly cracking Mike Schutte jokes. Mike's an easygoing kind of guy, as long as you don't push him too far.

The ventriloquist pushes him too far.

Gatvol, Mike jumps up from his barstool and shouts: 'If you don't stop making a fool out of me, I'm gonna moer you.'

The ventriloquist apologises profusely. Mike interrupts. 'I'm not talking to you, pal. I'm talking to that little poephol sitting on your lap.'

MAN OR MOUSE

Mike enters the Keg 'n Poacher in Brits, sits down and produces a mouse, a budgie and a tiny white piano from his pocket. 'Barman,' says Mike, 'check this out.'

The mouse walks over to the piano, starts hitting the keys with all its might as the budgie starts singing 'Hie' kommie Bokke.' The barman and barflies are amazed.

'If you give me all my dops for free for the rest of my life,' says Mike, 'you can have all three of them.'

The barman doesn't hesitate. 'Deal,' he says, as he starts pouring Mike a double Chivaz Regal.

Kallie, sitting in the corner with Jimmy, can't believe his eyes and walks over to Mike: 'What a poephol. You could've got millions for those animals man. You got rooked my ou.'

Mike laughs, hitting a thick middle finger against his forehead. 'Wat staan hier op my voorkop, huh? It's that stupid barman that's got rooked. That mouse is a blerrie ventriloquist.'

VIAGRA

IRON MAN

Warning! Be careful about mixing medications if you are taking Viagra. If you're on iron pills when you sluk the little blue pill, for example, you'll spin right around and point North.

LOG ON

Have you heard about the Viagra computer virus?
It turns your floppy disk into a hard drive.

BIG BUG

Did you hear about the oke who put Viagra in the fuel-tank of his VW Beetle?
It turned into an E-Type Jaguar.

DEEP THROAT

What happens if you get a Viagra pill stuck in your throat?
You get a stiff neck.

LAY-OFF

Did you hear about the strike at the Viagra factory?
The workers downed their tools.

UP AND AWAY

You know what's really amazing about Viagra?
It's the only product that doesn't get sent back to the factory if there's been a cock-up.

CASHING IN

There's good news and bad news about the wonder drug, Viagra. The bad news is that you have to be rich to be able to afford it. And the good news? If you're hard up, you don't need it.

BIG MAMBA

Did you hear about the black mamba that swallowed a jar of Viagra?
It ended up as a walking stick.

SUPERSEX

Still in love with life at the age of 83, Abie manages to persuade his doctor to put him on a course of Viagra.

It works.

Unable to believe his luck, Abie strips off his trousers and parades down the corridor of the old-age home, yelling, 'Super Sex! Super Sex!' at every female he sees.

Finally, one little old lady pricks up her ears, whips out her glasses, and takes a good look at Abie as he stands before her.

'Super Sex!' he yells, one more time.

And the little old lady says, 'Thanks. I'll take the soup.'

MEMBER OF THE BAR

What happens when you give Viagra to a lawyer?

He gets taller.

HARDCORE

These crooks hijacked a shipment of Viagra when it arrived at the Durban harbour.

The police are looking for four hardened criminals.

NO PROBLEM

This oke finally plucks up the courage to go and see his doctor about an embarrassing personal problem.

'Doctor,' he says, gazing down at the floor, 'you have to help me. I'm having a problem with my sexual performance.'

The doctor nods understandingly, and then he says: 'Relax. I've got great news for you. They've just come out with a wonder drug called Viagra. You take a small blue pill, and your hassles are history.'

The oke can't believe it. In fact, the oke doesn't believe it. There's only one way to find out. So the doctor does all the necessary tests, and then he gives the oke a prescription and sends him on his way.

A couple of months later, the doctor runs into his patient on the street. 'Doctor, doctor!' exclaims the man excitedly, 'I've got to thank you! This drug is a miracle! It's wonderful!'

'Well, I'm glad to hear that,' beams the physician. 'And what does your wife think about it?'

'Wife?' asks the man, 'I haven't been home yet.'

DOMESTIC BLISS

This oke finally scores his long-awaited prescription for Viagra, and goes home to get ready for the Big Event. He calls his wife on her cell. 'I'll be home in an hour,' she says. Perfect. The oke pops his pill, because the doctor told him to take it an hour in advance. The hour passes. His wife calls.

'This traffic is terrible!' she says. 'I won't be home for another forty-five minutes.'

Gritting his teeth with frustration, the guy phones his doctor. 'What should I do?' he asks.

'Hmmm,' says the doctor, 'it would be a shame to waste it. Do you have a housekeeper around?'

'Yes,' replies the man.

'Well,' says the doctor, 'I don't want to cause any problems, but why don't you, you know, I mean, you and the housekeeper ...'

'You must be crazy!' replies the man. 'Since when do I need Viagra with the housekeeper?'

BUYING SPREE

What's the difference between an Italian wife and a Jewish wife?

An Italian wife tells her husband to buy Viagra, a Jewish wife tells her husband to buy Pfizer.

(You don't get it? Pfizer is the company that makes Viagra.)

OFF HER ROCKER

Bored with the genteel pace of life at the Sunny Acres Retirement Home, Abie persuades his doctor to put him on a course of Old Man's Smarties. He pops his Viagra as instructed. Lo and behold! He feels like a new man. Then he feels like a new woman.

There isn't one around, so old Mrs Finklestein, sitting in her rocking chair in the Bingo Room, will simply have to do.

'Joyce,' says Abie, whispering in the old lady's ear, 'have I got a proposition for you.'

Joyce listens up, setting the volume on her hearing-aid to 11.

'For R20,' says Abie, 'I'll have sex with you on that rocking-chair. For R50, I'll have sex with you on that sofa over there. And for R100, I'll take you back to my room, light a few candles, and treat you to an evening of passion and romance that you'll never forget.'

Mrs Finkelstein thinks about it for a while. Then she reaches into her handbag and pulls out a R100 note.

'Aha,' says Abie, 'you want to spend the night in my room?'

'No,' says the old lady. 'I want five times in the rocker.'

EASY DOES IT

Forget about Viagra. There's a revolutionary new medication on the market. It's not just an aphrodisiac; it's also a laxative. Remember to ask for it by name.

Easy Come, Easy Go.

VRYSTAAT

IT'S TEN O'CLOCK

In America they say, 'It's 10 o'clock ... do you know where your children are?'

In England they say, 'It's 10 o'clock ... do you know where your wife is?'

In France they say, 'It's 10 o'clock … do you know where your husband is?'

In Bloemfontein they say, 'It's 10 o'clock … do you know what time it is?'

MY OTHER CAR IS A TRACTOR

Why are Fiat Unos so popular in the Free State?

Because you can drive them with an elbow out of each window.

DRY SPELL

'It's so dry in the Free State,' said Vaal Gys, 'that all the babies are on powder milk. Ja. We don't dry them, we just dust them off.'

NOG YS!

Die Vrystaatse ondersteuners kuier die trein stukkend op pad Potch toe vir 'n Curriebekerwedstryd teen die Mielie-boere in die vroeë vyftigs. Naderhand is die ys op, en die kondukteur word opgekommandeer om nog ys te loop haal.

Die derde kas Klippies sneuwel kort duskant Bothaville, en kort-kort skree die manne, 'Meneer die conducter, bring nog ys!' Die kondukteur maak so, en maak weer en weer so.

Die trein fluit skril toe dit Potch se stasie binnestoom, en weer skree die manne, 'Nog ys!'

Die kondukteur stap die kompartement binne met twee blokkies ys in 'n glas. 'Manne', sê hy, 'dis die laaste batch. Nog een stukkie ys dan gaan daai lyk ontdooi.'

WEDDINGS

VAN'S NEW SUIT

Van is wearing his brand-new suit one morning, as he pushes a wheelbarrow full of manure around his plot outside Brakpan. Frik jogs by, sees Van, and yells out, 'Hey Van, why are you wearing your brand new suit on the plot, hey?'

Van waves at him and says, 'Man, I'm getting married this afternoon, but I've got to manure my lawn first. So I thought I'd save a bit of time by putting my suit on early. Then I only have to change my vest and my underpants, and I'm ready for the wedding.'

MIK

'n Vrou wat dink die pad na 'n man se hart is deur sy maag, mik 'n bietjie hoog.

TROULIED

Watter lied word gespeel as man en vrou trou?
Die troumars
As twee moffies trou?
Aandlied van die voëls.
As twee vrouens trou?
Die padda wou gaan opsit …

RSVP

How does a Jewish wedding guest interpret the RSVP on an invitation card?

'Remember Send Vedding Presents.'

ORGANISASIE

Die oom en tannie sit op die stoep van hulle huisie in die aftreeoord en bespreek almal wat daar verbyloop. Daar stap 'n ou oom en sy vrou verby.

'Ek hoor hy't sy protestantklier laat uithaal,' sê die oom.

'Ja, en sy't glo haar vrolike dele laat verwyder,' sê die tannie.

'Nou hoe gaan hulle dan 'n organisasie bereik?' vra die oom.

HERE COMES THE BRIDE

Scientists have discovered an amazing substance that is capable of reducing a woman's sex-drive by up to 90 %.

It's called wedding cake.

THE BIG PICTURE

It's their first night together for the deliriously happy newlyweds. The new bride steps out of the bathroom, freshly showered and wearing her fluffy pink robe.

The proud husband says, 'My dear, we are married now, you can open your robe.'

So she opens her robe. The new husband is momentarily speechless.

'Oh, oh, aaaahhh,' he exclaims, 'you are so beautiful! Let me take your picture.'

'MY picture?' asks the bride. 'Like this? What for?'

'So I can carry your beauty next to my heart forever,' he says.

The new bride smiles for the camera. Her husband snaps the shutter, and then he heads into the bathroom to shower. He comes out wearing his fluffy blue robe. 'Why are you wearing a robe?' asks his wife. 'We're married now, remember?'

So he opens his robe. She stares at him, momentarily speechless. Then she runs off.

'Where are you going?' he asks.

'To get the camera,' she says. 'I want to take a picture!'

'So you can carry my beauty next to your heart forever?' he asks, boldly striking a pose.

'No,' she answers. 'So I can get it ENLARGED!'

I KNEW YOU WOULD SAY THAT

Hier's 'n lekker storie om jou gehoor tydens 'n huweliks-onthaal mee uit te vang. Jy kan die grap inkleur nes dit jou pas.

Suzie kry 'n date met 'n Engelse rugbyspeler tydens die Britse Leeus se toer in Suid-Afrika. Suzie is mal oor die ou, maar sy't 'n probleem: sy kan glad nie Engels praat nie.

'Moenie worry nie,' sê haar ma, 'ek kan ook nie die rooitaal praat nie, maar ek het 'n manier ontdek om die probleem te bowe te kom. Wat die Engelsman ookal vir jou sê, sê net elke keer "I knew you would say that." Op die manier kan jy nie verkeerd gaan nie. In elk geval sal die Engelsman net wil vry, so dis nie nodig om meer as dit te sê nie.'

Suzie gaan staan voor die spieël en sy oefen 'I knew you would say that' miljoen keer oor. Toe sy seker is sy het dit, lui die voordeurklokkie en daar staan die Engelsman. Hy kyk die sexy Suzie so op en af en sê, 'You look absolutely divine', en Suzie sê in perfekte Engels, 'I knew you would say that.'

Haar ma smile trots, knipoog vir Suzie en sy en die Leeu is daar weg. Later op die dansbaan sak die Engelsman se hand soepel van Suzie se rug af na haar been tot net onderkant haar kort minirokkie. 'I have never touched anything softer in my entire life', sê die Engelsman.

Suzie smile sexy en sê, 'I knew you would say that.'

Nog 'n rukkie later skuif die Engelsman se hand saggies boontoe, die slag tot op haar boudjies. Hy streel hulle so saffies en sê, 'Bill Gates will only discover the true meaning of software once he's felt what I'm feeling right now.'

Suzie druk haar kop liefderyk teen die Engelsman se skouer en sê, 'I knew you would say that.' En so gaan dit aan, al verder, of is dit nou al nader ... en die Engelsman raak al speelser, en uiteindelik sit hy sy hand ...'

Die grapverteller handhaaf so paar sekondes stilte, asof hy dit ernstig oorweeg of hy met die grap moet voortgaan of nie. Dan sê hy:

'Luister mense, dis 'n briljante joke die, maar hy's 'n bietjie dicey. Ek glo nie ek moet voortgaan nie. Wat dink julle?'

As jy 'n lekker gehoor het gaan hulle skree:

'Nee man, gaan aan, vertel!'
En dis wanneer jy sê: 'I knew you would say that!'

GETTING TO KNOW YOU

It was lust at first sight for the good-looking young couple who met on the dance floor of the disco. Love followed a little while later, and under its dizzy spell, he held her in his arms and said: 'Will you marry me?'

'Marry you?' she laughed over the thump-thump-thump of disco music. 'But I don't even know you!'

He looked her in the eyes.

'Don't you see?" he said. 'That's exactly the point. We don't need to know anything about each other right now, except that we're madly in love. We can learn everything else as we can go along.'

It was the craziest, most romantic idea either of them had ever considered. The very next day, they got married at the registry office, and off they went to a tropical island for their honeymoon. It was, of course, sheer bliss.

One morning, the newlyweds were lying by the pool, soaking up the sun. He got up off of his towel, climbed up to the 10-meter board and did a perfect swallow dive, followed by three rotations in jack-knife position. He straightened out and cut the water like a knife.

After a few more demonstrations, he came back and lay down on the towel. 'That was incredible!' she said.

'Well,' he shrugged, 'I used to be an Olympic diving champion.' He kissed her lovingly on the cheek.

'You see, I told you we'd learn more about ourselves as we went along.'

She got up, jumped in the pool, and started doing laps. After about 30 laps she climbed back out and lay down on her towel, hardly out of breath.

'That was incredible!' he said. 'Were you an Olympic endurance swimmer, by any chance?'

'No,' she answered. 'I was a hooker in Venice, and I worked both sides of the canal.'

WHO WEARS THE PANTS?

The married couple retire to their hotel room on their wedding night. The man, who is much larger than the petite woman, takes off his pants and throws them over to his wife, saying, 'Put these on.'

The woman replies, 'But they're much too big for me!'

'Put them on anyway,' orders the man.

She puts them on. They fall to the floor.

'I can't fit into these!' she complains.

'That's right,' says the man. 'So just remember who wears the pants in this relationship.'

The woman then takes off her panties. She throws over to her husband. 'Put these on,' she says.

He holds them in his hands. 'I can't get into these!' he says.

'That's right,' replies his wife. 'And you won't be able to in the future unless you change your attitude!'

AGSTE MAN

Tolla was vir die soveelste keer in sy lewe seremonie-meester by 'n troue. Hy begin toe so:

'Ek voel vandag soos Elizabeth Taylor se agtste man. Ek weet wat om te sê, ek weet hoe om dit te sê, maar ek weet wragtag nie hoe om dit interessant te maak nie.'

STICKY SITUATION

Young Koos and his bride Sannietjie, having limited funds, returned to her parents after the wedding for their honeymoon night.

Next morning, the family gathered for breakfast and lunch without them.

As the family sat down to supper that night, the head of the household asked his wife and their eight-year-old son, 'Have any of you seen the newlyweds?'

The mother replied that she had not seen Koos and Sannietjie since the previous day.

The bride's kleinboet replied that he had last seen Koos at about ten o'clock the previous night, when he had stuck his head out of the door and ask him if he knew where there was any Vaseline.

The parents, a little embarrassed, waited for the rest of the story.

'Well?' the father finally said, as the boy continued eating.

'Oh,' said the boy. 'I couldn't find any Vaseline, so I gave him my model airplane glue.'

WEDDING TOASTS

I was once a guest at a wedding that was proceeding rather calmly and formally, until the best man stood up and uttered one word that shocked the entire reception hall into silence.

That word was 'Fornication'.

After a dramatic pause, the best man continued: 'Fornication like this, we need the very best champagne!'

Of course, we got it, and the rest of the reception was a riot. Here are a bunch of other toasts that are guaranteed to give any wedding day that extra touch of sparkle:

To the groom: Here's to all the kisses you've snatched … and vice versa!

As you slide down the banister of life, may the splinters never point the wrong way.

Here's to you and yours, and to mine and ours.
And if mine and ours
Ever come across to you and yours,
I hope you and yours will do
As much for mine and ours
As mine and ours have done
For you and yours!

May your arguments be as long-lived as your New Year's resolutions.

Here's to the girl with the long blonde hair,
She made 'em laugh, she made 'em stare.
She lost her cherry, but that's no sin,
'Cause she still got the box that the cherry came in!

No man is complete until he is married – then he's finished!

Here's to you as good as you are,
Here's to me as bad as I am.
As bad as I am, as good as you are,
I'm as good as you are, as bad as I am!

To the ships of our seas, and the women of our land,
May the former be well captained and the latter be well manned.

A piece of cowboy advice: 'There's two theories to arguing with a woman. Neither one works.'

May the woman you marry be the love of your life,
And may the man that she marries be the love of your wife!

Here's to you, here's to me,
May we never disagree.
But if we do, the hell with you,
Here's to me!

Here's to you and here's to me,
And here's to love and laughter,
I'll be true as long as you,
But not a minute after.

Here's to the bride and mother-in-laws;
Here's to the groom and father-in-laws;

Here's to the sisters and brother-in-laws;
Here's to the brothers and sister-in-laws;
Here's to good friends and friend-in-laws;
May none of them need an attorney-at-law!

Here's to you two from we two, for we two hope you two like we two as much as we two like you two, but if you two don't like we two as much as we two like you two then to hell with you two and here's to we two!

May all your children have wealthy parents!

Here's to your health if your blood's good,
And here's to your blood if your health's good,
Here's to your blood and here's to your health,
And here's to your bloody good health.

Perchance to dream, perchance is right, you won't get a chance to dream tonight.

I'd rather be with the people here today, than with the nicest people in the world!

Here's to today. Here's to tonight. We shot the stork, so it's allright.

I've drunk to your health in taverns, I've drunk to your health in my home.
I've drunk to your health so many damn times, I've almost ruined my own.

To the groom: now that you are a married man, forget all your mistakes.
No sense two people remembering the same thing!

Remember, the key to a long and happy marriage is to always say those three little words: 'You're right, dear!'

WINNIE

IRON LADY

Winnie Madikizela-Mandela was on a visit to the United Kingdom. While there, she was invited to a cocktail party which was to be attended by Margaret Thatcher. When Winnie saw the ex-Prime Minister on the other side of the room, she barged past everyone, causing several drinks to be spilled on the way.

Finally, she stood brazenly in front of Maggie and declared, 'I hear they call you the Iron Lady.'

'I have been referred to by that name, yes,' replied Maggie. 'And who, may I ask, are you?'

'I am the Iron Lady of South Africa!' bragged Winnie, waving her fist in the air.

'I see,' replied Maggie, 'and for whom do you iron?'

HARD LABOUR

The judge asked Winnie what she wanted from the divorce.

'I want half,' said Winnie.

So the judge gave her 13 years and six months.

EAU DE WINNIE

What's Winnie's latest perfume range?

Light My Tyre.

WORKERS

LUNCHTIME

There were these three construction workers. One was Mexican, one was English, and the other was Mike Schutte. They were sitting on the scaffolding of their building one day, and they were about to tuck into their lunch.

The Mexican looked in his lunchbox and said, 'A taco. Man, if I get a taco one more time I'm going to jump off this building!' The Englishman looked in his lunchbox and said, 'Crumpets. You know, if I get crumpets one more time I'm going to jump off this building!'

Then Mike Schutte looked in his lunchbox and said, 'Vetkoek. Ek sweer, as ek weer 'n keer vetkoek kry, spring ek van hierdie gebou af. Wragtig!'

The next day they all got the same lunch. So they all jumped off the building. Kaput.

Later, their wives get together to reflect on this terrible tragedy. The Mexican's wife says, 'If he had just told me he didn't want tacos, I would have made him something different.'

The English guy's wife says, 'If he had only told me he didn't want crumpets, I would gladly have made him something else.'

Then Mike Schutte's wife says: 'I don't understand. He made his own lunch.'

KNOCKING-OFF

There were these three okes who worked in a factory. One was Van, the other was Vusi, and the third was Piet. One day Van says, 'Have you okes noticed how the boss is leaving work a little earlier every day?'

The other okes nod. They've noticed. Piet says, 'I've got an idea, manne – next time we see the boss knocking off early, let's knock off early too.'

They agree. Next day, the boss leaves his office an hour early. So Piet goes home and watches television. Vusi goes home and has a couple of beers. Van goes home, walks into his bedroom, and sees the boss in bed with his wife. Without making a sound, Van closes the door and leaves.

Back at the factory the next day, the okes start talking about knocking off early again. 'No ways,' says Van.

'Why not?' ask Piet and Vusi.

'Because yesterday I almost got caught, man!'

WORK FOR ALL

Madiba is addressing a Cosatu gathering. 'My friends,' he booms, 'it is you, the workers, and you alone, who have made this country what it is!'

A worker at the back pipes up: 'Mister President! It is not fair to blame only us. What about the criminals, the hijackers and the rapists?'

HAMMER AND TONGS

Kallie and Mike are hard at work on their latest brilliant project. Building a house. Mike is busy mixing cement, while Kallie is hard at work putting wooden panels in place.

Kallie picks up a nail, looks at it, and hammers it in. He picks up another nail, looks at it, and throws it away. Picks one up, hammers it in. Picks another, throws it away.

Mike watches this for a while, and then yells, 'Hey Kallie, why are you throwing half those nails away?'

'Because those ones were pointed on the wrong end!' he replies.

Mike shakes his head. Sometimes he can't believe how stupid his buddy is.

'You idiot!' he says. 'Those are for the other side of the house!'

YOUR MOMMA!

SO FAT

Your momma's so fat, she had to have her ears pierced by harpoon.

Your momma's so fat, she needs a hula hoop to keep up her socks.

Your momma's so fat, she sets off car alarms when she runs.

Your momma's so fat, she uses the Equator for a belt.

Your momma's so fat, she has to take her bath in the Vaal Dam.

Your momma's so fat, she went skydiving and caused a total eclipse of the sun.

Your momma's so fat, I&J use her pantyhose to catch tuna.

Your momma's so fat, when she stood still at the airport, they painted a flag on her butt.

Your momma's so fat, when she fell in love she broke it.

Your momma's so fat, she had her baby pictures taken by satellite.

Your momma's so fat, she went to the movies and sat next to everyone.

Your momma's so fat, she's on both sides of your family.

Your momma's so fat, they tie a rope around her shoulders and drag her through a tunnel when they want to clean it.

Your momma's so fat, when she bungee jumps she brings down the bridge.

Your momma's so fat, when her beeper went off, they thought she was backing up.

Your momma's so fat, she shows up on radar.

Your momma's so fat, her cereal bowl came with a lifeguard.

Your momma's so fat, they held a circus inside her dress.

Your momma's so fat, when the police showed her a picture of her feet, she couldn't identify them.

Your momma's so fat, she's got to iron her pants on the driveway.

Your momma's so fat, she fell and got stuck in the Grand Canyon.

Your momma's so fat, the National Weather Agency has to assign names to her farts.

Your momma's so fat, I swerved to miss her but ran out of petrol.

SO STUPID

Your momma's so stupid, she sold her car for petrol money.

Your momma's so stupid, when I asked her to buy me a colour TV she asked, 'What colour?'

Your momma's so dumb, she locked herself in a motorcycle.

Your momma's so dumb, she put ice cubes in the freezer to keep the refrigerator cold.

Your momma's so stupid, she sits on the TV, and watches the couch.

Your momma's so stupid, when she missed the number 44 bus, she took the number 22 twice instead.

SO UGLY

Your momma's so ugly, she looked out of the window and got arrested for mooning.

Your momma's so ugly, they filmed 'Gorillas in the Mist' in her shower.

SO OLD

Your momma's so old, that when God said 'Let there be light', she hit the switch.

Your momma's so old, that when she was in school there was no history class.

Your momma's so old, her birth certificate says 'Expired' on it.

Your momma's so old, her birth certificate is in Roman numerals.

SO POOR

Your momma's so poor, when I saw her kicking a can down the street, I asked her what she was doing, and she said, 'Moving'.

Your momma's so poor, when she goes to KFC, she has to lick other people's fingers.

Your momma's so poor, your family ate cereal with a fork to save milk.

ZOOS

TRUNK CALL

Mike Schutte goes to the zoo to see the elephants. But he can't see them anywhere. So he calls the zookeeper over and he says, 'Hey! Where are the elephants?'

The zookeeper shrugs, 'They're inside the elephant house, making love.'

Mike looks at the brown paper bag in his hand, and he says, 'Do you think they'll come out if I offer them a peanut?'

And the zookeeper says: 'I don't know, Meneer. Would YOU?'

THIS LITTLE PIGGIE

Mike is driving down the road in Potgietersrus, minding his own business. Suddenly, he sees a baby warthog standing in the middle of a mealie-field. Mike slams on the brakes, rushes over, and gently carries the frightened animal to his car.

A little while later, Mike is stopped by a cop. The cop looks in the passenger seat and says, 'Hey, what are you doing with this animal in your car?'

Mike shrugs and says, 'I found him in the middle of a mealie-field in Potgietersrus.'

'I don't care where you found him,' the cop barks. 'I want you to take this blerrie warthog to the zoo, and I mean IMMEDIATELY!'

Mike says okay, and he zooms off. The next day, the same cop sees Mike driving down the same road. He pulls him over and looks in the passenger seat. Same warthog. The cop explodes with fury.

'MAN, I THOUGHT I TOLD YOU TO TAKE THIS ANIMAL TO THE BLERRIE ZOO!'

Mike looks at the cop. 'I did take him to the zoo,' he says. 'We had such a lekker time that I'm taking him to the rugby now.'

POOR TASTE

A lion in the Jo'burg zoo was lying in its quarters, lazily licking its arse under the midday sun.

'What an docile old animal,' said a visitor to the zoo keeper.

'No ways!' said the zookeeper. 'It's a very aggressive animal. In fact, just a few moments ago it dragged an Aussie tourist into the cage and completely devoured him.'

'So why is it just lying there licking its arse then?' asked the visitor.

'Poor thing is trying to get the taste out of his mouth,' said the keeper.

ZOOMA

What do you call a female politician who's in charge of a zoo?

A Zooma.

ZUMA

DR ZUMA

There once was a doctor named Zuma
Who started a terrible rumour
That if you should smoke
After having a poke
All your bodily parts would go 'WOEMMMAAA!'

There once was a sickly old puma
Who lived on his own in the zooma
The keeper arrived
And said, 'You're alive!
But wait till you meet Dr Zuma.'

BIG FAT ZERO

What does 'Zuma' stand for?
Zero Understanding of Medical Affairs.

BABY BOOM

Madiba and Dr Zuma are on their way to visit a hospital in Bapsfontein. 'I wonder if there were any great men born in this town?' wonders Madiba.

'Aikona,' says Dr Zuma. 'Only babies.'

CRAZY WORLD

Graffiti teen 'n muur in Kaapstad:
God loves Dr. Zuma.
En daaronder:
God loves Winnie Mandela.
En daaronder:
The Gods Must Be Crazy.

HORSES FOR COURSES

Dr. Zuma en Minister Alfred Nzo word genooi om tydens 'n ou-Kaapstad herdenkingsdag saam op 'n perd deur die Moederstad se strate te ry as deel van 'n hele optog.

Hulle stop by Van Riebeeck se standbeeld om toesprake te lewer, en maak die perde aan 'n paal vas tussen 'n klompie ander perde. Na die verrigtinge stap Dr Zuma van perd na perd, terwyl sy elkeen se stert oplig.

'Wat maak djy?' vra Alfred Nzo.

'Ek soek onse perd,' sê Dr Zuma.

Minister Nzo frons en vra, 'Nou vir wat soek djy vir hom so?'

Dr Zuma sê, 'Onse perd hy es anders as die ander perde. Toe ons vanmôre so deur Adderleystraat ry toe hoor ek iemand sê, 'Check daai perd met die twee poepholle.'

WHERE THERE'S SMOKE, THERE'S FIRE

Having take a unilateral decision to ban smoking in public places, Dr Zuma sent one of her top officials to conduct a street survey on the subject. Armed with a questionnaire, he took to the streets of Gauteng. Here is his report, exclusive to this book:

OFFICIAL: Excuse me, sir, do you smoke?
MAN: No, but I used to.
OFFICIAL: What made you give up?
MAN: I got fired for smoking on the job.
OFFICIAL: And what line of work are you in, sir?
MAN: I'm a petrol-station attendant.

OFFICIAL: Mevrou, hoe oud is u?
OLD LADY: Ses-en-taggentag.
OFFICIAL: Rook u?
OLD LADY: Ja, ek rook.
OFFICIAL: Trek u die rook in?
OLD LADY: Ja, maar gelukkig blaas ek nie weer uit nie.
OFFICIAL: En u, jong dame?
YOUNG LADY: Ek rook ook.
OFFICIAL: U trek seker nie in nie?
YOUNG LADY: Nee, maar ek trek graag uit!

OFFICIAL: Aa, Mike Schutte. Do you smoke, Mike?
MIKE: I smoke, ja. Only packets of twenties.
OFFICIAL: Why only twenties?
MIKE: 'Cause thirties are too strong. In fact, I'm gonna smoke a cigarette right in front of you, so you can tell your Doctor Zuma she's not gonna stop me.
            (Mike puts a cigarette in his mouth and tries to light a match. The match doesn't light. He tries another and another, still it won't light. Finally he only has one match left. He strikes it, and it works. He lights his cigarette, and puts the burnt match back into the match box.)
OFFICIAL: Why keep the burnt match, Mike?
MIKE: 'Cause it's the only one that works!

OFFICIAL: Excuse me, sir! I'm conducting a survey for the Department of Health. Do you smoke?

MAN: Do I smoke? Do I SMOKE? I'll have you know that I've never bought a cigarette in my life.

OFFICIAL: I see. So you're strongly opposed to smoking, then.

MAN: No, I'm just strongly opposed to buying my own cigarettes. You wouldn't happen to have a Gunston Plain on you, by any chance?

OFFICIAL: Sorry, no.

OFFICIAL: Sir! Sir! Do you mind if I ask you a question?

YUPPIE: Go ahead.

OFFICIAL: I was just wondering what you felt about smoking.

YUPPIE: It's a filthy, disgusting habit.

OFFICIAL: I see. And what is your attitude towards people who use snuff?

YUPPIE: They're a danger to society. I believe they should be locked up without the option of a fine.

OFFICIAL: But I thought I saw you using snuff only a couple of minutes ago.

YUPPIE: Snuff? Me? You must be crazy. That was just cocaine.

OFFICIAL: Verskoon my juffrou, rook u?

JUFFROU: Natuurlik ja, dink jy ek stink altyd so?

OFFICIAL: Weet u kêrel u rook?

JUFFROU: Nee, maar hy weet ek stink.

OFFICIAL: Dink u mense moet in openbare plekke rook?

JUFFROU: Natuurlik ja, dan kan niemand ruik ek stink nie.

OFFICIAL: Doen u iets om u asem beter te laat ruik?

JUFFROU: Ja, ek borsel my tande.

OFFICIAL: Met Colgate?

JUFFROU: Nee, met Klipdrift.

OFFICIAL: Ah, here's a little boy. How old are you, son?

YOUNG BOY: Ten.

OFFICIAL: You don't smoke, do you?

YOUNG BOY: No, but my oupa is smoking right now.

OFFICIAL: Where's your oupa?

YOUNG BOY: In the crematorium.

OFFICIAL: Excuse me, constable, do you smoke?

CONSTABLE: Ja, I have to smoke.

OFFICIAL: You have to smoke?

CONSTABLE: Ja, I'm a dagga tester for the Police.

OFFICIAL: I'm sure Dr Zuma wouldn't like that.

CONSTABLE: Well, if you want to know the truth, I pass her a zol every now and again.

OFFICIAL: What? You want to tell me Dr Zuma smokes dagga?

CONSTABLE: No, I didn't say that. I just know that she likes staying in touch with the grassroots of politics.

OFFICIAL: Aaah, here comes Prof. Chris Barnard, our heart-transplant pioneer. Good morning, Professor. You seem to be in a great hurry.

PROF. CHRIS: Ja man, I've just implanted a pacemaker in a man's chest, and I'm on my way to go and do the next one.

OFFICIAL: Tell me Prof. do you smoke?

PROF CHRIS: Unfortunately I do.

OFFICIAL: Can I see what you smoke?
(The Prof. searches his pockets.)

PROF CHRIS: Here, let me see ... oh, here it is ...
(He looks at the box and frowns.)

PROF CHRIS: Now what blerrie cigarettes are these? ... PACEMAKER? PACEMAKER?? PACE-MAKER??! Oh shit, don't tell me I implanted my packet of Lex ... wragtag!!! Mariuuuuus!! We did it again!!!

OFFICIAL:	Aaah, here's Jimmy Abbott. Do you smoke?
JIMMY:	Ja, I smoke.
OFFICIAL:	But why are you so fat then?
JIMMY:	'Cause I never exhale.
OFFICIAL:	Good day, sir. Do you smoke?
SIR:	Only with very good reason.
OFFICIAL:	And what is your reason for smoking, sir?
SIR:	It annoys the hell out of Dr Zuma.

SLAPSTICK

I don't know why people keep saying all these nasty things about Dr Zuma. As far as I'm concerned, she does the work of two men. Laurel and Hardy.

SCHUSTER UNPLUGGED!

A PORTRAIT OF THE ARTIST AS A YOUNG OKE

In many ways I had a wonderful life as a child. I grew up in the Orange Free State. I don't know why they called it that – there's no oranges, nothing is free and it's in a terrible state. Still, I love the place.

Okay, we were poor – there was no place outside to hang our nappies so my mom had to hang them inside the house. It made the most beautiful rainbow in the kitchen. Our neighbours called us the Rainbow Nation long before the New South Africa.

My brother and I were twins. There was no money, so when we were born my mom said, 'Let's drown the ugly one.' That's how I learnt to swim. I was really ugly. My mom carried me upside down for three years before she realised which side was up. She didn't push the pram; she pulled it.

As a teenager I had these ugly pimples on my face. Thousands of them. One day I fell asleep in the school library and when I woke up a blind oke was busy reading my face.

I was very thin. My school blazer only had one stripe. When I stuck my tongue out they thought I was a zip. One day when I bent forward my ruggraat cut the elastic of my underpants.

My dad was very strict. We got a hiding every day. We begged him to move to us all to Transvaal, 'cause they only get hidings on Saturdays. My dad worked in a shoe factory. He made shoes from bananas. They called them slippers.

My mom was a plumber. They called her a tap dancer. My dad walked me to school every morning. It was handy 'cause we were in the same class. My dad never learnt to drive a car. He didn't have to because we had an automatic.

Our favourite pastime was playing snakes and ladders on my grandma's varicose veins. My grandma worked for Boswell and Wilkie circus for a few years. They put a handkerchief behind her and she would bend over backwards and pick it up with her teeth. For an encore she picked up her teeth. She tried to commit suicide once. She put the revolver against her left breast and tried to shoot herself in the heart. So she shot off her knee-cap.

My grandpa was a stuntman in Hollywood, so we never saw much of him. With one foot on each horse he did fine, until he came to a fork in the road one day. Then we saw even less of him.

I started playing rugby at a very young age. I started playing for the first team but systematically worked my way into the third team. Our rugby jerseys were a dark green with a yellow stripe across the breast. There was no money for a rugby jersey so I put on my dark green school jersey and went to lie on a freshly painted loading zone.

My first position was scrumhalf, but I soon developed an inferiority complex – every time the scrum went down I thought they were skinnering about me. So they moved me to prop. I played tighthead. One day an oke tackled me with a stiff arm, and then I played loosehead. I didn't do very well. The captain said I wasn't a prop's arse. The vice-captain made me feel better when he said, 'You're wrong – he is.'

They moved me to lock. I was very short so I only jumped in the short lineouts. One day a hooker hit my one front tooth clean out of my mouth. I went down on my knees looking for it. The ref asked, 'What are you doing?' I said, 'I'm looking for my tooth.'

'Why do you want your tooth?' he asked. I said, 'I'd like to keep it for a souvenir, it was a moeruvva good punch.'

We never won a single game. Every time the captain said, 'Take up your positions', we went to stand behind the posts. One day I ran into the kitchen and shouted, 'Ma, I've just scored a try!' My mom said, 'Fantastic, who won?' I said, 'I don't know, they're still playing.'

Nowadays I go to every single rugby match at Ellis Park. I never pay to go in: I just walk in back to front and they think I'm going out. I always sit next to this oke from Bez Valley, and his wife. Last Saturday he was alone, so I asked, 'Where's your wife?' He said, 'My wife died.'

I said, 'Well, why didn't you give her ticket to one of your friends?' He said, 'They've all gone to the funeral.'

HOW I GOT INTO SHOWBIZ

As a student at the University of the Free State many years ago, I used to play rugby to take my mind off my studies. In fact, I was so good at taking my mind off my studies, that I made it into the university's first rugby side, popularly known as the Shimlas. Okay, we weren't exactly the Amabokkebokke, but we did go out of our way to play the game to the best of our ability.

On one memorable occasion, we went as far out of our way as Italy, where we toured with great success and even played a match against the Italian international side. It was at a party after this match that I got my first real taste of the Big Time. Not in rugby, but in showbiz.

I was telling the following story to the partygoers, when a reporter from the Bloemfontein newspaper, *Die Volksblad*, took my picture and sent it back home, along with a comment that I should think of giving up rugby and becoming an entertainer instead. I took the guy's advice, and the story has been a favourite of mine ever since.

Here it is:

I'LL BE FRANK WITH YOU

At the height of the apartheid years, the world's greatest entertainer, Frank Sinatra, was invited to perform a series of concerts in South Africa. The money was good and the wildlife sounded exciting, so Frank thought, 'To hell with politics, to hell with the blacklist. I'm going to do this my way. I'm going to South Africa.'

Just a week before he was due to fly out, however, Frank received an invitation to appear in Las Vegas at triple the fee. Frank was in a quandary, until he remembered that he had an Italian cousin who could have passed for his twin brother in the right light. Or even the wrong light. Who was going to know the difference, all the way down there at the bottom end of Africa?

Frank phoned up his cousin, who went by the name of Enrico Oechielie, and said, 'Hey couz, how would you like to earn yourself one million dollars?'

'One million dollars!' gasped Enrico. 'Who do you want me to bump off, Frankie?'

'No one,' sighed Frank. 'It's not that kind of job. All you gotta do is go to South Africa and pretend to be me. You already look like me, so all you gotta do is talk like me and sing like me for a coupla days. Got that?'

'Sure Frankie!' said Enrico. 'For you and a million dollars, I do anything. But I got a just two questions.'

'Shoot.'

'Shoot? I thought you said it's a not that kind of a ...'

'I mean, fire away. I mean ... you know what I mean.'

'Sure, Frankie,' said Enrico, slowly sliding his weapon back into its holster. 'My first question is, well, you are the romantic singer, Frankie, and I have always been the opera singer. No way I can-a sing like Frank Sinatra. So how are the people going to believe I am you when I am up there on the stage pretending to be you?'

'Come off it, couz,' said Frank. 'Those South Africans haven't had an international entertainer of format on their soil for years. They wouldn't know Pavarotti from Elvis Presley. Just get up there and sing. As long as you look like me, they'll be happy. What's your second question?'

'Uh, Frankie, where the heck is this South Africa place?'

It wasn't long before Enrico discovered the answer to that one. Stepping off the plane at Jan Smuts Airport, he was greeted by thousands of wildly cheering fans, delighted to have a real star within their reach at last.

'Frankie! Frankie! Frankie!' they chanted, as the concert

promoter rushed forward to shake Frankie's hand and welcome him to the Republic. Overwhelmed by the reception, Enrico blew kisses to the crowd and returned their fervent waves. Then he suddenly thought to himself, 'Wait a second. These people aren't cheering and waving at me. They're cheering and waving at Frank Bloody Sinatra!'

A rush of anger went to Enrico's head, and he told the promoter in no uncertain terms, 'Listen, there's a been a big mistake. I'm-a not-a Frank Sinatra. I just a look like him. I am-a the famous Italian opera singer, Enrico Oechielie!'

To prove his point, Enrico started singing an aria – 'La donna e' Mobile'. Of course, the promoter thought Frankie was just having a bit of fun, so he roared with laughter, slapped Enrico on the back, and herded the famous entertainer towards his limousine.

As he stepped through the doors of the International Arrivals hall, the excited crowd started chanting again: 'We want Frank! We want Frank! We want Frank!'

Enrico clenched his fists, glared at the fans through his sunglasses, and roared, 'I am-a not a Frank Sinatra! I am-a Enrico Oechielie, the famous Italian opera singer!'

To prove his point, he burst into a short aria, 'Funiculi Funicula'. The crowd went ballistic, believing they had just been treated to a spontaneous rendition of Frankie's latest hit single. Enrico shrugged, climbed into the limo, and headed for his hotel.

At Sun City, Enrico was ushered into reception, where Sol and the entire hotel staff welcomed him with a spirited rendition of Shoshaloza. Sol rushed over to Enrico, plonked a traditional Zulu grass hat on his head, wrapped a leopard skin around his shoulders, thrust a knobkierie into his right hand and said, 'Frank! Old buddy! Welcome to South Africa.'

Enrico worked himself free from Sol's embrace and said: 'I am-a telling everybody I am-a not-a Frank Sinatra! I am-a Enrico Oechielie, the famous Italian opera singer!'

To prove his point, he sang a heart-wrenching version of 'O Sole Mio'. Then he picked up his briefcase and said,'Now please, take-a me to my hotel room, I need-a to rest.'

So Enrico was ushered to his hotel room on the sixth floor of the main hotel at Sun City. As he walked through the doors of the room, he was faced with the sight of a stunningly beautiful, leggy, luscious, and totally nude blonde lying on the bed. Enrico froze in his tracks. His jaw dropped.

The blonde opened her arms and said, in the sexiest voice Enrico had ever heard: 'Hello, Frankie baby. I've been waiting for you.'

She beckoned at him, blew him a kiss, and continued: 'Come here, big boy. Let's do it MY way.'

Enrico looked at the blonde for a second, put his hand in the air and said, 'I am not-a ...'

He paused. Then, from the bottom of his heart and soul, he burst into loud and lusty song, 'Strangers in the night, la la la la la laa, lovers at first sight ...'

EK LAAIK MIKE

Me and ou Mike Schutte go back a long way. In fact, I knew him when he was still a featherweight.

Since then, of course, he's been a heavyweight champ, a professional wrestler, a debt collector, a comedian, a recording artist, and a TV and movie star. But I've always known him best as plain old, big old, loveable old Mike Schutte.

Here's what happened when I set out to interview him for a radio talkshow one day ...

ME: Mike Schutte. Is that your real name?

MIKE: No, it's Jakob Mike Schutte.

ME: Jacob with a 'k'.

MIKE: No, stupid. Jakob with a 'J'. Otherwise I would have been Kakob.

ME: Where do you come from originally, Mike?

MIKE: Jo'burg.

ME: Which part?

MIKE: All my parts.

ME: You married for the fourth time recently. How's it going?

MIKE: Fine thanks, yourself?

ME: I meant how's it going with your marriage?

MIKE: Okay, but I have to be honest. Sometimes I just don't understand my wife.

ME: What do you mean, Mike?

MIKE: Well, last night, Nellie says to me, 'Mike, take off my broeks.' I swear, I almost gave her a klap.

ME: Why was that?

MIKE: Because I wasn't wearing her blerrie broeks.

ME: So how was the honeymoon, hey Mike?

MIKE: Lekker. I was in Durban.

ME: Don't you mean, 'We were in Durban'?

MIKE: No. Only me. She's been in Durban already.

ME: Do you make a happy couple?

MIKE: Ja, but she's blerrie lazy. I got to do everything in the house. Wash the dishes, wash the washing, wash the floors.

ME: What about your wife?

MIKE: No man, she washes herself.

ME: What's your favourite pastime, Mike?

MIKE: Drive-in.

ME: You like the movies?

MIKE: No, I like the drive-in. Last night Nellie and I were just getting lekker hot in the car, and you know what she says?

ME: No, what did she say?

MIKE: She says 'Mike, do you wanna get in the back seat?'

ME: So?

MIKE: So I said 'No, I wanna stay here in front with you.'

ME: Let's talk about your boxing career, Mike. Who had the greatest influence in your boxing career?

MIKE: Aag, there was a lot of them. Ali, Alan Toweel, Kallie Knoetze, Anneline Kriel.

ME: Anneline Kriel? What did she teach you?

MIKE: A helluva lot more than those other okes.

ME: What did you regard as your best punch?

MIKE: My right hook.

ME: What was so good about that?

MIKE: I hit it with my left hand.

ME: You've gained a lot of weight since those days, Mike.

MIKE: Ja. But I went to the doctor last week and he said he's putting me on a diet.

ME: What diet?

MIKE: He said I must sleep on an empty stomach every night.

ME: So?

MIKE: So I put my wife on a diet. But it didn't work. So now I'm on a garlic diet.

ME: A garlic diet?

MIKE: Ja. I eat a moeruva lot of garlic every day. Now my breath is so vrot, that everybody checks me out from doer in the distance, and then I look thin.

ME: How's your old friend Kallie Knoetze doing nowadays?

MIKE: He's okay. I saw him in hospital the other day.

ME: What were you doing in hospital?

MIKE: I was there for my wisdom teeth.

ME: Did they pull them out?

MIKE: No, they put them back.

ME: So how's Kallie?

MIKE: He's okay. He was in hospital for a boil and the nurse had to prick it. Unfortunately, the nurse got confused, and did it the other way round.

ME: Eina. Is he okay now?

MIKE: Ja, he's fine. But those nurses in hospital, hell, they're stupid. One day I shouted, 'Hey nurse, I wanna have a crap.' You know what she tunes me? She tunes me it's bad manners to say that.

So she tunes me if I wanna crap I must say number 1, and if I wanna pee, I must say number 2. Then they push ou Kallie in next to my bed and he's got a lot of pain and he tunes me, 'Hey ou Mike, I wanna have a crap.' So I shout to that stupid nurse and I tune her 'Hey nurse, ou Kallie wants to kak, but he hasn't got a number yet.'

READY OR NOT

The following story has to be my all-time favourite. The person telling the story needs to affect a heavy Indian accent.

If you can't find a heavy Indian, I suggest you pop over to your video store and rent one of my early epics, 'Oh Schucks It's Schuster'. Better still, buy your own copy at the CNA! Stick it into your VCR and listen carefully to my old pal, Raasbanja. Here's the story:

'Are you ready?', the co-pilot asks his captain on board an SAA flight to India.

'No, man, I'm Patel,' answers the captain. A voice comes through from the control tower: 'Captain Patel, what's your height and your position please?'

Patel says: 'I'm five foot six and I'm sitting right in front of the plane.'

The plane takes to the air. As it levels out, Captain Patel speaks into the mike.

'Ladies and gentlemen, this is your captain Rashid Patel speaking. Welcome on board South African Airways flight 220 to New Delhi. Presently we are flying at a height of 25 000 feet, but for you I'll make it 20,000. I hope you'll have a very enjoyable flight, so sit back and relax and thank you very much for flying South African Airways.'

Half an hour goes by. The aircraft is cruising along comfortably when Captain Patel says, 'Ladies and gentlemen, this is your Captain speaking again. We seem to have developed a slight problem with engine number four and all, but not to worry, we've still got three left. So sit back, relax and thank you very much for flying South African Airways.'

Two hours go by without a problem. Then there's a problem. Says the Captain, 'Ladies and gentlemen, I'm sorry to have to inform you that engine number three has now packed up. However, there's no need to start panicking, as my careful calculations tell me we've still got two engines left. So please don't worry, just sit back and relax and thank you very much for flying South African Airways.'

You guessed it. Forty minutes later Captain Patel takes the mike again, this time with a slight air of panic in his voice, 'Ladies and gentlemen, I don't know what's wrong but these bloody Boeing engines keep cutting out on me. We've now lost engine number two which means we've got just one keeping us in the air. But still there's no need to start panicking and all, so why don't you just sit back, relax and thank you very much for flying South African Airways.'

Another hour goes by. Just when the passengers have begun to sit back, relax, and fly South African Airways, up pops Patel again.

'Ladies and gentlemen, I'm sorry to have to tell you that our one and only remaining engine has also packed up, which means we will shortly be doing an emergency landing in the Indian Ocean. Now all those passengers who can swim, please move over to the left-hand side of the plane'.

'Those passengers who cannot swim, please move over to the right-hand side of the plane'.

There's a loud crash as the aircraft hits the water. It takes some time before it comes to a standstill. The captain's voice comes over the p.a. system for the last time, 'Ladies and gentlemen, this is your captain speaking. As you will probably have noticed by now, we have just made an emergency landing in the sea. Now will those passengers on the left-hand side of the plane who can swim please proceed to the emergency exit immediately and start swimming like hell.

'And to those passengers on the right-hand side of the plane who cannot swim at all I'd like to say, thank you very much for flying South African Airways!'

SLEG TROEP

I used to do a skit on stage between this feeble-minded troepie in the army and the captain. It went down very well, and I'd like to include it for the sake of scholars who might want to use it during a school concert.

The skit was originally done in Afrikaans, but I've translated it into English for everyone to understand.

I played the part of the troepie, and well-known Afrikaans entertainer Danie Niehaus was the army captain.

The skit kicks off with the troepie standing guard outside the little guard hut just outside the base camp. The captain walks towards the troepie who has both hands on the barrel of his gun, and his head resting on the barrel, fast asleep. The captain bends down and shouts into the troep's ear:

CAPTAIN: Troep!!

There's a beat, and then the troepie says: 'Amen,' pretending that he was praying. He slowly raises his head and opens his eyes, looking into the angry face of the captain:

TROEP: Uh ... hullo.
CAPTAIN: Hullo, captain!
TROEP: Hell, that's lekka. I only got here and I'm
                   already a captain.
CAPTAIN: Salute me, you idiot!

The troep salutes with both hands, and the gun falls to the ground. The captain is furious.

CAPTAIN: You ought to be ashamed of yourself treating your gun like that!

The captain picks up the gun and starts inspecting it:

CAPTAIN: Look at the state your gun is in, man! Tomorrow this gun will be so clean that I'll be able to see my face in the butt.
TROEP: Uh, thanks. That's kind of you.
CAPTAIN: Tell me troep, what's the first thing you do before cleaning your gun?
TROEP: Uh, I check out the serial number.
CAPTAIN: (Puzzled) Why would you check the serial number?
TROEP: To make sure I'm not cleaning another poephol's gun.

The captain puts his hands behind his back, and starts pacing up and down the stage.

CAPTAIN: In this part of the world it is law that you clean your gun every day. You follow me?

The troep gives a dumb look.

CAPTAIN: And that you'll spit and polish your boots every day. You follow me?

The troep takes the captain literally and starts following him, pacing behind him, up and down. The captain is unaware of this.

CAPTAIN: And that you will respect your seniors, you follow me?!

The captain has stopped and the troep shouts from behind his back right into his ear:

TROEP: Jaaa!!

The captain gets a heng of a fright. He jumps around.

CAPTAIN: What the devil do you think you're doing?!
TROEP: You said I got to follow you.
CAPTAIN: Captain said I got to follow captain!
TROEP: Aag, you can sommer say 'you'.
CAPTAIN: Seems you've got a problem with your military ranks! Tell me troep, one star is a ... ??
TROEP: Uhhh ... Lieutenant.
CAPTAIN: Two stars is a ... ?
TROEP: Uhhh ... First Lieutenant.
CAPTAIN: Three stars is a ...
TROEP: Moeruvva lot of stars!
CAPTAIN: Three stars is a captain, you idiot! In other words, I am a ... ?
TROEP: Real little windgat!

There's a few seconds' silence. The captain narrows his eyes.

CAPTAIN: Tell me, troep. How long have you been in the army?
TROEP: Two weeks.
CAPTAIN: What I'd like to know is what the devil are you doing in the army?!
TROEP: Ja, that's what I'd also like to know.
CAPTAIN: No, I'll tell you what you're doing here. You sit on your backside in an office the whole day long licking stamps!
TROEP: Not a heng. That's why we got a captain.
CAPTAIN: We'll soon see what you've been doing in the army. Atteeeeeention!

The troep comes to attention.

CAPTAIN: Shoulder arms!

The troep gives the captain a dumb look. Then he lifts his gun, and starts hitting his shoulder against it, like one would shoulder an opponent in a rugby match. The captain places the gun in the correct 'shoulder arms' position against the troep's shoulder.

CAPTAIN: Present arms!

The troep puts the gun between his legs, and throws both his arms on the captain's shoulders.

CAPTAIN: What the hell are you doing?!
TROEP: You said I must present arms.
CAPTAIN: You damn idiot! This is 'present arms'!

He takes the gun from the troep, and demonstrates. He hands it back to the troep, who starts practising the moves.

CAPTAIN: We'll have to start right from the beginning. The first thing you've got to know is … troep, are you listening?

The troep isn't listening. He is too intrigued with his gun, swinging it around and practising moves.

CAPTAIN: Troep, listen to me!

No use. The troep carries on with his moves.

CAPTAIN: Troep! Forget about the damn gun!

TROEP: Sure!

He slings the gun to one side. The captain is desperate.

CAPTAIN: Tell me, what have you got against the army?
TROEP: Uhhh … they put us on these lorries, then they drive us off into the bush, miles away, then we got to stay there for seven days without any food. The only thing we can eat is grass.

CAPTAIN: You should remember, troep, you're not here on a holiday, you're here to defend your country!

TROEP: Ja, but not to blerrie eat it up!

The captain loses his cool, grabs the troep and starts pushing him around. Music up and curtain closes.

FLUIT-FLUIT

Ek ry een dag in Voortrekkerstraat in Belville, en ek stop by 'n verkeerslig.

Hier staan 'n ou so lekker slap teen 'n paal en leun terwyl hy sy slap chips eet, en so tussendeur die etery fluit hy een van my eerste rugbyliedjies, 'Die Rugbyonthaal'.

Dit laat my nogal goed voel, en ek sê: 'Ou pêl, dis my song daai, like jy dit?'

Hy sê: 'Watter song?'

Ek sê: 'Daai een wat jy nou net gefluit het. Ek het die woorde geskryf.'

Hy sê: 'So what? Ek het nie die woorde gefluit nie.'

THE PLUMBER

I phoned this plumber once, and pretended to be this lady who got her big toe stuck in the tap of the bath. I put up a hell of a spiel, and begged him to come out to my house and help me with my dilemma. He bluntly refused, saying that he could only make it in two days' time.

I screamed, became hysterical, pretended to be writhing in agony, but he kept on saying there's no way he could come out today. Finally I said, 'How can you be so heartless? I'm a beautiful young girl of twenty-one, I've got my big toe stuck in the tap and I'm lying in the bath completely naked and you refuse to help me!'

He paused for a while, then said in a flash, 'Wat's jou adres? Ek's nou daar!'

BOLS TO YOU

During my second movie, 'You Must be Joking Too', I played the part of a traffic cop and stopped people on the highway to do an alcohol test. We filmed this prank at about ten in the morning, which was a highly unlikely time for any normal person to have consumed alcohol.

This one oke, I think he was Greek, got very upset when I bent forward, sniffed inside his car and said in a very cheeky and boorish voice, 'Sir, I detect with my inquiring nostrils a heavy whiff of a certain nasty substance in your 'vrot' breath, called alcohol. In fact, I can tell you with forensic accuracy that you have been devouring a large amount of brandy earlier this morning.'

His face turned bloodshot red and he jumped out of his car in a flash shouting, 'Balls!'

'No', I said, sniffing again, 'not Bols ... definitely Viceroy!'

FREE KOEKSISTERS

The most dangerous scene I ever filmed was the one at the Boksburg Lake with the AWB Republic Day festivities in May 1989. I was disguised as an Indian gentleman, handing out free koeksisters and pretending to be propagating Nationalist Party policy. At that time there was a fierce opposition from the AWB towards the NP for their liberal politics.

I remember wanting to shake the hand of this one oke. He jumped away from my outstretched hand shouting, 'I don't shake the hand of the antichrist, especially if he's a f****n charro!'

I stuck my hand out again and said in my best Indian accent, 'Hey man, I want to be your friend and all.'

He was furious, hit my hand away and snarled, 'I'll kill you, you f****n koelie!'

He put his hand inside his briefcase, and I was convinced that my last seconds on earth had dawned, thinking that he was about to draw his .38 special. But what he actually did was to take his camera out of his briefcase, hand it to his wife, and then started attacking me with the briefcase over my head with all his might.

I endured a few heavy knocks, but finally ran away, realising that this oke would have no problem killing me right there on the spot. I returned after a while, elated at the prospect of having this dramatic, truly old South African incident on film.

Problem is, I have to have the written permission of the person I caught out, and when I revealed myself to this oke he was even more furious. He started calling me names that even Quentin Tarantino would never consider using in his movies, and bluntly refused to sign the release form.

I'll go back to this oke for his written permission to use that piece of film material once the Rainbow Nation has become a reality in his screwed mind ... which is unlikely to happen in my lifetime.

PAP NAT

I was once asked to deliver a speech for some National Party function. This was in about 1989. Imitating the SABC's parliamentary correspondent of the day, Riaan Nel, I started my speech like this:

'In die Volksraad het Helen vandag weer vir PW kwaad gemaak.

'Magnus Malan het oorlog gemaak, Barend du Plessis het geld gemaak en Andries Treurnicht het hom amper vuilgemaak toe Chris Heunis sê hy wil nog 'n gebied oopmaak.

'Kobie Coetzee het vrede gemaak en vir Minister Hendrik Schoeman gevra om 'n paar grappe te maak. Almal het hulle natgemaak, en Helen Suzman het drooggemaak. Daarna het sy tee gemaak wat ter tafel gelê is saam met die potjiekos deur Pik gemaak.

'Aan die einde van die dag se verrigtinge het Dawie de Villiers die oond skoongemaak.'

That got quite a laugh. Then I went on to imitate the SABC's financial correspondent of the day, Jerry Schuitema.

'Goeienaand. Die goudprys toon 'n oorskot, die handelsbalans toon 'n agterskot en op die Durban se Plaza het jy vandag net tien rand betaal vir 'n kerriekot.

'Daar was vandag weer visse in die fiskale beleid, monikke in die monitêre beleid maar steeds geen doel in PW se beleid nie.'

My audience shuffled around uncomfortably, and I started doing Eugene Terreblanche.

' … en nou word daar gesê, Meneer die Voorsitter, daar is die KP en daar is ons regses, en nou het die KP ons gekoop, AWB ingesluit.

'Maar dan kan ek net sowel sê, Meneer die Voorsiter, daar is die NP en daar is die PFP maar daar is nie meer kiesers nie.

'Net so is daar vandag FW en daar is PW, maar daar is nie meer hare nie!'

At this point I was removed from the stage forcefully and was never asked to speak at an NP function again.

OH SCHUCKS, IT'S ME!

I did a radio show many years ago in which I caught people out over the telephone. It was great fun, and proved to be very popular with the radio audience.

I was constantly looking for new victims for my show, and got a lot of input from the public. One day a good friend of mine told me about what a great character his aunt was. Her name was Ant Mien, she was about sixty-five, a fiery character and known for her very short temper and her constant use of expletives.

At the time she was in charge of her late husband's brickworks just outside Pretoria, and used to deliver bricks to the building sites herself, driving a heavy duty truck. Her tongue was feared by everyone, and even more so her physical strength. This friend of mine told me about numerous incidents where she physically attacked anyone who stretched his luck just a wee bit too far. I couldn't wait to phone her.

I dialled the number, disguised my voice and pretended to be an upset builder who was unhappy with the quality of bricks which had been delivered to my building site. The interview lasted about ten seconds.

I was still in the middle of my introduction when she interrupted and shouted: 'If you got a blerrie problem meneer, come and see me yourself! For the moment you can take this f****n telephone and stick it up your arse!', and slammed the phone down. I knew immediately that I would have to change the tone of the prank if I wanted anything at all out of this lady, and that I should change my tactics.

So I phoned her again, this time playing the role of the boss of the builder who had just spoken to her. I was very decent and apologised for the fact that the builder was a bit harsh. I said that the builder was in tears over the whole incident, and told her that the builder would like to apologise to her personally.

She agreed, and I pretended to hand the phone to the builder, and put up my builder's voice again, saying: 'Mrs. Robberste, I am very sorry for upsetting you over the telephone like that. I want you to forgive me.

'Ja', she said, 'just don't f****n do it again.' Then I said: 'Personally I am also hurt about what you told me to do with the telephone, and would feel much better about the whole matter if you would also apologise to me.'

There was a long silence before she said, 'Just refresh my memory and tell me what I told you to do with the telephone.' I said, 'You told me to take the phone and stick it up my arse.'

Another silence followed, and then she said, 'Okay, I'll apologise. You can take it out now.'

YES, JIMMY REALLY DID NEUK ME

Jimmy Abbott was another character. Should I say, is another character, 'cause whenever I see him in his Gauteng Lions' rugby jersey occupying three seats at Ellis Park, I think back on that same day with the AWBs. People constantly ask me whether his attack on me in the movie was for real. Quite frankly, I crapped myself.

To see this mass of 180 kilograms loading onto you with the force of a sumo wrestler, and not knowing whether he will appreciate the joke once I reveal myself, was a nightmare of a thought. Normally I get away with it once I shout, 'It's ou Leon!', but one never knows what goes on inside that huge ex-boxer head.

Fortunately Jimmy is not the vrot oke he sometimes pretends to be, and although he didn't appreciate the joke on the day, we've had many laughs about the incident since.

On one occasion I asked him exactly what went through his head at that moment and he said, 'As jou pruik nie afgeval het nie, en ek nie gesien het hoe bles jy is nie, het ek jou daai dag heeltemaal opgemoer. Maar my ma het my geleer om respek te hê vir die oues van dae.'

O CAR-AMBA!

I was once asked by a well-known car dealership to do a gig for the launch of a new motor vehicle. Now, it's always good to prepare something really special for an occasion like this.

The first thing I did was write down the name of every single car on the market that entered my mind. Having done this, I schemed for hours how I could work the names of the different cars into my routine.

Then the idea hit me: I would tell my audience that I used to be a second-hand car salesmen, but had this great ambition to become a rugby commentator. So I hopped over to the SABC's Topsport one day and told them I had this talent to broadcast rugby. They said, 'Prove it', and stuck me behind a microphone for my voice test.

Because I worked with cars every single day of my life, I got the names of the cars all mixed up with the names of the rugby players. The result went something like this:

Goeiemiddag en hartlik welkom hier by CURRIE MOTORS ... ee, ek bedoel welkom hier by die CURRIE-BEKERWEDSTRYD.

Hier op Ellispark skyn DATSUN ... eee, ek bedoel skyn DIE SON.

Ek sit hier bo in die kommentaarhok, en op die oomblik gaan hier nog NISSAN ... eee, gaan hier nog NIKS AAN nie.

Hier onder die hoofpawiljoen is daar 'n klompie polisiemanne met hulle HONDA BALLADE ... eee, hulle HONDE WAT BLAF.

En daar kom die manne nou uitgedraf. Ou Tommie Laubscher sukkel so bietjie om weg te kom want hy't 'n MERCEDES BENZ ... ek bedoel hy't 'n MOERSE PENS. Die man word nie maerder nie, nee hy word ALPHETTA ... eeee, hy word AL VETTER.

Die man wat agter Laubscher draf is FERRARI van die VW ... eee, FERREIRA VAN DIE WP.

Die losskakel het die bal gestel en die skeidsregter vra, 'Is jy reg?' En die losskakel sing: 'ALLES REG, ALTYD REG, TOYOTA.'

Dan skop hy af, maar die FORD ESTCOURT ... eee, ek bedoel die SKOP IS KORT.

Daar is 'n skrum op die middellyn, en die skeidsregter sê vir die voorspelers, 'KOMBI... ee, KOM HIER.' Hy sê vir die agterspelers, 'STANZA' ... ek bedoel 'STAAN DAAR.' Hy sê vir FERRARI, 'MOENIE DAAR STAAN EN IDLE NIE' ... ek bedoel hy sê vir FERREIRA, 'MOENIE DAAR STAAN EN NIKS DOEN NIE.'

Nou het die manne gesak vir die skrum maar die hele ou spul val inmekaar. Hulle sak weer maar die skrum val weer inmekaar. Dit gebeur BMW … eee, dit gebeur WEER EN WEER. Die skrumskakel vra, 'Wie se bal is dit?' en die skeidsregter sê, 'Dis HYUNDAI' … ek bedoel, 'DIS JOUNE DAAI.'

Hy sit die bal in die skrum in, maar skielik klap die vuiste! Nou groet die manne mekaar! Ollie gryp vir Olo aan sy kraag en hy sê, 'Moenie met my kom KAWASAKI SUZUKI!' … eeee, 'Moenie met my kom TWAK SOEK NIE!' En dan slaan hy hom vol op die BUICK … ek bedoel die BEK. Hy gryp sy mond vas en hy skree, 'ISUZU!' … eee, 'EITSJOE!' Olo skree vir Ollie, 'Hoekom slaan jy my, ek kan nie VIR STANNIC VERDISKONTEER!' … ek bedoel, 'Ek kan nie VERSTAAN NIE DIS VERDOMP SEER!' Dan kyk hy vir Ollie en hy vloek hom en hy sê, 'Jou MASERATTI' … ek bedoel, 'Jou PA SE TO TIE.'

Die skeidsregter vra vir Olo, 'Het jy seergekry?' en Olo sê, 'MITSUBISHI' … eee, 'NET SO BIETJIE.'

Die noodhulpmanne draf op en hulle gee hom 'n pil, maar hy spoeg dit uit want dis 'n OPEL … ou pil.

Die skeidsregter gaan vir Ollie afstuur, maar Ollie sê vir hom, 'Ek is jammer, meneer.' Die skeidsregter sê, 'Moenie by my kom CADILLAC nie' … ek bedoel, 'Moenie by my kom GATLEK nie.'

En Teichmann vra vir die skeidsregter, 'Meneer hoekom stuur jy vir Ollie af?' en die skeidsregter sê, 'Dit het VAUXHALL met jou te doen nie' … eee, 'Dit het NIKS MET JOU TE DOEN NIE.'

Uiteindelik kan die manne skrum, die bal is uit en daar trek FERRARI … eee, FERREIRA! Hy maak sy rug krom en hy gee FIAT! … eee, hy gee VET! Maar hier van die kant af kom Lomu en hy laai hom op met 'n HI-ACE! … ek bedoel hy MAAI HOM AF MET 'n HIGH TACKLE!'

Dan blaas die eindfluitjie en die mane is FORD … eeee die manne is FORT na die kleedkamer!

POMP AND CIRCUMSTANCE

Back in the days before he had a change of heart about the surgical profession, Professor Chris Barnard once told an interviewer that the heart was really nothing more than a pump. I was working for the SABC's Afrikaans Radio Service at the time, and I couldn't resist the opportunity to have a little fun at the Prof's expense. This is what I came up with ...

'I would like to say that there is a misconception about the heart, in so far as the heart is actually not a heart, it is a pump. Ja die hart is 'n pomp. Therefore if I talk about my young wife Karen, I shouldn't say "Karen is a girl after my heart". No, I should say she's a girl after my pomp.

'Also, for example, we shouldn't be talking about the little town of Hartenbos. No, we should call it Pomp-in-die-bos. There's also this place in the Transvaal that is called Hartebeesfontein. That's wrong. It should be called Pomp-'n-beesfontein.

'There's this Afrikaans song that says 'My hart verlang na die Boland'. I suggest that we rename this song and call it 'My pomp verlang na die Boland'.

'The other night my young wife Karen put it so beautifully after she put out the light. She put her hand on my pomp and said, "Chrisjan, I love you because you've got a pomp of gold".'

OMROEPER SE WAT?

Ek het maar in die begin van my uitsaaidae gesukkel. Eendag stotter en stamel ek met die nuuslees. Toe ek klaar is, sê daai skerpsinnige klein Paul Eilers, 'Schuster, jy's nie 'n omroeper se gat nie.' Fanus hoor dit, en sê, 'Jy's verkeerd. Hy is!'

NOMMER TWEE

Ek en een van my base by die SAUK, het nie veel ooghare vir mekaar gehad nie, veral nie hy vir my nie, en veral nie toe ek bietjie sukses begin smaak nie.

Eendag is ek besig met nommer twee op die toilet. Hy klop hard aan die deur en skree, 'Schuster, jy's laat vir jou vergadering!'

Toe sê ek, 'Sorry, meneer, maar ek kan net een k*k op 'n slag hanteer.'

BILTONG AND SPAGHETTI

On another occasion travelling to Bloemfontein by car, I was caught on the N1 speeding. Two cops, one coloured, one white, jumped in front of my car and stopped me. I thought. 'Oh-oh, this means trouble.'

The coloured oke walked over to my window, checked me out and said, 'Jy's mos daai actress wat die mense so bedonder.'

I tried to make a joke out of it, but this oke was very serious: '178 in a 120 zone, swaer, jy's in groot moeilikheid. Klim uit die kar, meneer.'

I had stacks of biltong in the car, and handed him a bag. 'This is for you guys who perform such a noble job.' He had already written the ticket, so my gesture wasn't meant as a bribe – it was merely a present for these guys who work under very difficult and often thankless circumstances (ha ha!).

My brother, who was with me at the time, took a 'Hie' Kommie Bokke' CD and handed that to the cop too. He looked at the biltong in his one hand, looked at the CD, then looked at me and asked, 'Meneer, wil meneer nie nog 'n slag oor daai spaghetti neuk ry nie'.

LEKKER VAKANSIE

Ek stop een Desember vakansie op Richmond in die Kaap om vol te maak. Daar's agt kinders in die kar – vier van my eie en elkeen het 'n pêl.

Soos ek uitklim, so neem hulle oor – my laaitie hop van agter af oor en neem my sitplek in om met die stuurwiel te speel. Die ander baklei en stry laat die hare waai en die snot spat. Dis 'n verskriklike gedruis in daai kar.

My vrou gil, en begin naderhand huil. Die petroljoggie check my so uit terwyl ek moedeloos langs die kar 'n Camel opsteek. Hy sê, 'Meneer, as djy nie vasigtag is nie, spyker djy djouself nog yt 'n seat yt.'

PEANUT GALLERY

There was this oke in the audience one night at a show I did in Welkom. The oke was lying spread-eagled over two seats in the back of the theatre.

He looked motherlesss and was bleeding from the head and nose, as if he'd been involved in a henguvva bar fight. Everytime I told a joke he went 'Aaaaarrrghhhh!'

This was terribly irritating for me and the audience. I tried to silence the heckler by saying things like, 'Go sit in your car and bark at the burglars,' but he just kept on going 'Aaaaarrrgggghhhhhhh!'

Finally I said, 'Tell me, asshole, where do you come from?'

And he said, 'From the balcony. Aarrgghhh!'

ME AND OU JIMMY

The most frequent question I get asked is, 'Did Jimmy Abbot really neuk you in that scene from *Oh Schucks It's Schuster*?'

Let me put it to you this way. Ek is nie so gebore nie, ek is so gedonner.

RAASBANJA

Kallie Knoetze was another one of my candid camera highlights. I'll never forget the day I pitched at his farmstall, Die Bek se Padstal outside Brits, disguised as this cheeky Indian Raasbanja (raas baie) with twenty chickens in a crate tied onto my old Valiant's roof.

On arrival Kallie wasn't there, but his old farmhand, Jakob, assured me that he would be arriving soon. To kill time I started checking his watermelons that were displayed outside the farmstall, testing them for ripeness. Whenever I felt a watermelon wasn't ripe enough, I would throw it onto the ground, to the horror of old Jakob. I knew that as soon as Kallie pitched, all hell would break loose, and this watermelon bit was actually the ideal opportunity to set Mr Knoetze up in a big way.

And so it was: Kallie got out of his bakkie, saw the broken watermelons lying on the ground, and stormed in my direction, with Jakob going absolutely ballistic trying to explain to him the mad antics of this ridiculous Indian. Kallie produced the best unscripted one-liners I have experienced in any movie, and I had a great battle trying to contain my laughter.

This scene was filmed in 1986 shortly after oom PW had delivered a speech about nation building etc., and at a stage when things were starting to get really hot Kallie shouted at the top of his voice, 'PW Botha sê aanmekaar "bou 'n nasie, bou 'n f****n nasie" maar hoe de f*k bou mens 'n f****n nasie met iemand soos jy?!'

This scene was filmed a few years after Kallie lost a major boxing bout against the American John Tate, to the great disappointment of the SA boxing supporters, and it was rumoured at the time that Kallie had been partying heavily in Sun City the night prior to the fight.

This was a very touchy issue for Mr Knoetze, and when this cheeky Indian raised the matter, Kallie's patience was stretched to the limit. He clutched my neck with his big hands like a python would squeeze its prey, and pushed me against the watermelon stand in a fit of rage, drawing back that huge right fist, ready to donner this oke like he had never donnered anyone before.

I got a henguvva skrik and shouted, 'Asseblief Kallie, moenie slaan nie, dis net ou Leon!', not really knowing whether this would swing his fierce mood back to normality. Fortunately it did, and being the great sportsman that he is, Kallie shouted, 'Leon, jou bliksem! Ek sal jou mos vrekmaak jou vark!'

I was very satisfied with the material I had on celluloid, and Kallie was even more satisfied knowing that he was about to hit the limelight one more time. We sat on the stoep of his neatly kept smallholding for hours on that Saturday in '86, reminiscing about the good old days and sipping Castle quarts by the dozen until deep into the night.

KLASSIEKE KOMEDIE

Leon sit in die treinkompartement saam met Naas, 'n beeldskone jong meisie en 'n bejaarde ou dame.

Die trein gaan deur 'n tonnel, en dis nagswart binne die kompartement. Skielik is daar die geluid van 'n soen, gevolg deur die geluid van 'n harde klap deur iemand se smoel.

Die trein is uit by die anderkant van die tonnel, en niemand sê 'n woord nie, maar almal dink.

Die bejaarde ou dame dink, 'Mooi so, jong meisie. Naas het die kat in die donker probeer knyp, en toe gee jy hom 'n taai klap deur sy bek. Good for you.'

Die jong meisie dink, 'Snaaks dat Naas verkies om by die ou tannie aan te lê, en nie by my nie.'

Naas dink, 'Dis darem nie fair nie. Schuster soen die meisie, en sy klap my.'

Leon dink, 'Dit was nou lekker. Ek soen die agterkant van my hand, gee Naas 'n snotklap, en niemand sê 'n woord nie.'

ALL FALL DOWN

Finally, here's a prank that is guaranteed to bring the house down wherever it is played. (So try not to play it at your own house.) It always works a treat at wedding receptions, especially if you involve the groom and his best mates.

Ingredients:

1) Ten fris rugbymanne between 18 and 30. (It doesn't have to be ten, it can be less. But the more, the merrier.)
2) Ten small pieces of paper.
3) A hat.
4) One of my rugby CDs, or the book you're reading right now, to serve as a prize for the winner.

Prior to the event, you take your ten small pieces of paper, and write the name 'Naas Botha' down on nine of them. (Again, it doesn't have to be Naas, it's just that Naas works very well for me. It can be any rugby player of your choice.) On the tenth piece of paper you write the name of any other player, for example Gary Teichmann.

Put these pieces of paper into a hat.

At the event, take up the microphone and call ten guys to the front, telling them that they'll be doing a bit of scrumming on stage. Make sure the guys you involve are fit and healthy, and are preferably rugby players. They're always around, believe me.

Right, you've got them on the stage and you tell them that each oke is going to represent a well-known rugby player. You've got the names of ten rugby players in the hat, and each oke draws a name.

Each oke must look at the name on the piece of paper, and must then hand the piece of paper back to you. VERY IMPORTANT: NONE OF THE OKES MUST KNOW WHICH RUGBY PLAYER'S NAME ANY OF THE OTHER OKES HAVE DRAWN. You'll soon see why.

Once the okes have got their names, you explain the game to them. They've got to stand in a straight line, facing the audience. Then they have to bind like front row forwards would before they go down to scrum. In other words, they must put their hands behind the backs of the guys next to them, and get a firm grip on the oke's trousers.

The best way to get a firm grip is to get your thumb in under his belt, and grab his trousers with the rest of your fingers, exactly the way ou Ollie le Roux does it in a scrum Saturday after Saturday.

Now you tell the okes that you will be playing the part of a rugby commentator, during a live broadcast of a fictitious match. As soon as an oke hears his name during the commentary, HE HAS TO TRY AND HIT THE GROUND, using all his power to go down.

The guys supporting him on the sides should try and PREVENT him from going down, and the FIRST GUY TO SUCCEED IN GOING DOWN will win the prize, which HAS to be this joke book or one of my CDs. Why? Easy – so you can put all the blame on me.

Once all the okes have got their tight grips around one another's backs, you start commentating:

'The ball has been placed in the middle of the field, the referee looks at the two teams and blows his whistle. The ball is kicked off by ... Henry Honniball!'

(Make sure to pause every time you're about to mention a name – it creates great anticipation.)

'The man waiting for the ball is ... Mark Andrews.'

(You pause for a while, as if you're waiting to see whether there is a 'Mark Andrews'. Then you carry on.)

'He gets the ball and gives it to ... Gary Teichman!'

(The guy who is 'Gary Teichman' now tries to hit the ground, with his mates trying to keep him up. If he succeeds, you give him the CD or joke book, and he falls out. Tell the others there are still lots of CDs and joke books to be won. Of course you're lying, unless you would like to give each competitor a CD or joke book at the end. Sounds like a good idea to me. Now carry on with your commentary.)

'There's a scrum in the middle of the field and the ball

is put in by … Joost van der Westhuizen! The man who breaks free with the ball is … André Venter! He passes the ball to … Bobby Skinstad! He gives the ball to … NAAS BOTHA!

Now, what you'll experience is something you've never seen before. Nine grown men getting airborne, and then hitting the ground with tremendous impact. The entire audience will be in stitches! (To say nothing of the okes on stage.)

Which reminds me: DO NOT attempt this joke on a concrete floor! The okes could get seriously injured. Do it only on a plank floor, or on a floor which is covered by a thick carpet.

Have fun, and remember … there's only one Naas Botha! (And that's me!)